D1240714

BL metamorphosis

story and art by
Kaori Tsurutani

CONTENTS

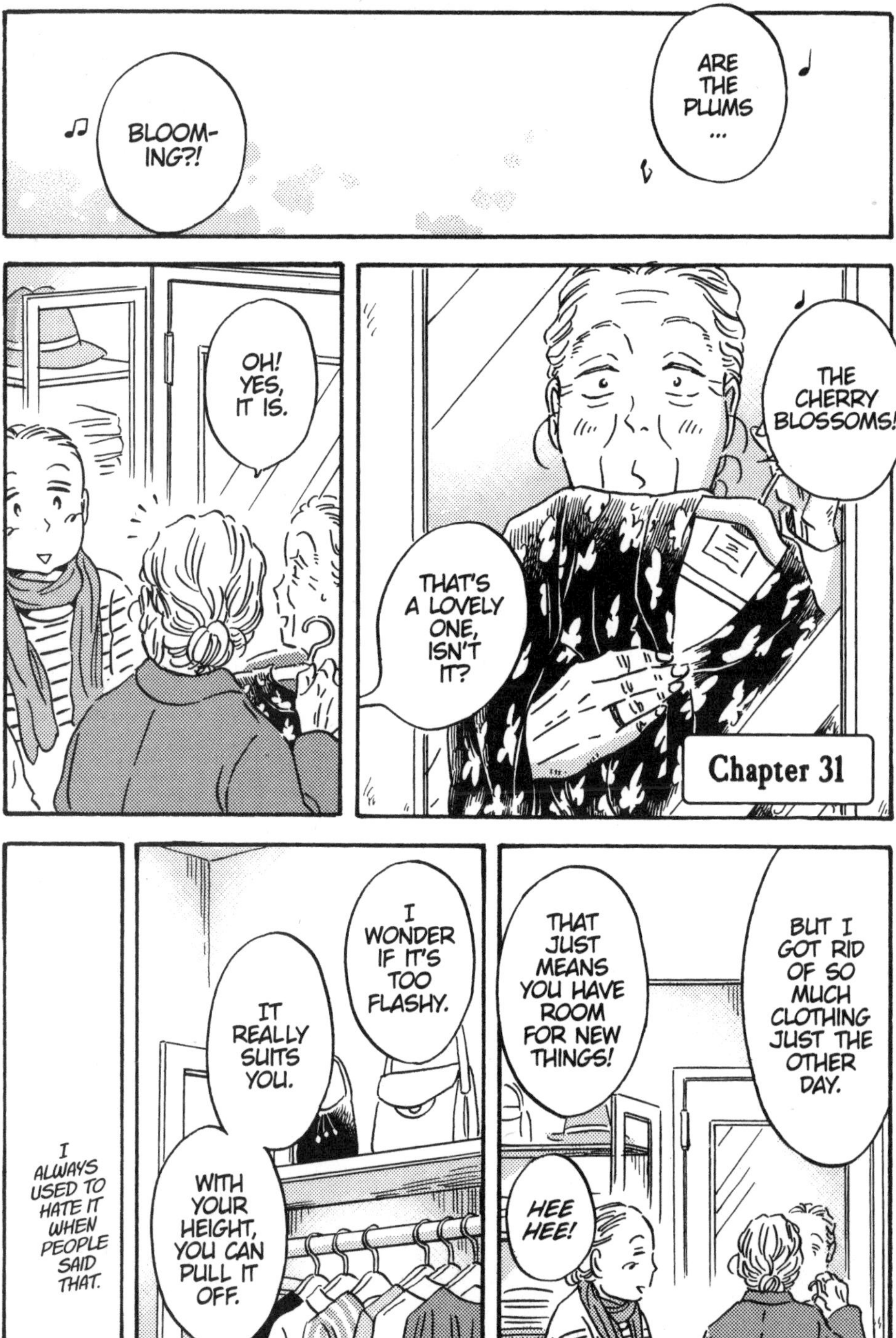
ARE THE PLUMS ...
BLOOMING?!
THE CHERRY BLOSSOMS!
THAT'S A LOVELY ONE, ISN'T IT?
Chapter 31
OH! YES, IT IS.
BUT I GOT RID OF SO MUCH CLOTHING JUST THE OTHER DAY.
THAT JUST MEANS YOU HAVE ROOM FOR NEW THINGS!
HEE HEE!
I WONDER IF IT'S TOO FLASHY.
IT REALLY SUITS YOU.
WITH YOUR HEIGHT, YOU CAN PULL IT OFF.
I ALWAYS USED TO HATE IT WHEN PEOPLE SAID THAT.

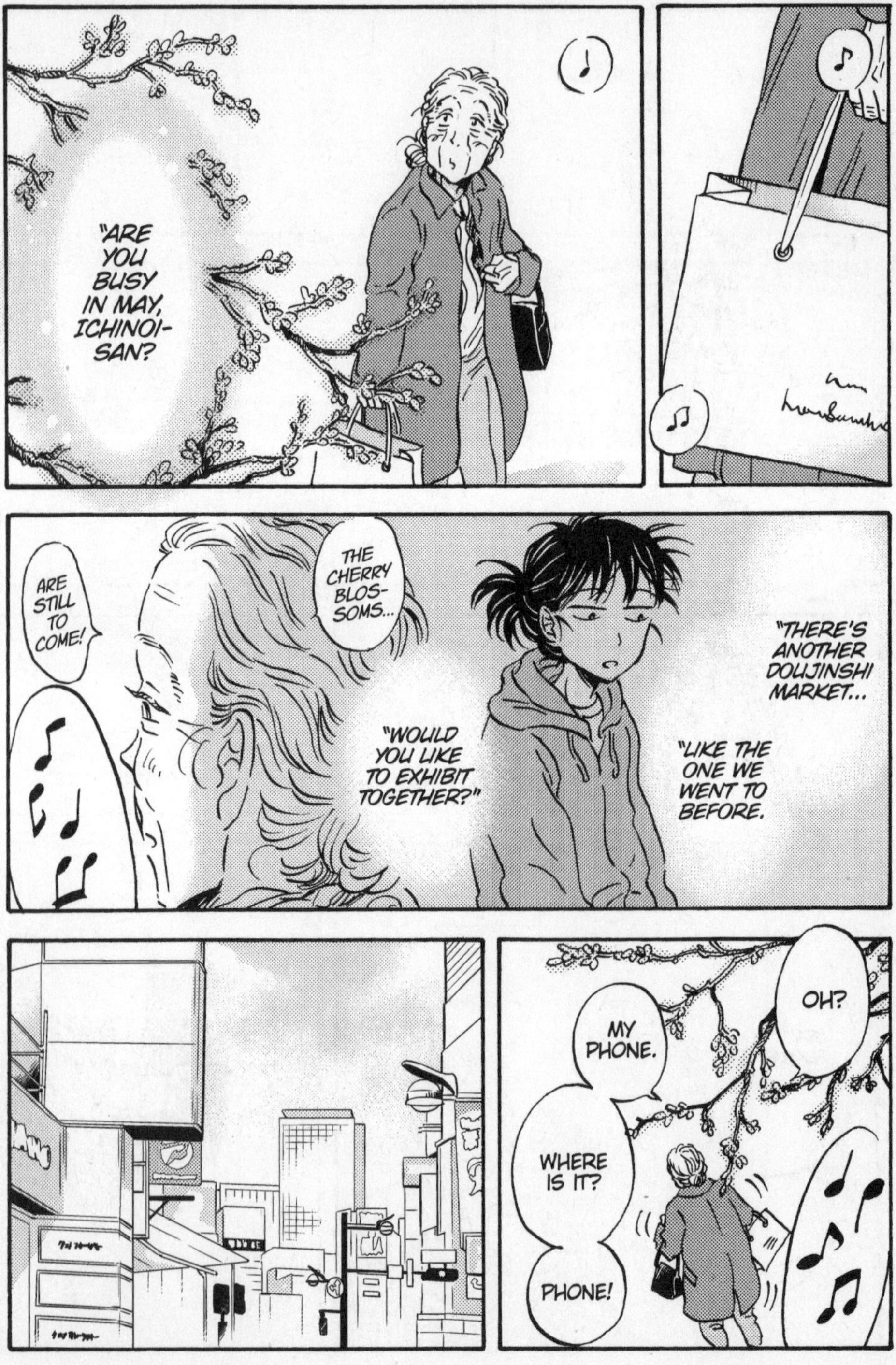
"ARE YOU BUSY IN MAY, ICHINOI-SAN?
"THERE'S ANOTHER DOUJINSHI MARKET...
"LIKE THE ONE WE WENT TO BEFORE.
THE CHERRY BLOSSOMS...
"WOULD YOU LIKE TO EXHIBIT TOGETHER?"
ARE STILL TO COME!
OH?
MY PHONE.
WHERE IS IT?
PHONE!

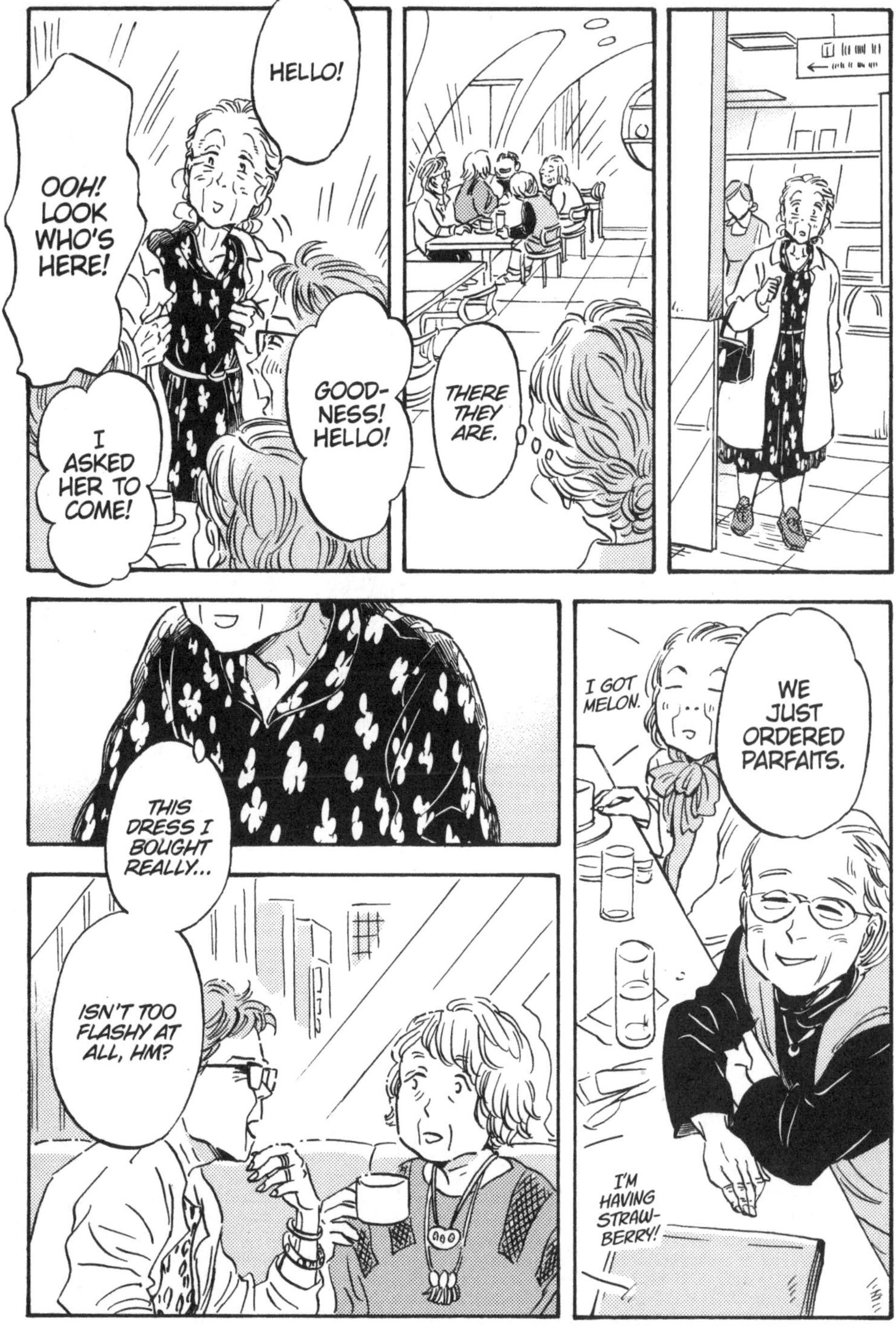
THERE THEY ARE.
HELLO!
OOH! LOOK WHO'S HERE!
GOODNESS! HELLO!
I ASKED HER TO COME!
WE JUST ORDERED PARFAITS.
I GOT MELON.
I'M HAVING STRAWBERRY!
THIS DRESS I BOUGHT REALLY...
ISN'T TOO FLASHY AT ALL, HM?

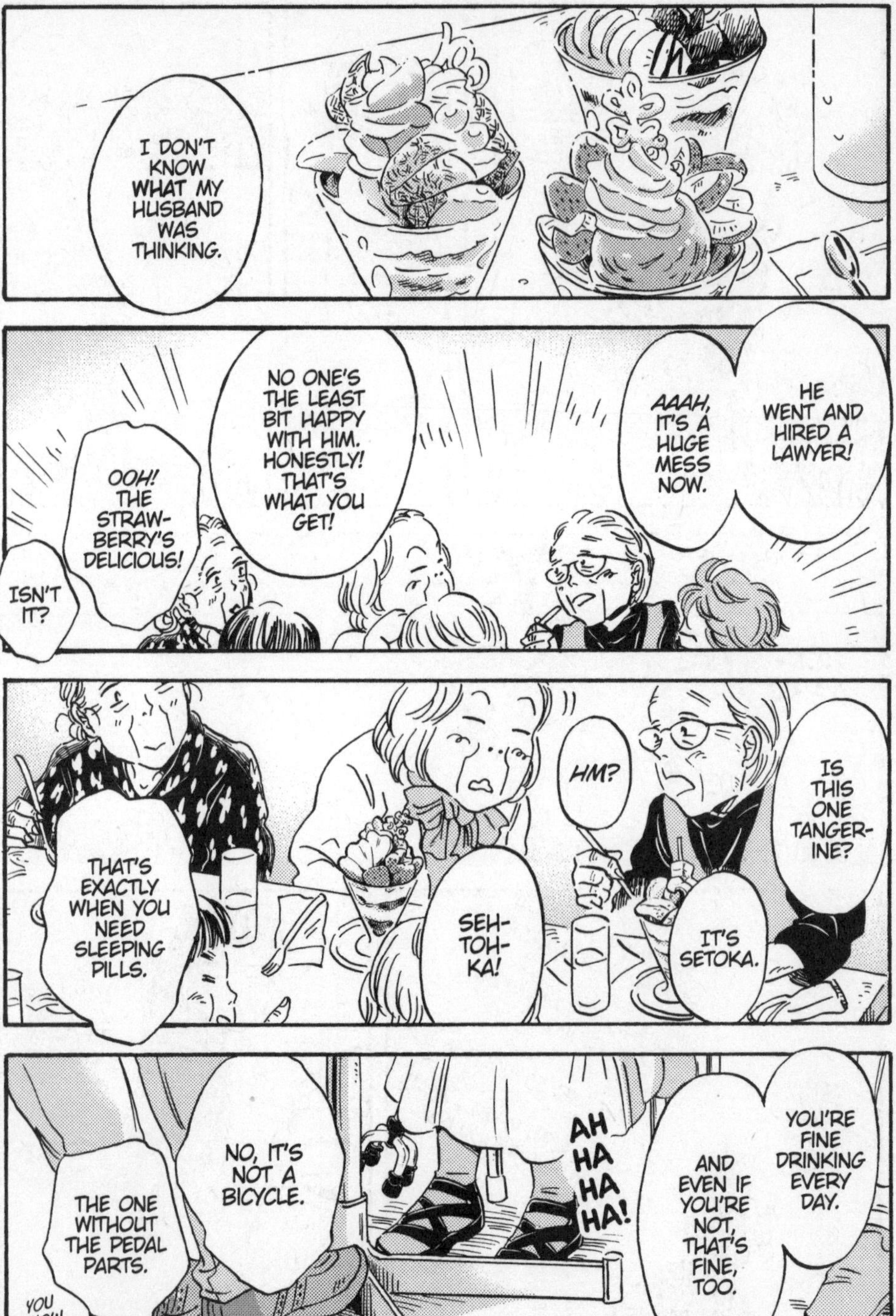
I DON'T KNOW WHAT MY HUSBAND WAS THINKING.
HE WENT AND HIRED A LAWYER!
AAAH, IT'S A HUGE MESS NOW.
NO ONE'S THE LEAST BIT HAPPY WITH HIM. HONESTLY! THAT'S WHAT YOU GET!
OOH! THE STRAW-BERRY'S DELICIOUS!
ISN'T IT?
IS THIS ONE TANGER-INE?
HM?
IT'S SETOKA.
SEH-TOH-KA!
THAT'S EXACTLY WHEN YOU NEED SLEEPING PILLS.
YOU'RE FINE DRINKING EVERY DAY.
AND EVEN IF YOU'RE NOT, THAT'S FINE, TOO.
AH HA HA HA!
NO, IT'S NOT A BICYCLE.
THE ONE WITHOUT THE PEDAL PARTS.
YOU KNOW.

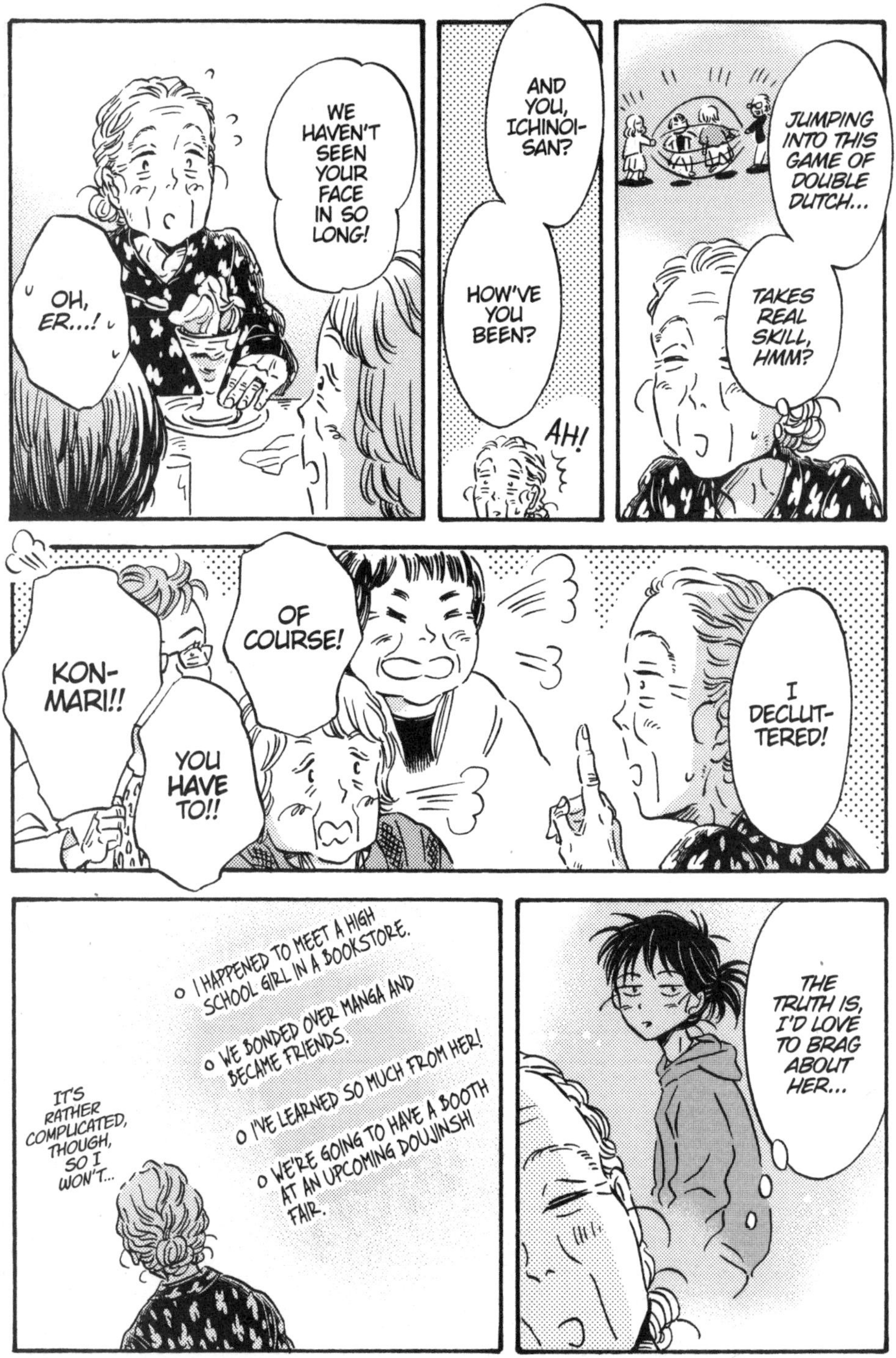
JUMPING INTO THIS GAME OF DOUBLE DUTCH...
TAKES REAL SKILL, HMM?
AND YOU, ICHINOI-SAN?
HOW'VE YOU BEEN?
AH!
WE HAVEN'T SEEN YOUR FACE IN SO LONG!
OH, ER...!
I DECLUT-TERED!
OF COURSE!
KON-MARI!!
YOU HAVE TO!!
THE TRUTH IS, I'D LOVE TO BRAG ABOUT HER...
○ I HAPPENED TO MEET A HIGH SCHOOL GIRL IN A BOOKSTORE.
○ WE BONDED OVER MANGA AND BECAME FRIENDS.
○ I'VE LEARNED SO MUCH FROM HER!
○ WE'RE GOING TO HAVE A BOOTH AT AN UPCOMING DOUJINSHI FAIR.
IT'S RATHER COMPLICATED, THOUGH, SO I WON'T...

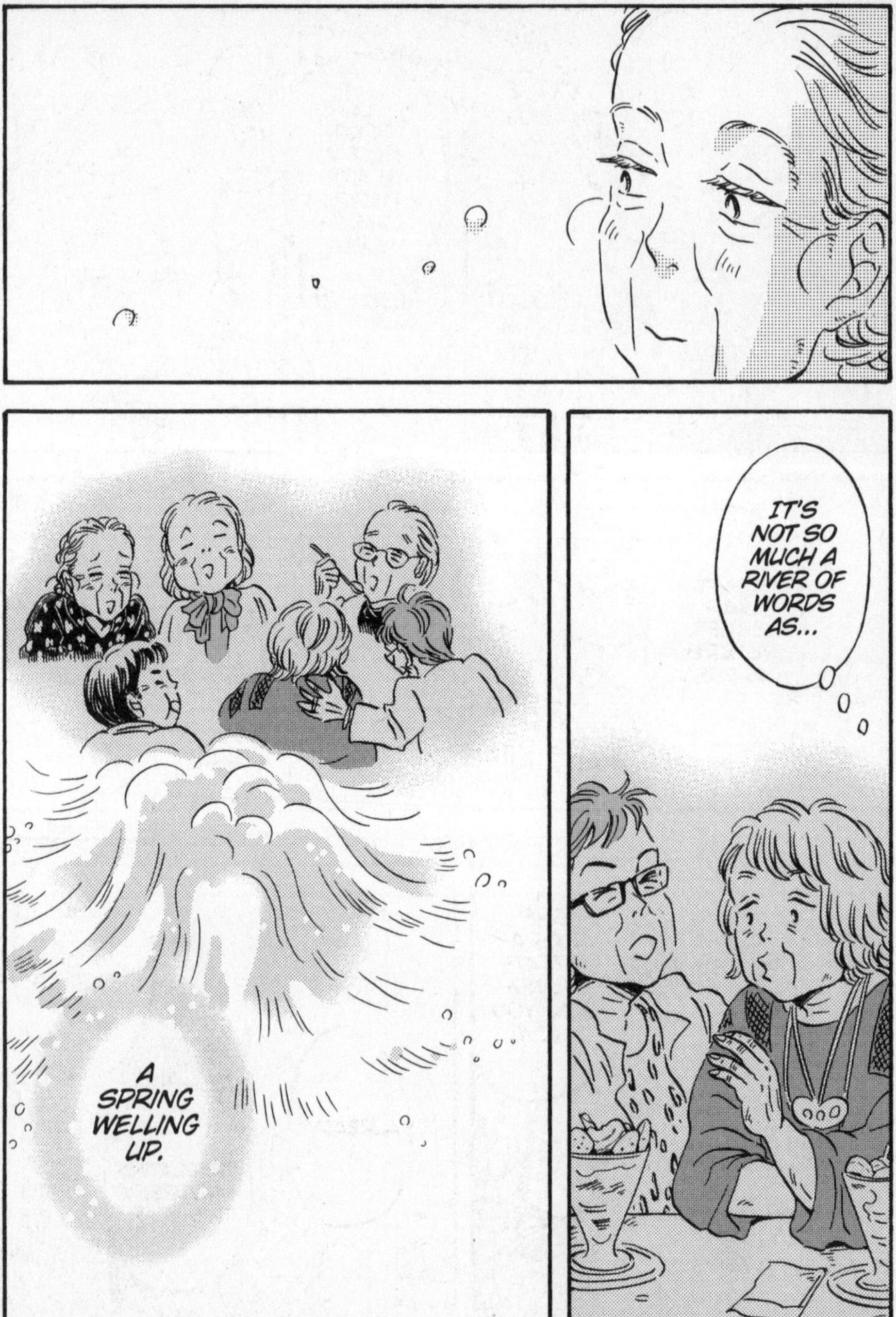
IT'S NOT SO MUCH A RIVER OF WORDS AS...
A SPRING WELLING UP.

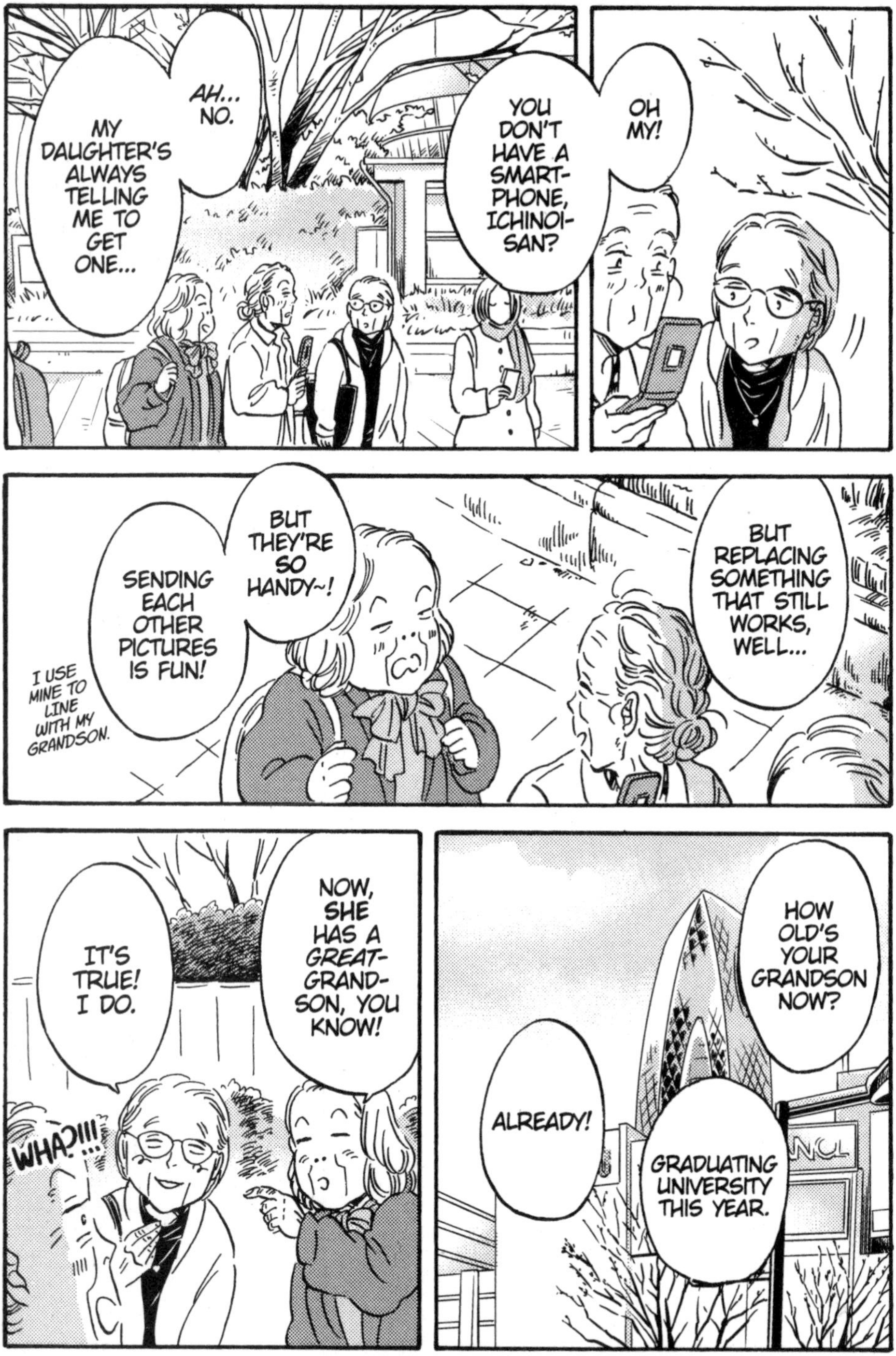
OH MY!
YOU DON'T HAVE A SMARTPHONE, ICHINOI-SAN?
AH... NO.
MY DAUGHTER'S ALWAYS TELLING ME TO GET ONE...
BUT REPLACING SOMETHING THAT STILL WORKS, WELL...
BUT THEY'RE SO HANDY~!
SENDING EACH OTHER PICTURES IS FUN!
I USE MINE TO LINE WITH MY GRANDSON.
HOW OLD'S YOUR GRANDSON NOW?
GRADUATING UNIVERSITY THIS YEAR.
ALREADY!
NOW, SHE HAS A GREAT-GRANDSON, YOU KNOW!
IT'S TRUE! I DO.
WHA?!!!...

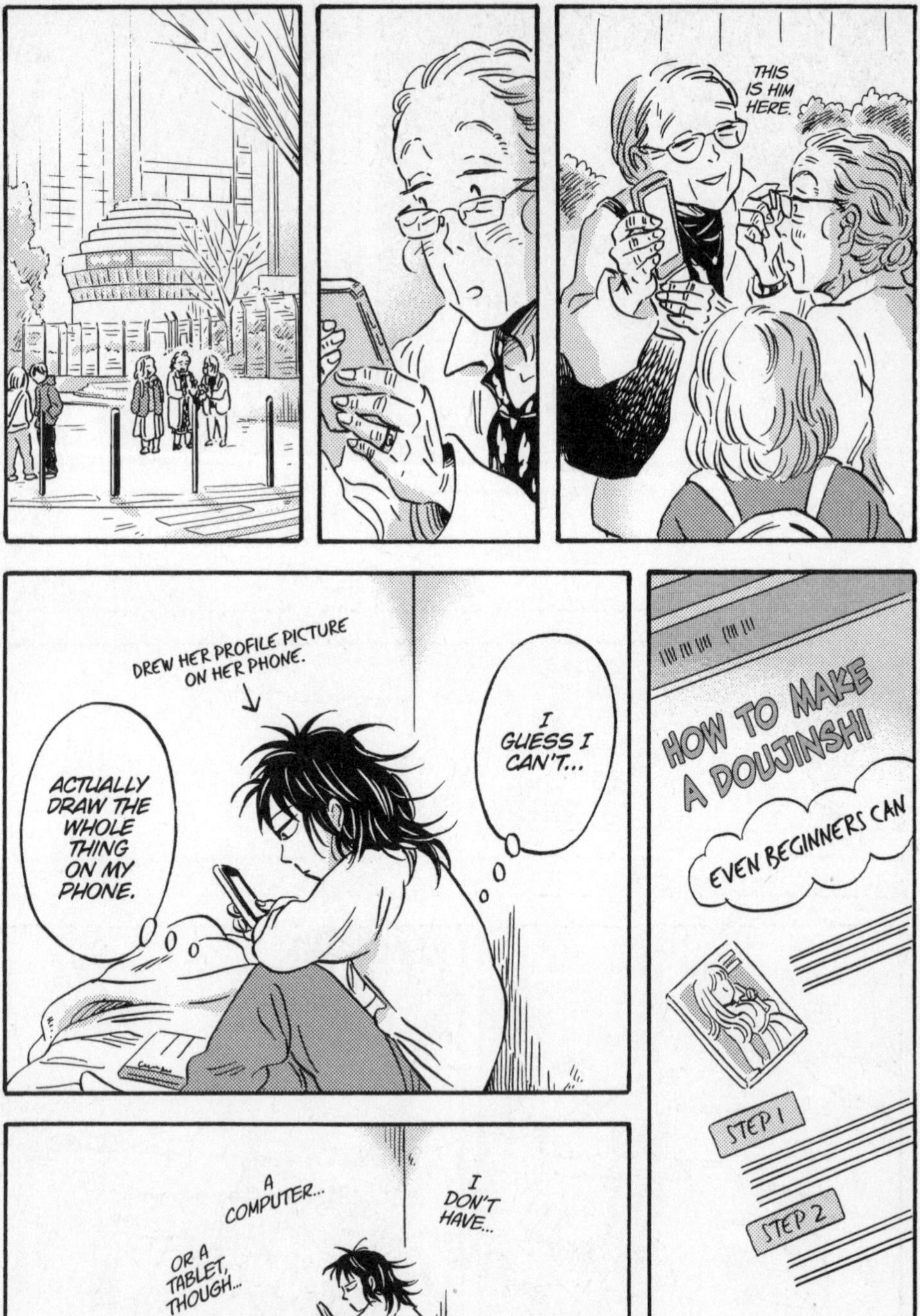
THIS IS HIM HERE.
HOW TO MAKE A DOUJINSHI
EVEN BEGINNERS CAN
STEP 1
STEP 2
I GUESS I CAN'T...
ACTUALLY DRAW THE WHOLE THING ON MY PHONE.
DREW HER PROFILE PICTURE ON HER PHONE.
I DON'T HAVE...
A COMPUTER...
OR A TABLET, THOUGH...

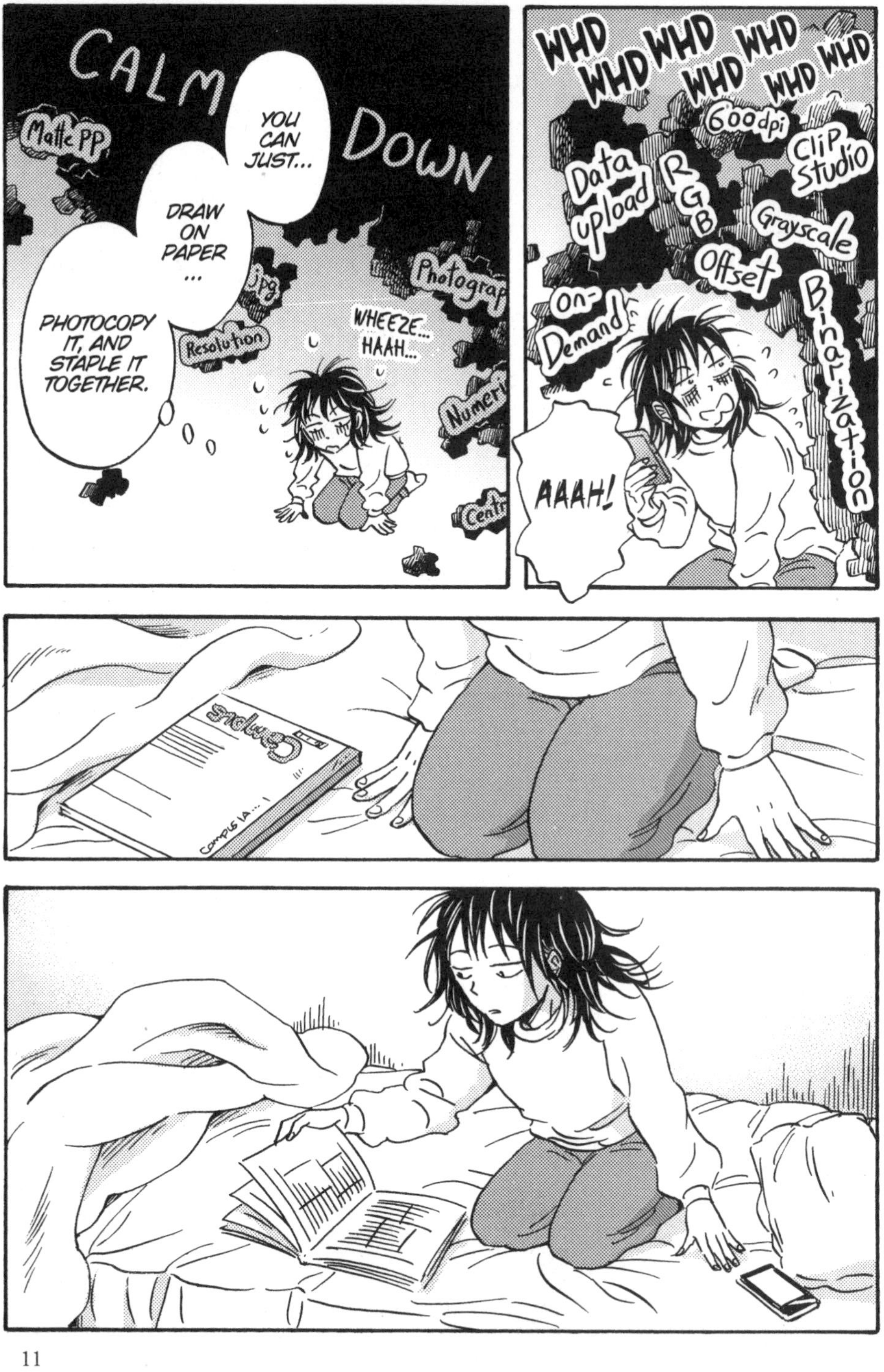
WHD WHD WHD WHD WHD WHD WHD WHD
600dpi
Data upload
RGB
CliP Studio
Grayscale
Offset
On-Demand
Binarization
AAAH!
CALM DOWN
YOU CAN JUST...
DRAW ON PAPER ...
PHOTOCOPY IT, AND STAPLE IT TOGETHER.
Matte PP
jpg
Resolution
WHEEZE... HAAH...
Campus

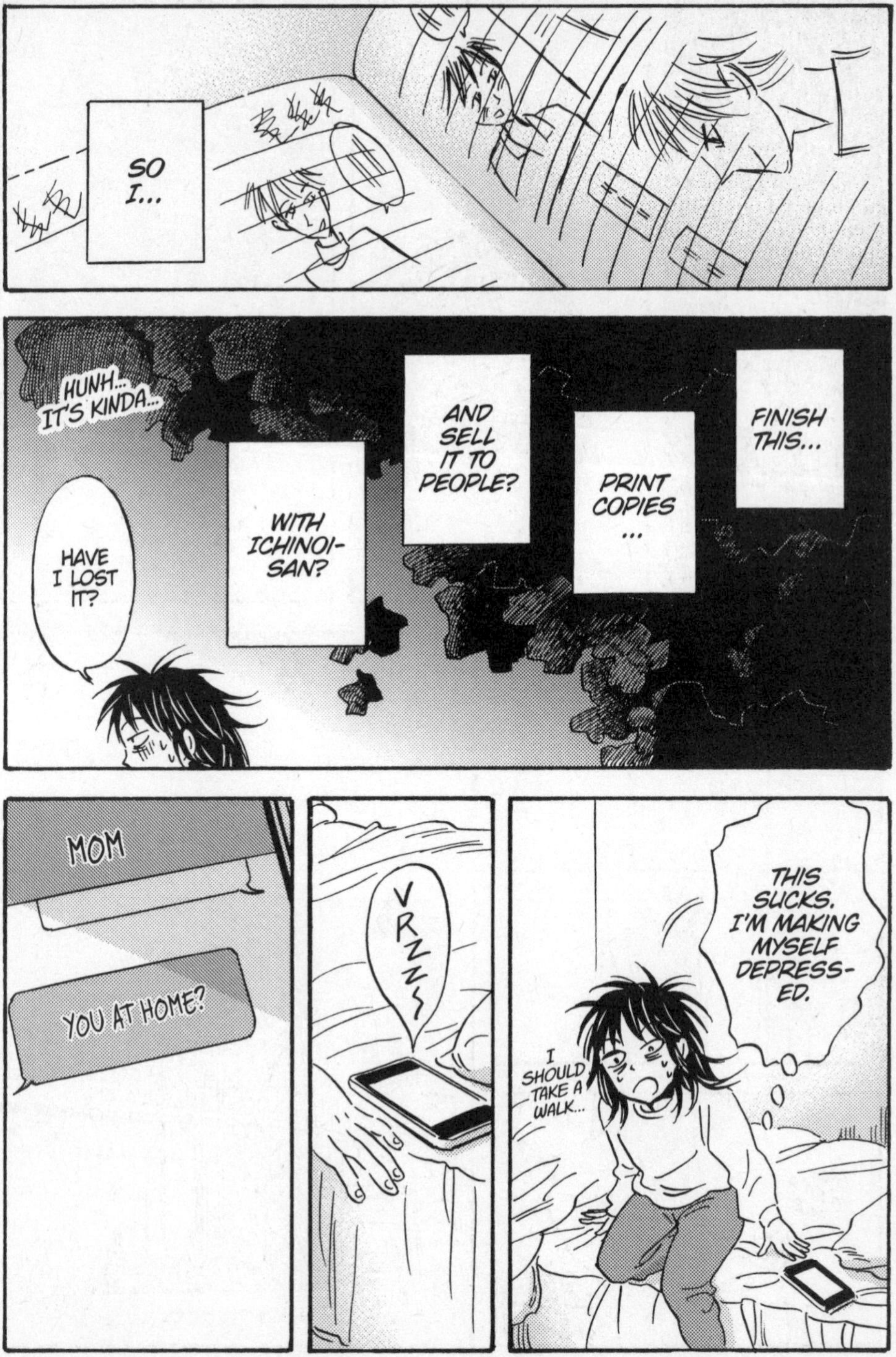
SO I...
FINISH THIS...
PRINT COPIES ...
AND SELL IT TO PEOPLE?
WITH ICHINOI-SAN?
HUNH... IT'S KINDA...
HAVE I LOST IT?
THIS SUCKS. I'M MAKING MYSELF DEPRESS-ED.
I SHOULD TAKE A WALK...
VRZZ
MOM
YOU AT HOME?

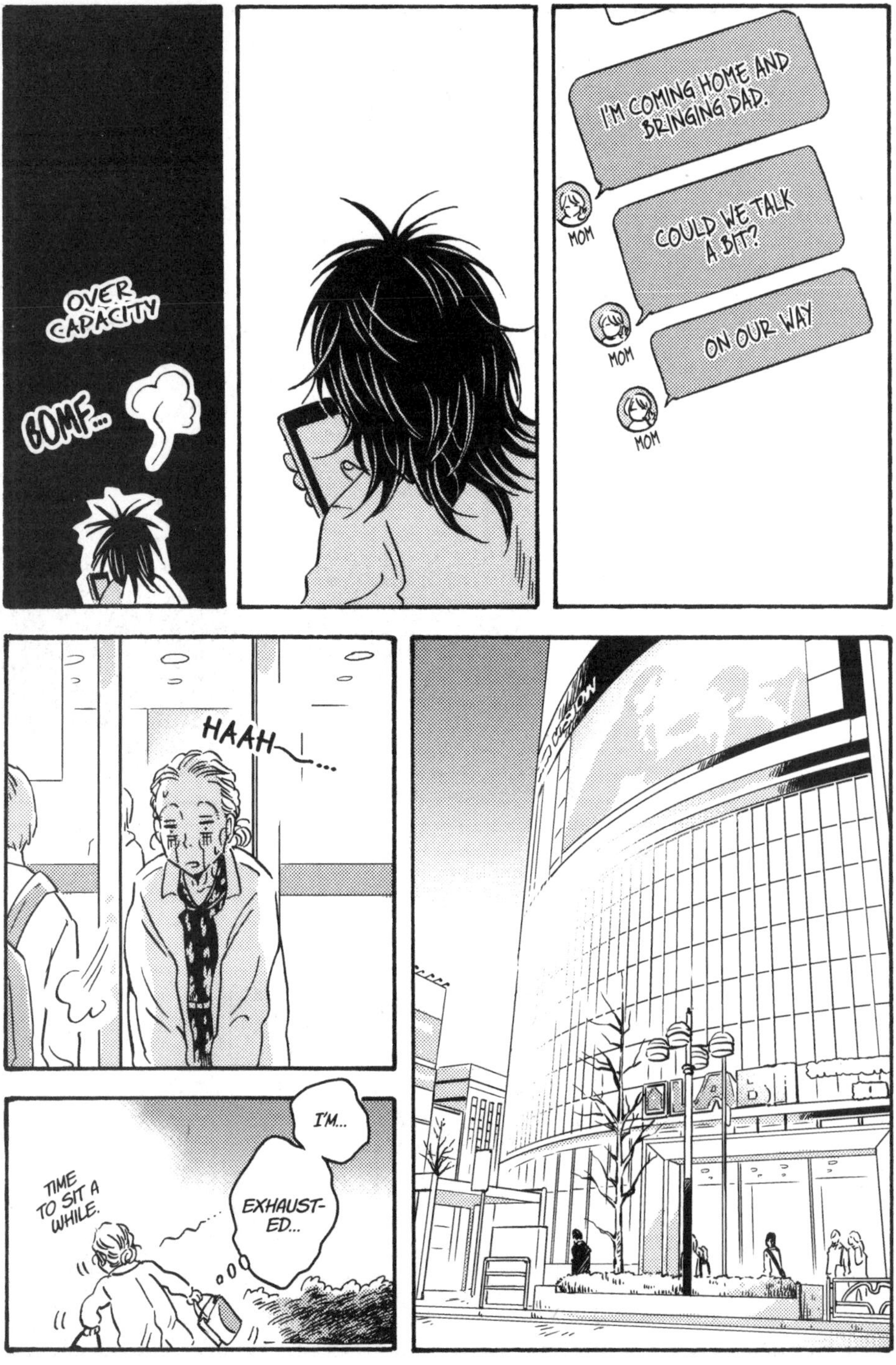
I'M COMING HOME AND BRINGING DAD.
MOM
COULD WE TALK A BIT?
MOM
ON OUR WAY
MOM
OVER CAPACITY
BOMF...
HAAH~...
I'M...
EXHAUST-ED...
TIME TO SIT A WHILE.

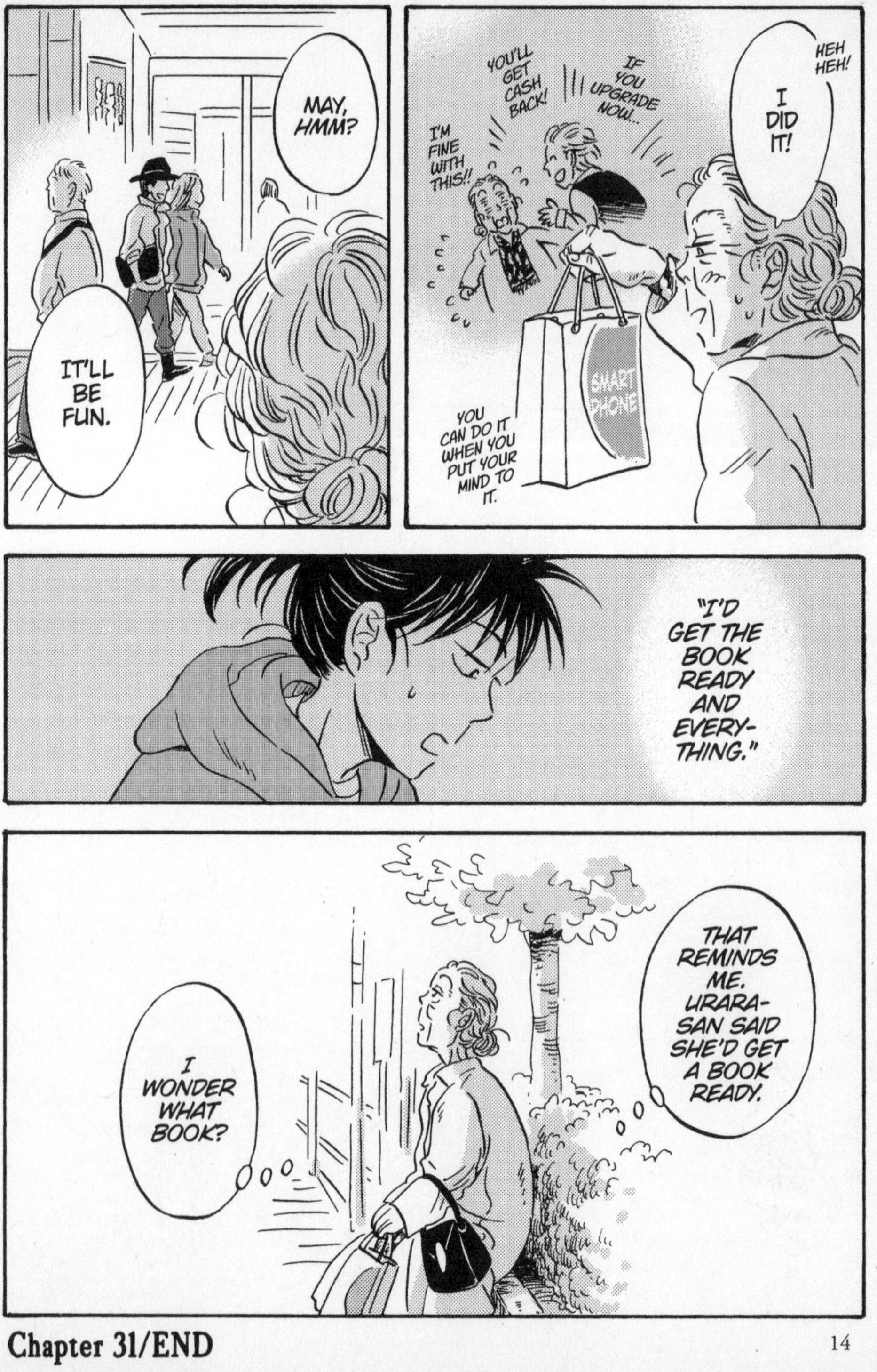
HEH HEH!
I DID IT!
IF YOU UPGRADE NOW...
YOU'LL GET CASH BACK!
I'M FINE WITH THIS!!
SMART PHONE
YOU CAN DO IT WHEN YOU PUT YOUR MIND TO IT.
MAY, HMM?
IT'LL BE FUN.
"I'D GET THE BOOK READY AND EVERY-THING."
THAT REMINDS ME. URARA-SAN SAID SHE'D GET A BOOK READY.
I WONDER WHAT BOOK?

Chapter 31/END

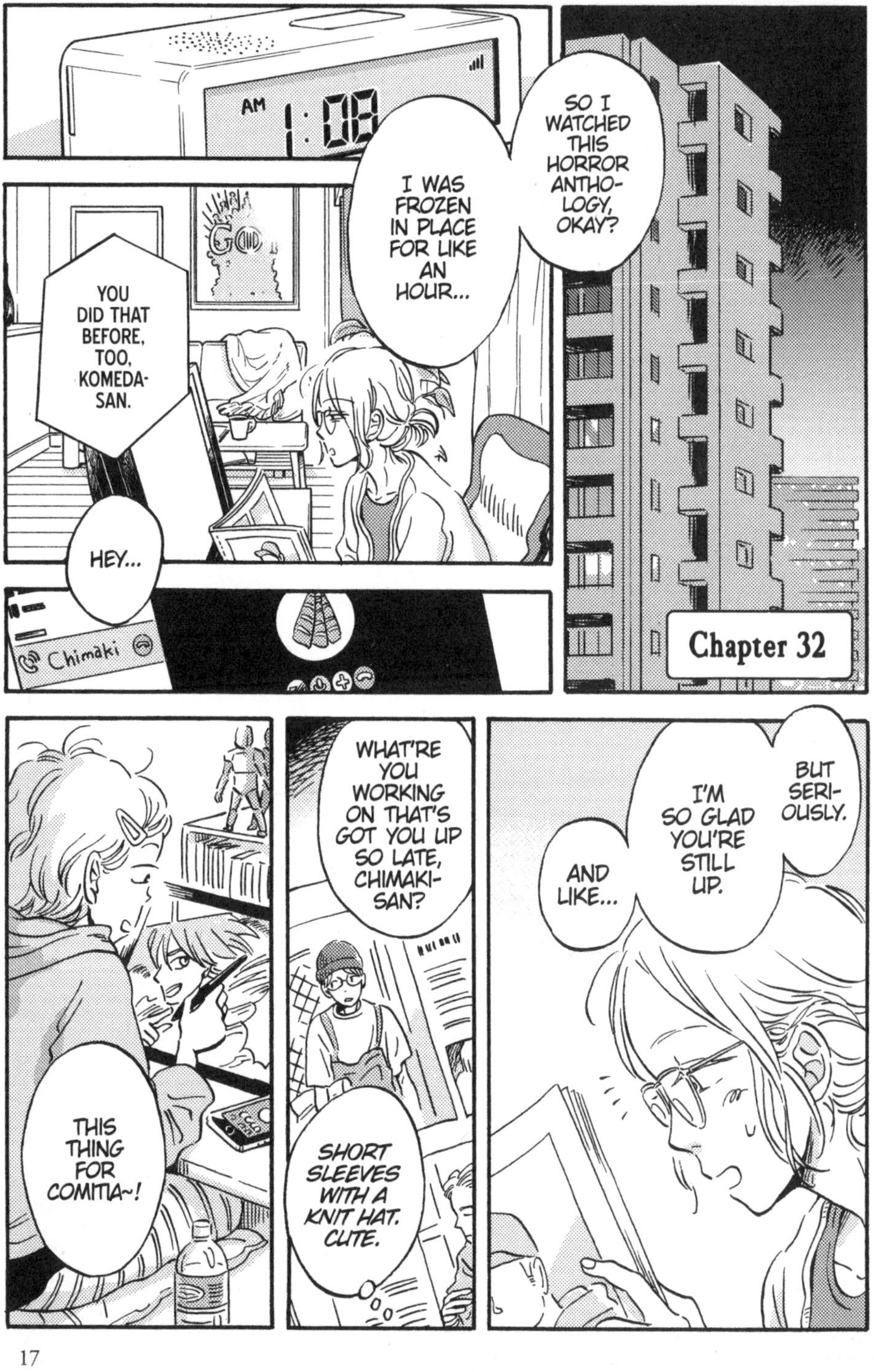
Chapter 32
SO I WATCHED THIS HORROR ANTHOLOGY, OKAY?
AM 1:08
I WAS FROZEN IN PLACE FOR LIKE AN HOUR...
YOU DID THAT BEFORE, TOO, KOMEDA-SAN.
HEY...
Chimaki
BUT SERIOUSLY.
I'M SO GLAD YOU'RE STILL UP.
AND LIKE...
WHAT'RE YOU WORKING ON THAT'S GOT YOU UP SO LATE, CHIMAKI-SAN?
SHORT SLEEVES WITH A KNIT HAT. CUTE.
THIS THING FOR COMITIA~!

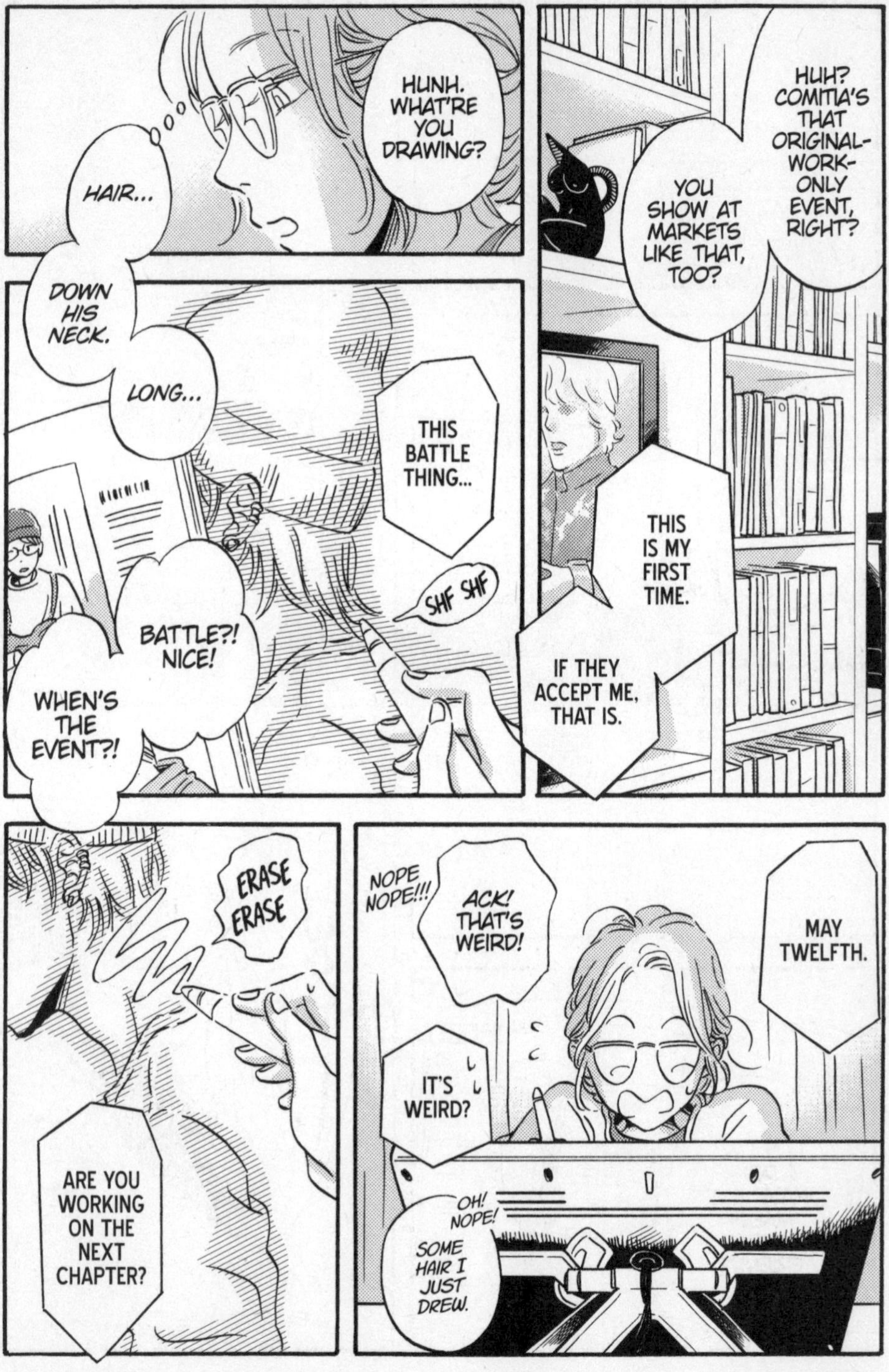

HUH? COMITIA'S THAT ORIGINAL-WORK-ONLY EVENT, RIGHT?
YOU SHOW AT MARKETS LIKE THAT, TOO?
THIS IS MY FIRST TIME.
IF THEY ACCEPT ME, THAT IS.
HUNH. WHAT'RE YOU DRAWING?
HAIR...
DOWN HIS NECK.
LONG...
THIS BATTLE THING...
SHF SHF
BATTLE?! NICE!
WHEN'S THE EVENT?!
MAY TWELFTH.
ACK! THAT'S WEIRD!
NOPE NOPE!!!
IT'S WEIRD?
OH! NOPE!
SOME HAIR I JUST DREW.
ERASE ERASE
ARE YOU WORKING ON THE NEXT CHAPTER?

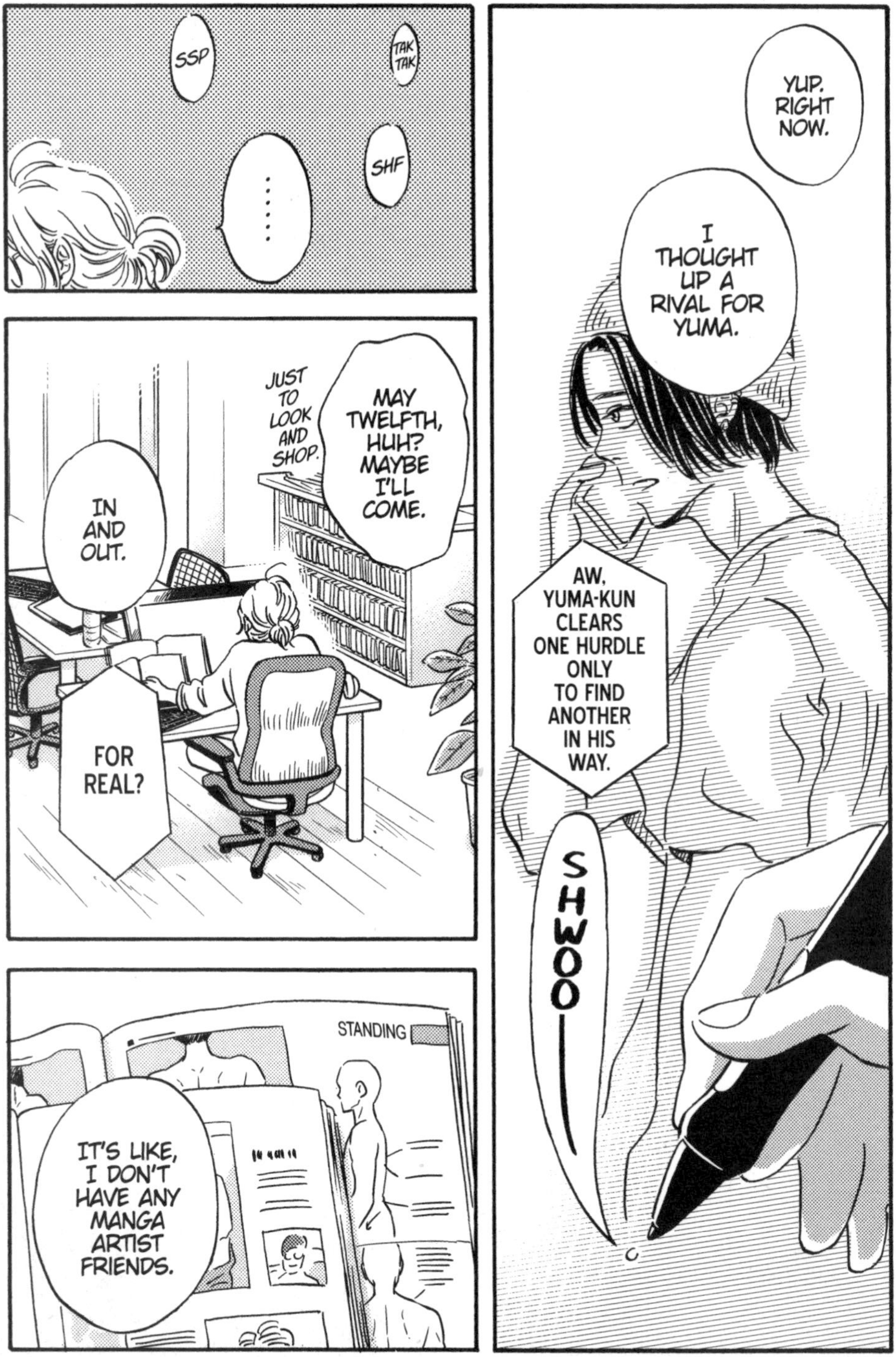
YUP. RIGHT NOW.
I THOUGHT UP A RIVAL FOR YUMA.
AW, YUMA-KUN CLEARS ONE HURDLE ONLY TO FIND ANOTHER IN HIS WAY.
SHWOO—
TAK TAK
SHF
......
SSP
MAY TWELFTH, HUH? MAYBE I'LL COME.
JUST TO LOOK AND SHOP.
IN AND OUT.
FOR REAL?
STANDING
IT'S LIKE, I DON'T HAVE ANY MANGA ARTIST FRIENDS.

I WANNA SEE OTHER PEOPLE WHO DRAW.
IN PERSON.
SOME-TIMES.
DID YOU WANT TO LEAVE SOME OF YOUR BOOKS IN MY SPACE, THEN?
FOR REAL?
ESSEN-TIALLY...
SPRING SEMESTER OF TWELFTH GRADE BEGINS TODAY.
THE TRUTH IS, THESE TWO WEEKS OF SPRING BREAK ARE IMPOR-TANT.
THAT MEANS...
WANNA STOP OFF ON THE WAY HOME?
BYE!

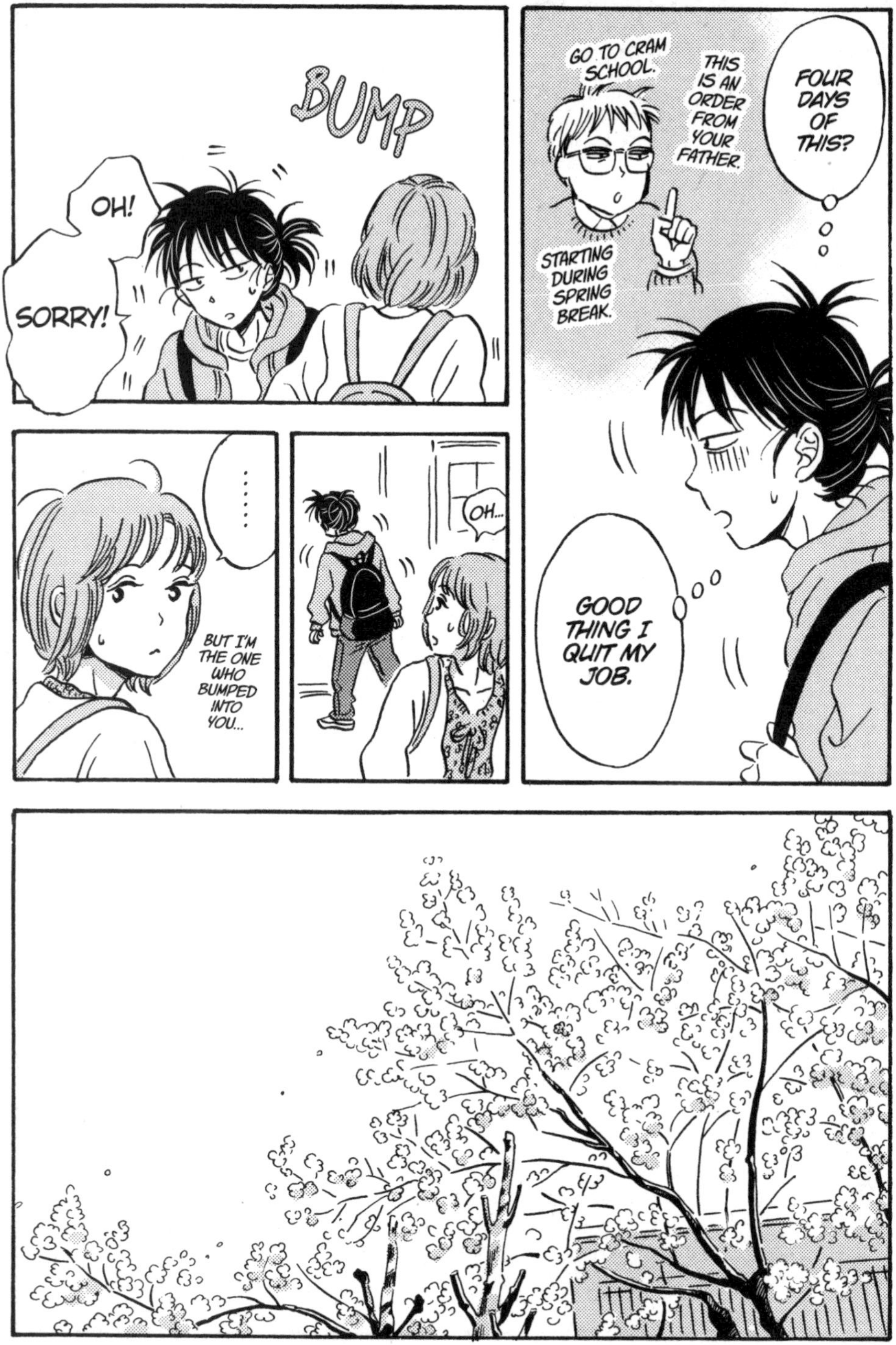
FOUR DAYS OF THIS?
THIS IS AN ORDER FROM YOUR FATHER.
GO TO CRAM SCHOOL.
STARTING DURING SPRING BREAK.
GOOD THING I QUIT MY JOB.
BUMP
OH!
SORRY!
OH...
......
BUT I'M THE ONE WHO BUMPED INTO YOU...

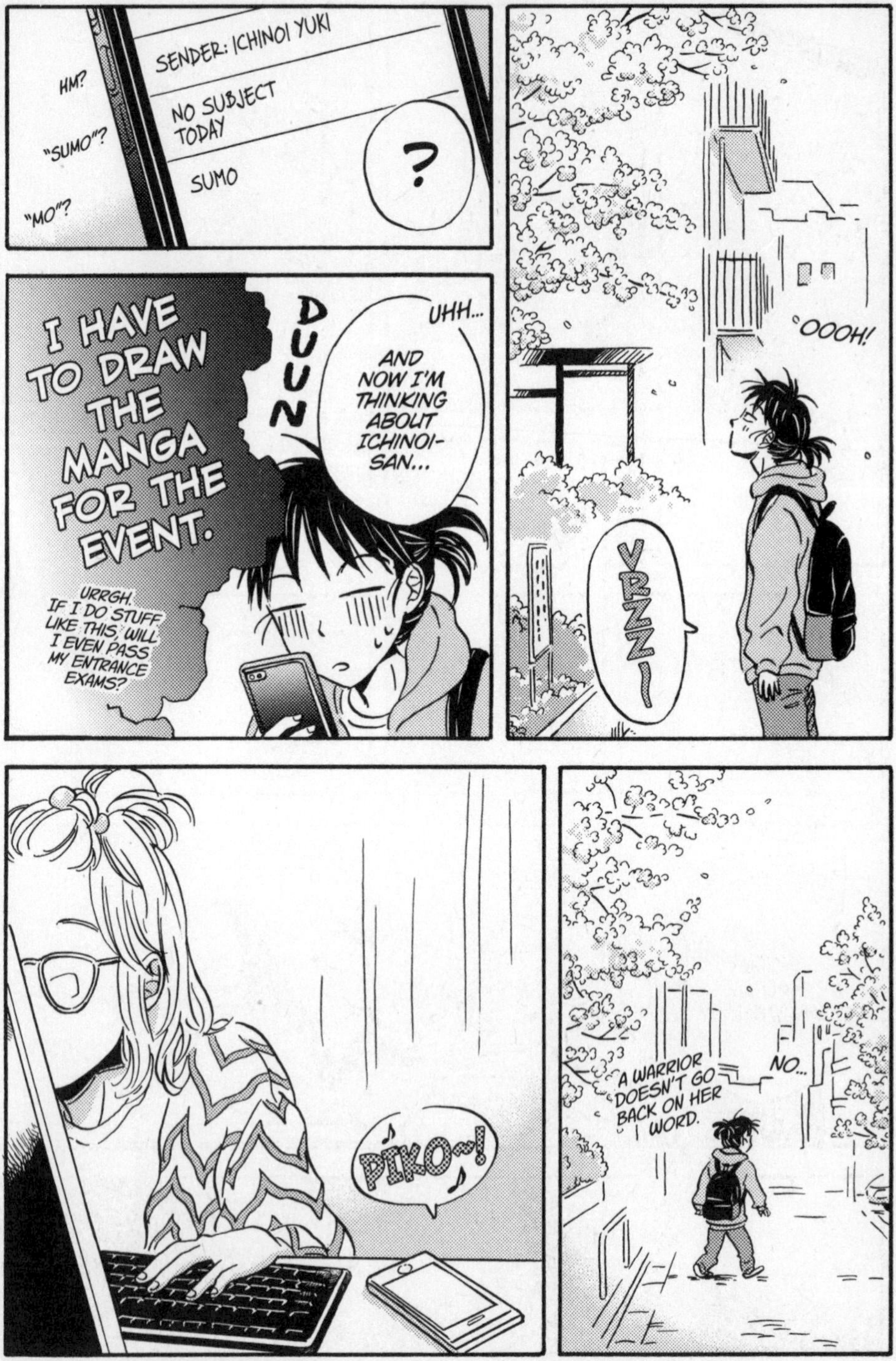
OOOH!
VRZZ
?
SENDER: ICHINOI YUKI
NO SUBJECT
TODAY
SUMO
HM?
"SUMO"?
"MO"?
UHH...
AND NOW I'M THINKING ABOUT ICHINOI-SAN...
DUUN
I HAVE TO DRAW THE MANGA FOR THE EVENT.
URRGH. IF I DO STUFF LIKE THIS, WILL I EVEN PASS MY ENTRANCE EXAMS?
NO...
A WARRIOR DOESN'T GO BACK ON HER WORD.
PIKO~!

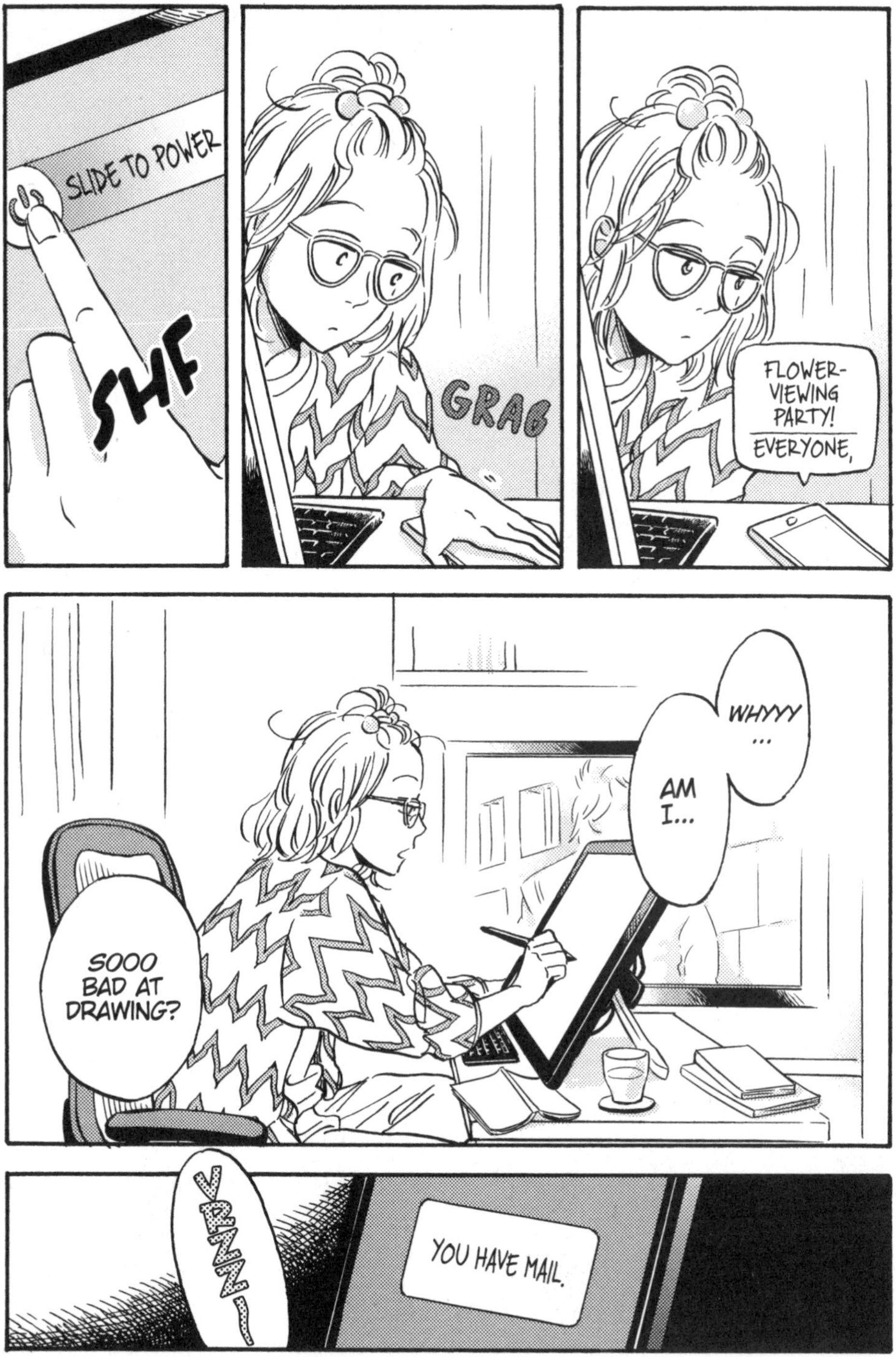
FLOWER-VIEWING PARTY! EVERYONE,
GRAB
SLIDE TO POWER
SHF
WHYYY...
AM I...
SOOO BAD AT DRAWING?
YOU HAVE MAIL.
VRNN—

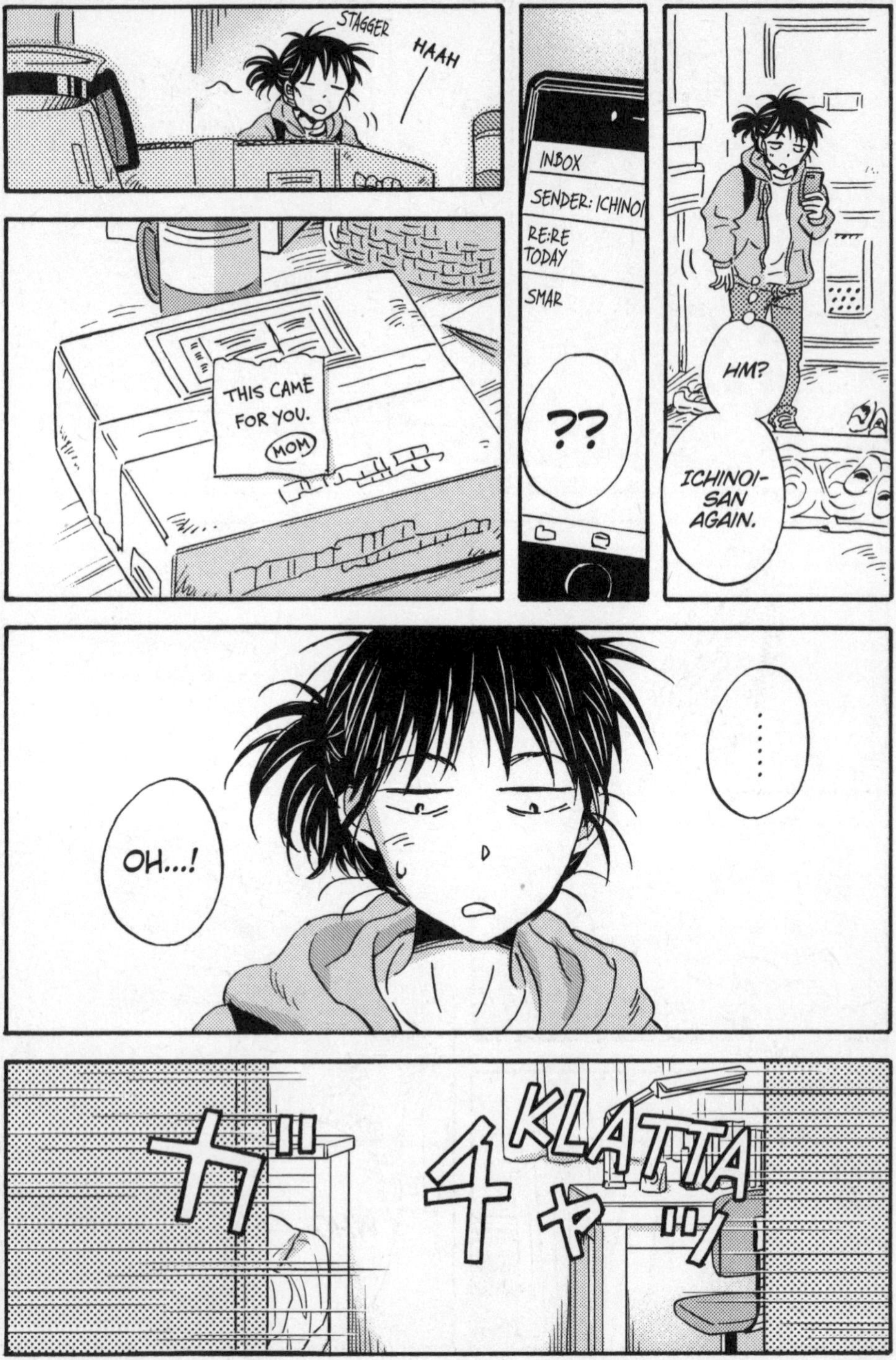
HM?
ICHINOI-SAN AGAIN.
INBOX
SENDER: ICHINOI
RE:RE TODAY
SMAR
??
STAGGER
HAAH
THIS CAME FOR YOU. MOM
......
OH...!
KLATTA

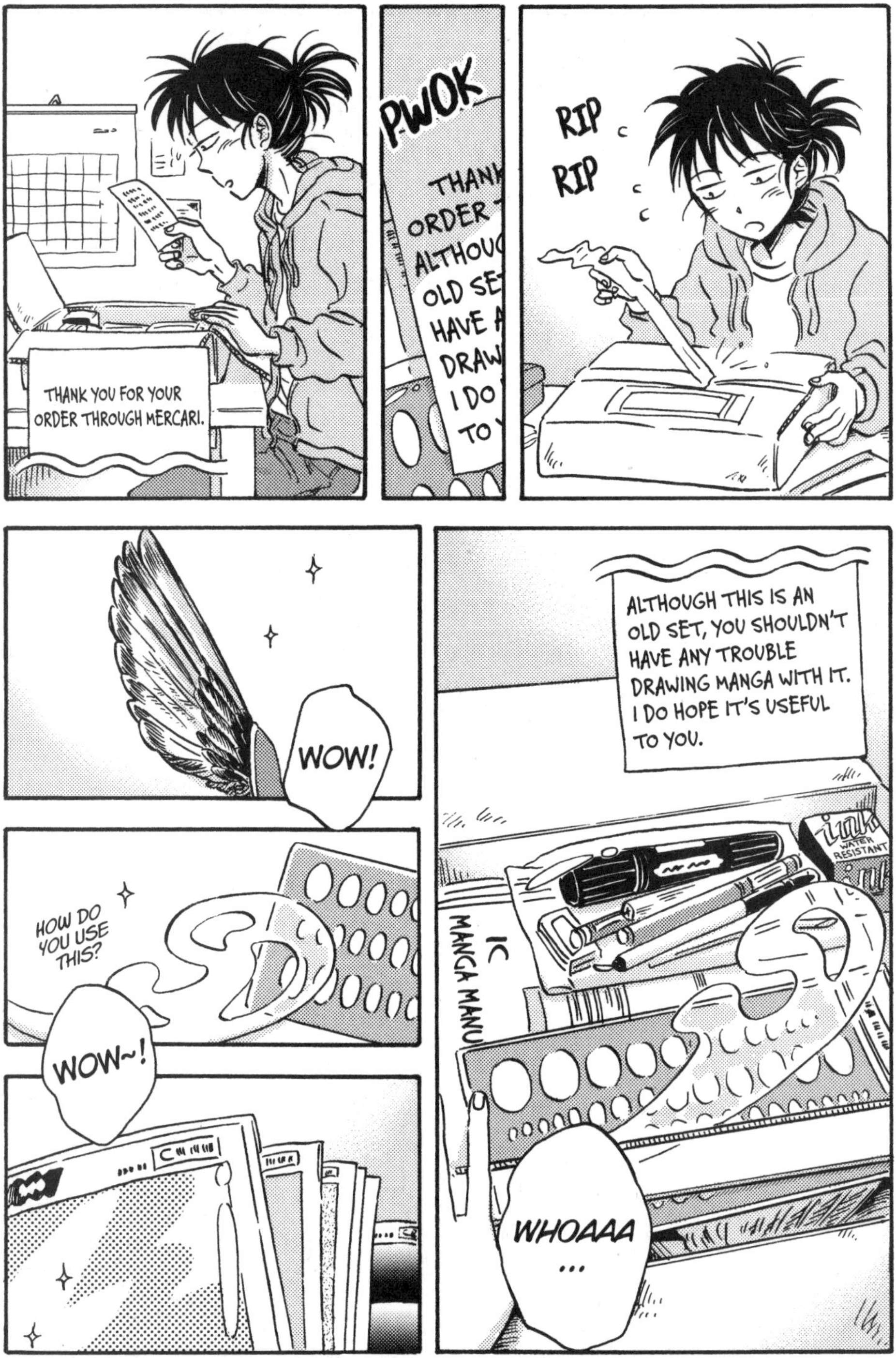
RIP
RIP
PWOK
THANK YOU FOR YOUR ORDER THROUGH MERCARI.
ALTHOUGH THIS IS AN OLD SET, YOU SHOULDN'T HAVE ANY TROUBLE DRAWING MANGA WITH IT. I DO HOPE IT'S USEFUL TO YOU.
ink WATER RESISTANT
MANGA MANU
WHOAAA ...
WOW!
HOW DO YOU USE THIS?
WOW~!

LIKE
THIS?

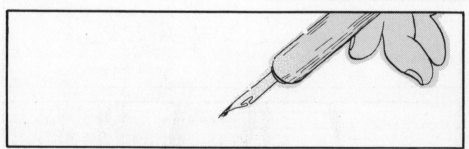

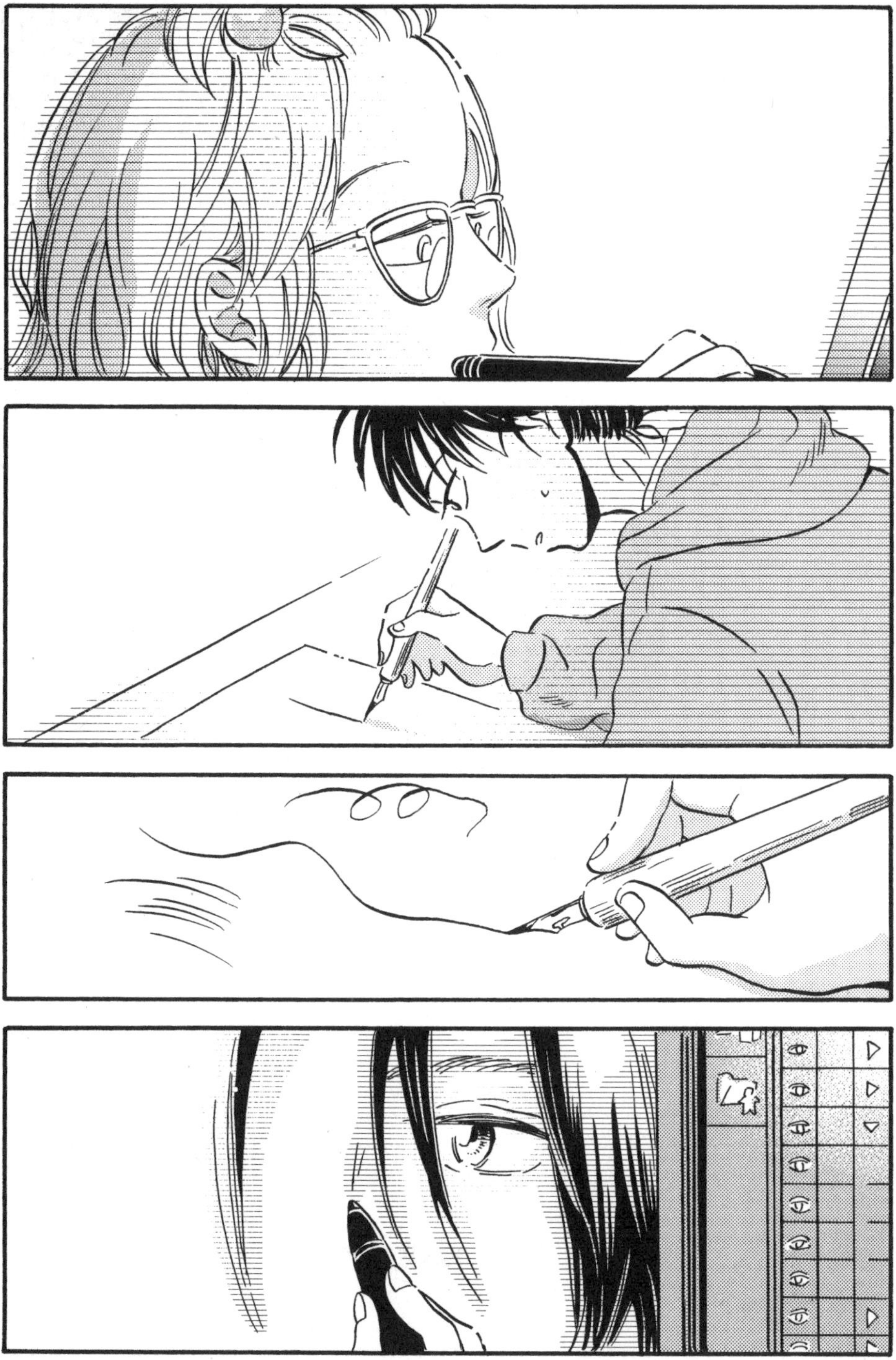

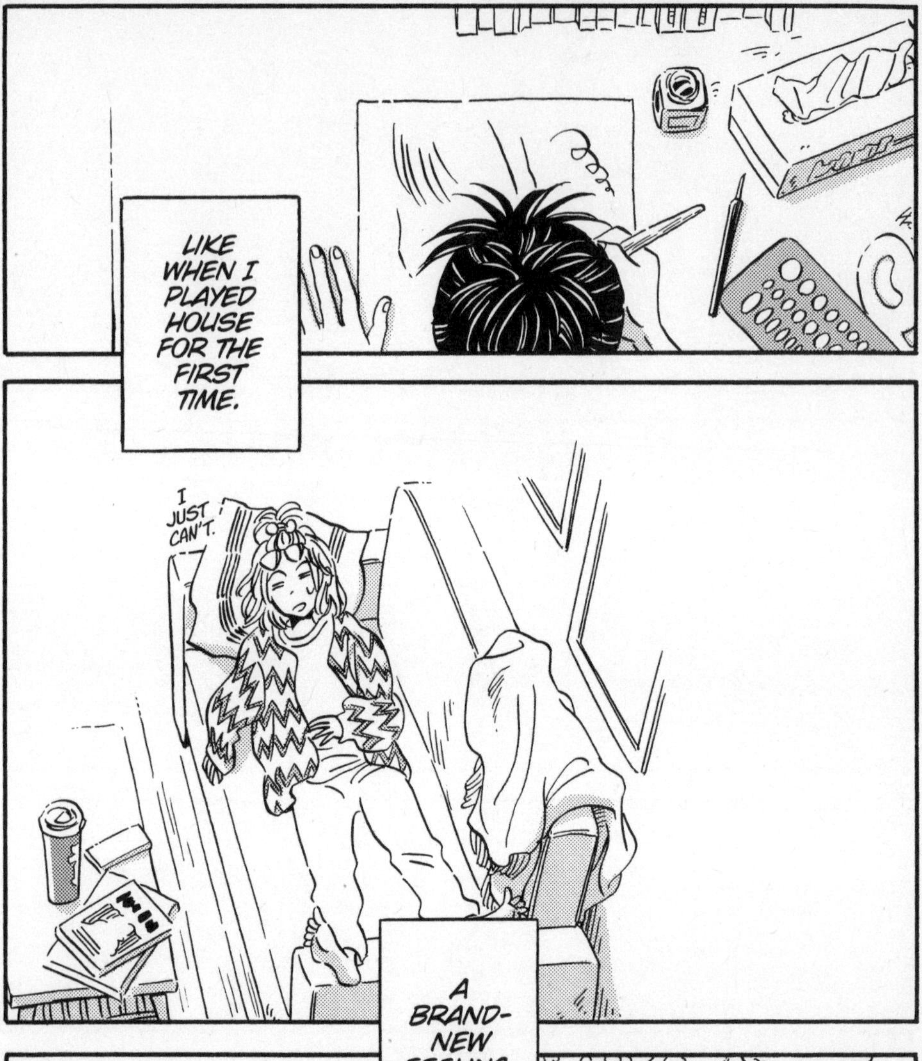
LIKE WHEN I PLAYED HOUSE FOR THE FIRST TIME.
I JUST CAN'T.
A BRAND-NEW FEELING.

Chapter 32/END

metamorphosis

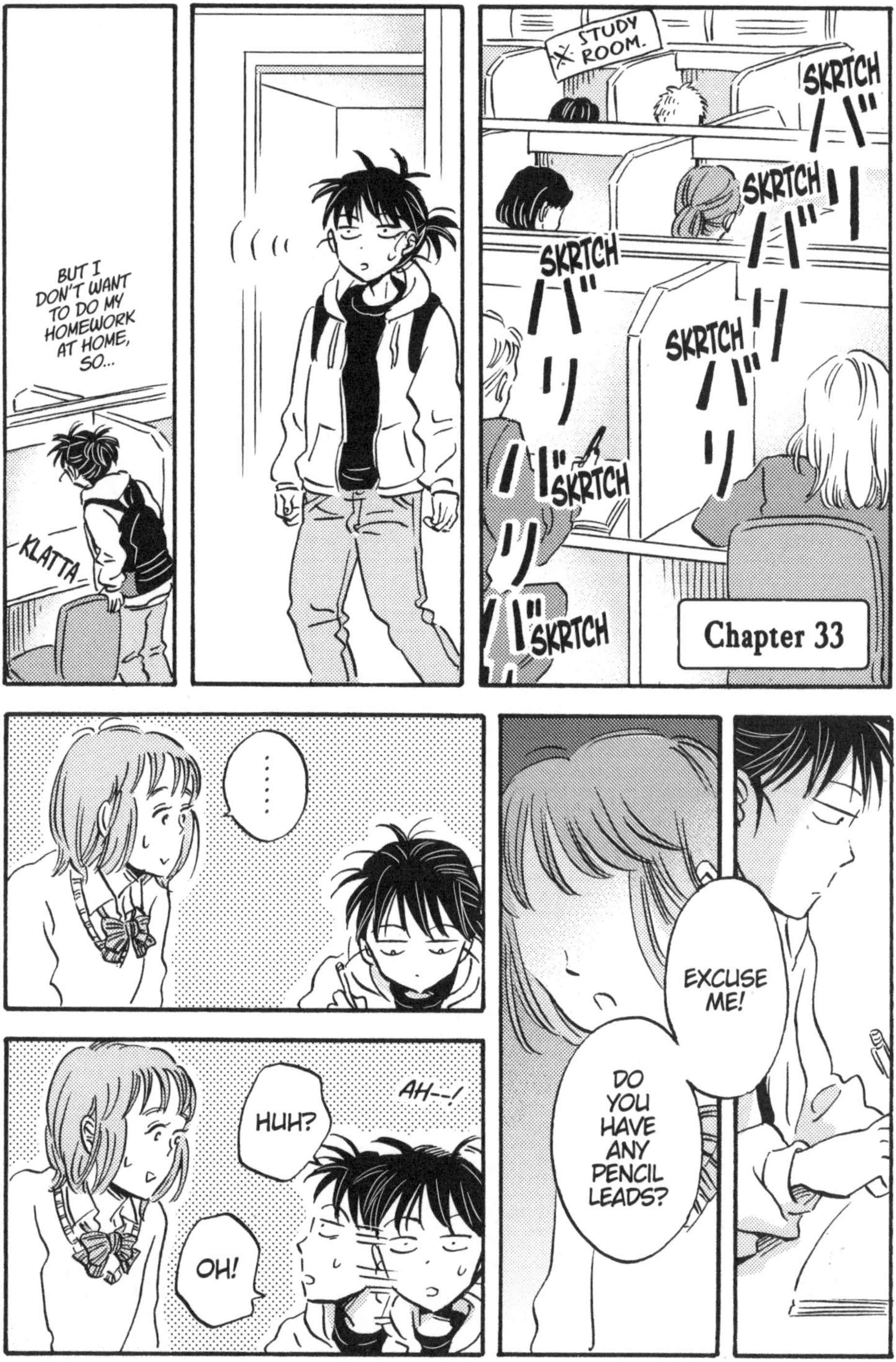
STUDY ROOM.
SKRTCH
バリ
SKRTCH
バリ
SKRTCH
バリ
SKRTCH
バリ
SKRTCH
バリ
SKRTCH
Chapter 33
BUT I DON'T WANT TO DO MY HOMEWORK AT HOME, SO...
KLATTA
EXCUSE ME!
DO YOU HAVE ANY PENCIL LEADS?
......
AH--!
HUH?
OH!

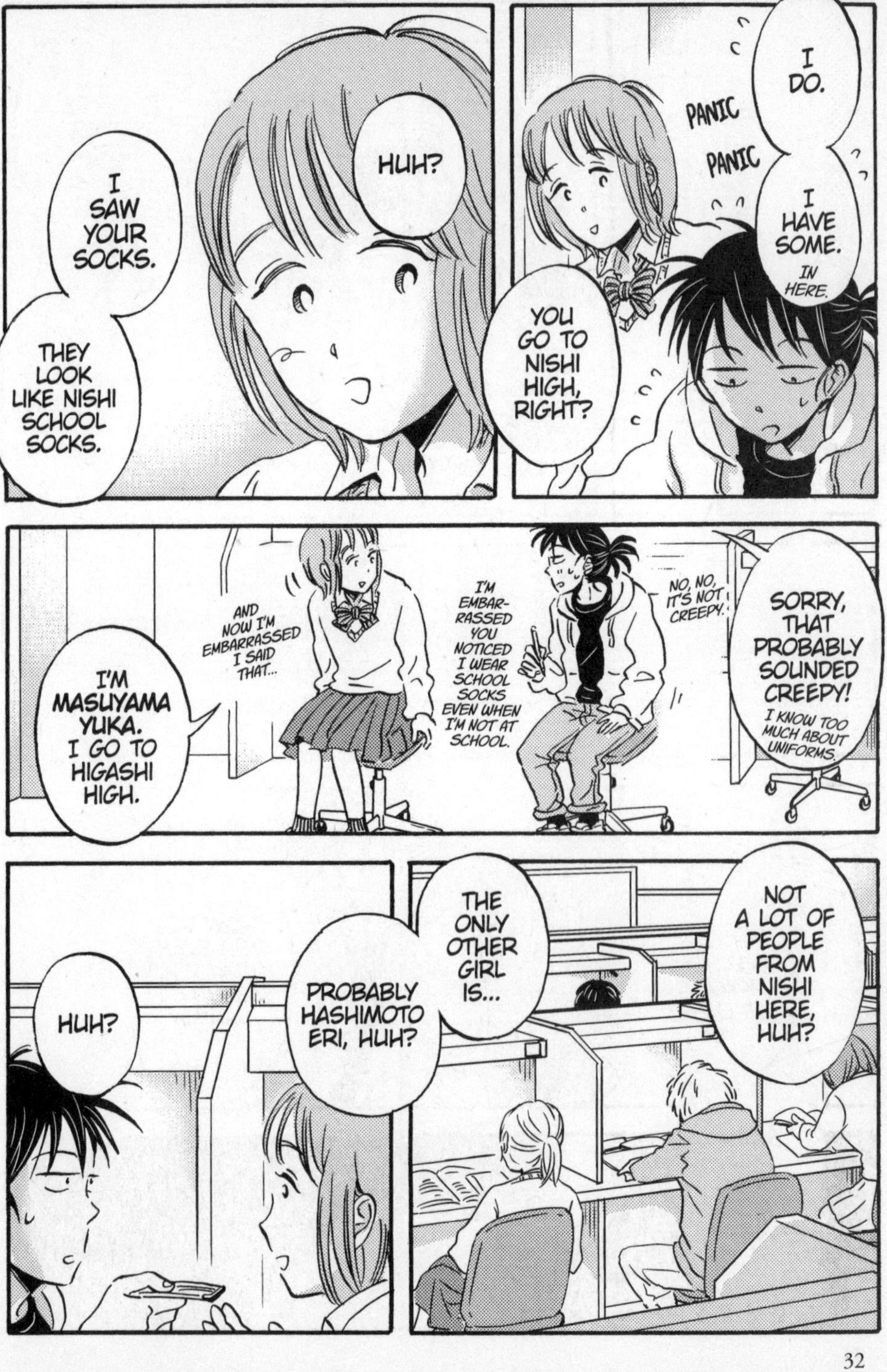
YOU GO TO NISHI HIGH, RIGHT?
I DO.
PANIC
PANIC
I HAVE SOME.
IN HERE.
HUH?
I SAW YOUR SOCKS.
THEY LOOK LIKE NISHI SCHOOL SOCKS.
SORRY, THAT PROBABLY SOUNDED CREEPY!
I KNOW TOO MUCH ABOUT UNIFORMS.
NO, NO, IT'S NOT CREEPY.
I'M EMBARRASSED YOU NOTICED I WEAR SCHOOL SOCKS EVEN WHEN I'M NOT AT SCHOOL.
AND NOW I'M EMBARRASSED I SAID THAT...
I'M MASUYAMA YUKA. I GO TO HIGASHI HIGH.
NOT A LOT OF PEOPLE FROM NISHI HERE, HUH?
THE ONLY OTHER GIRL IS...
PROBABLY HASHIMOTO ERI, HUH?
HUH?

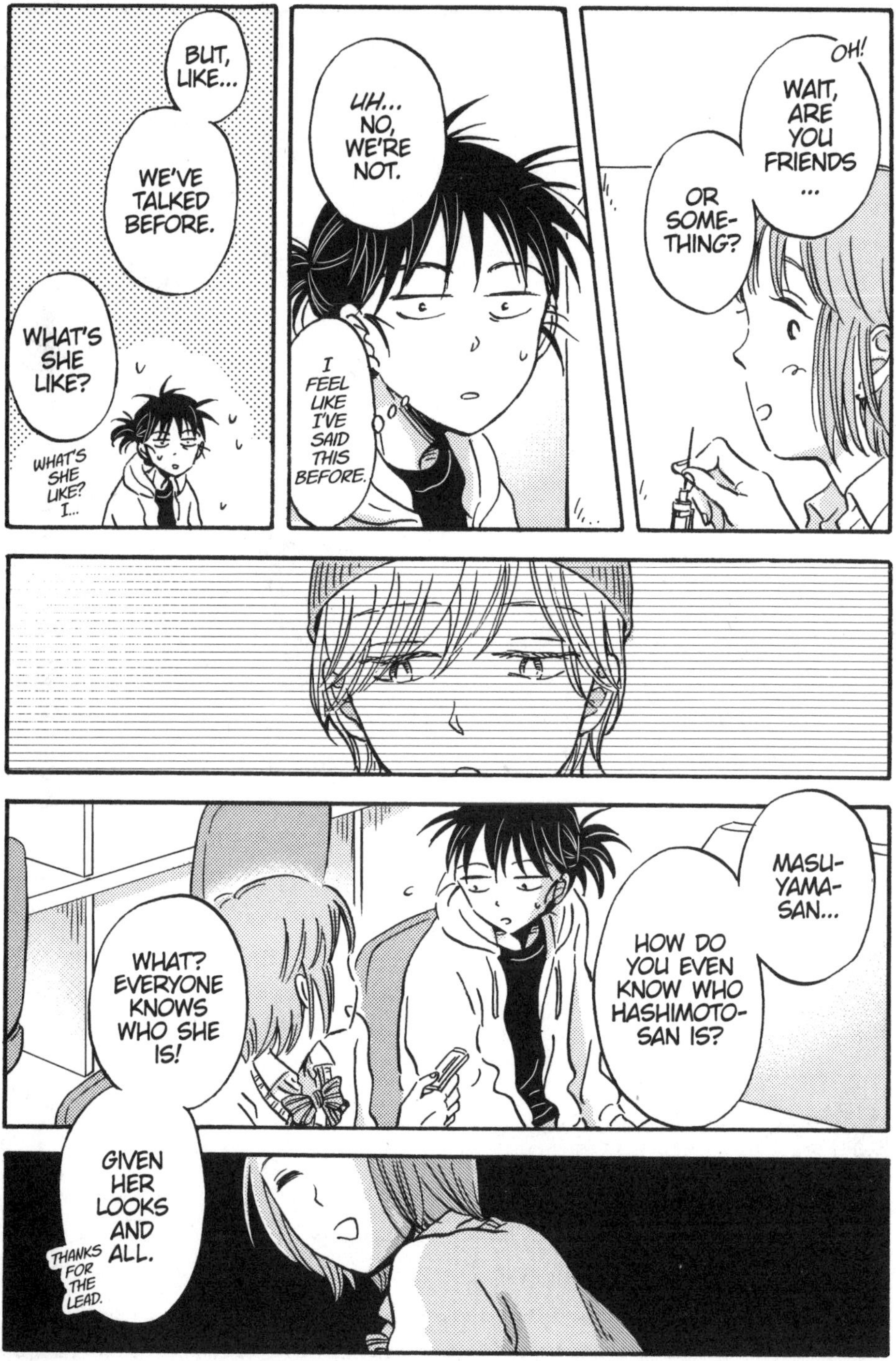
OH!
WAIT, ARE YOU FRIENDS ...
OR SOME-THING?
UH... NO, WE'RE NOT.
I FEEL LIKE I'VE SAID THIS BEFORE.
BUT, LIKE...
WE'VE TALKED BEFORE.
WHAT'S SHE LIKE?
WHAT'S SHE LIKE? I...
MASU-YAMA-SAN...
HOW DO YOU EVEN KNOW WHO HASHIMOTO-SAN IS?
WHAT? EVERYONE KNOWS WHO SHE IS!
GIVEN HER LOOKS AND ALL.
THANKS FOR THE LEAD.

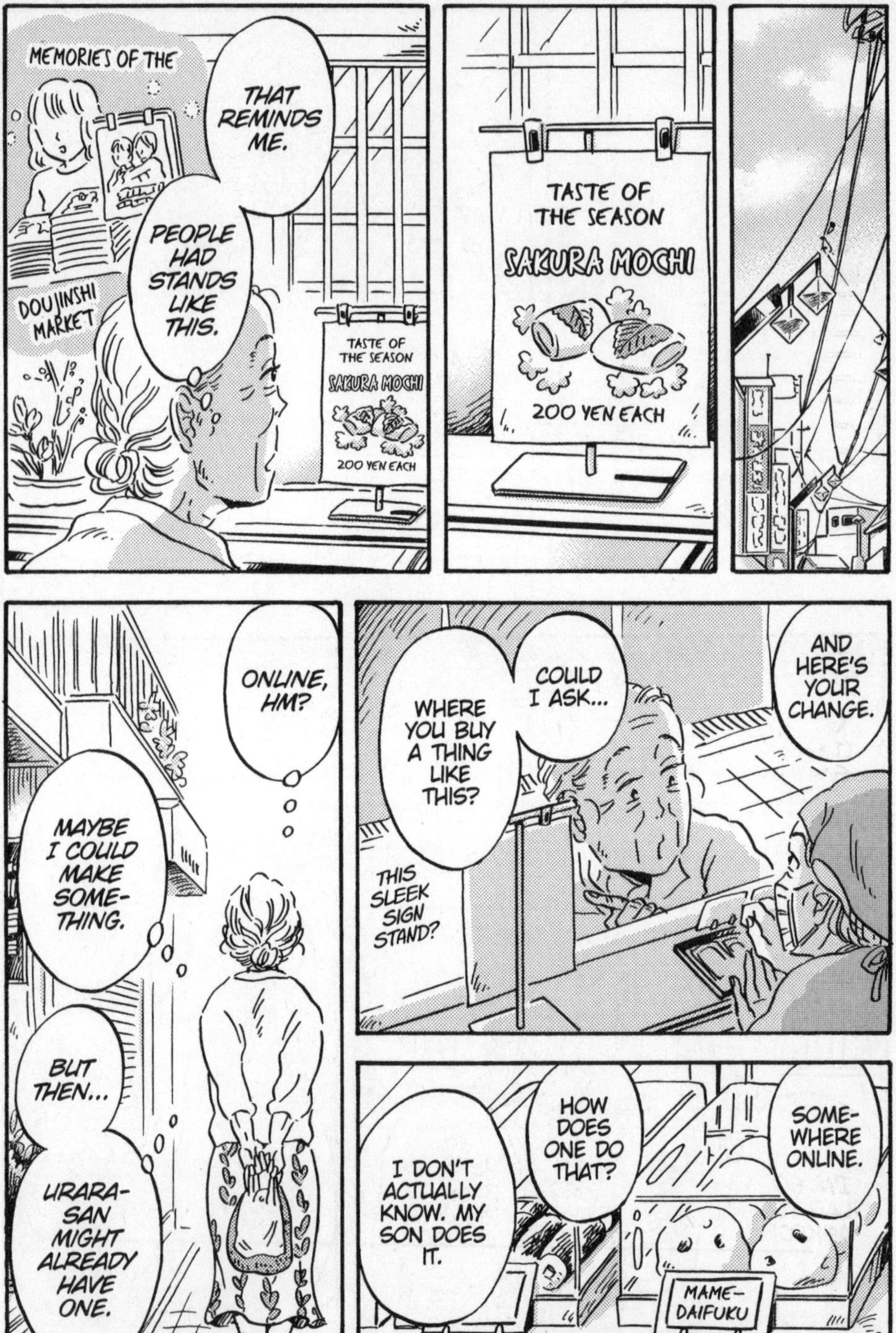
TASTE OF THE SEASON
SAKURA MOCHI
200 YEN EACH
THAT REMINDS ME.
PEOPLE HAD STANDS LIKE THIS.
MEMORIES OF THE DOUJINSHI MARKET
TASTE OF THE SEASON
SAKURA MOCHI
200 YEN EACH
AND HERE'S YOUR CHANGE.
COULD I ASK...
WHERE YOU BUY A THING LIKE THIS?
THIS SLEEK SIGN STAND?
SOME-WHERE ONLINE.
HOW DOES ONE DO THAT?
I DON'T ACTUALLY KNOW. MY SON DOES IT.
MAME-DAIFUKU
ONLINE, HM?
MAYBE I COULD MAKE SOME-THING.
BUT THEN...
URARA-SAN MIGHT ALREADY HAVE ONE.

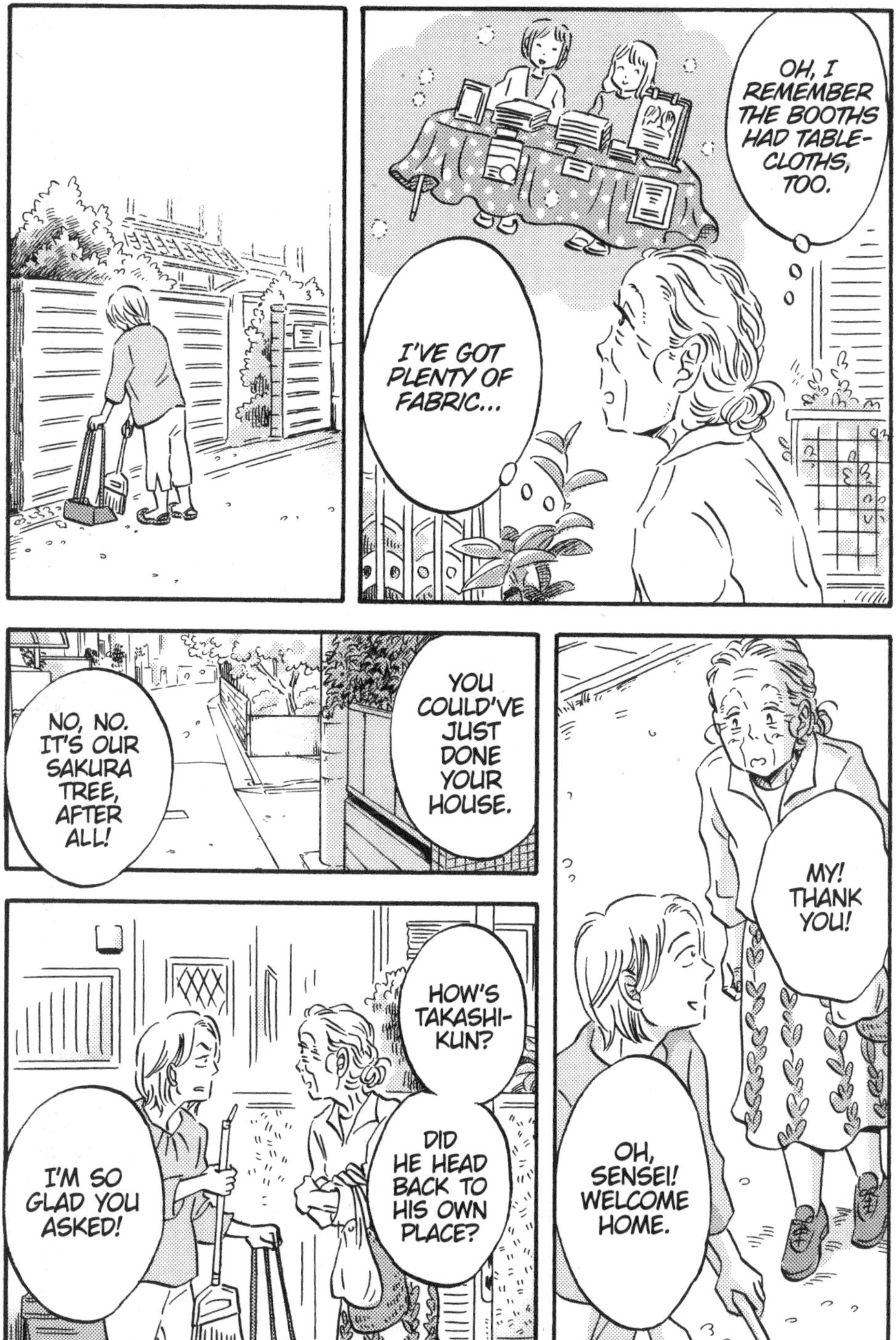
OH, I REMEMBER THE BOOTHS HAD TABLE-CLOTHS, TOO.
I'VE GOT PLENTY OF FABRIC...
OH, SENSEI! WELCOME HOME.
MY! THANK YOU!
YOU COULD'VE JUST DONE YOUR HOUSE.
NO, NO. IT'S OUR SAKURA TREE, AFTER ALL!
HOW'S TAKASHI-KUN?
DID HE HEAD BACK TO HIS OWN PLACE?
I'M SO GLAD YOU ASKED!

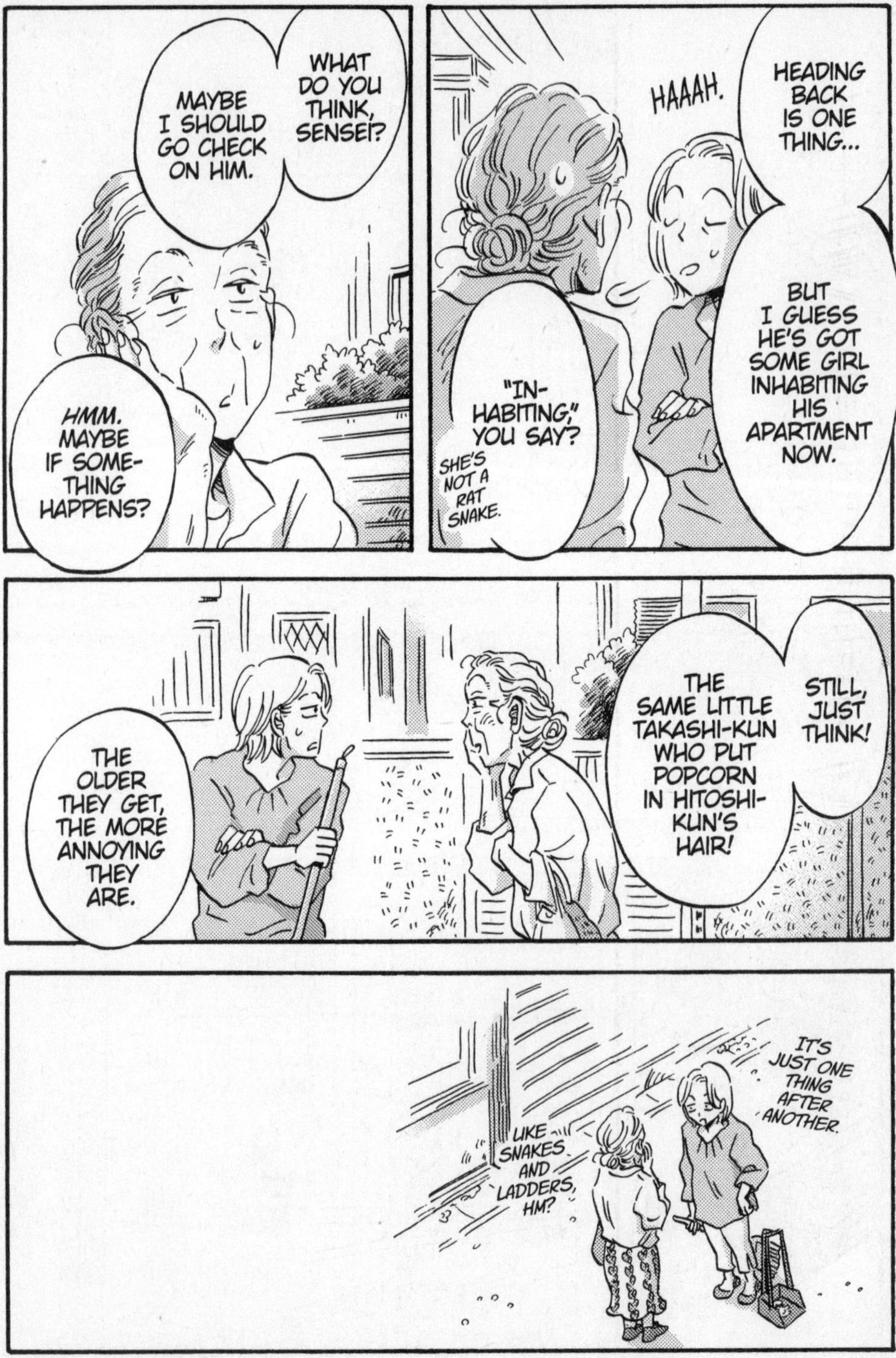
HEADING BACK IS ONE THING...
HAAAH.
BUT I GUESS HE'S GOT SOME GIRL INHABITING HIS APARTMENT NOW.
"IN-HABITING," YOU SAY?
SHE'S NOT A RAT SNAKE.
WHAT DO YOU THINK, SENSEI?
MAYBE I SHOULD GO CHECK ON HIM.
HMM. MAYBE IF SOME-THING HAPPENS?
STILL, JUST THINK!
THE SAME LITTLE TAKASHI-KUN WHO PUT POPCORN IN HITOSHI-KUN'S HAIR!
THE OLDER THEY GET, THE MORE ANNOYING THEY ARE.
IT'S JUST ONE THING AFTER ANOTHER.
LIKE SNAKES AND LADDERS, HM?

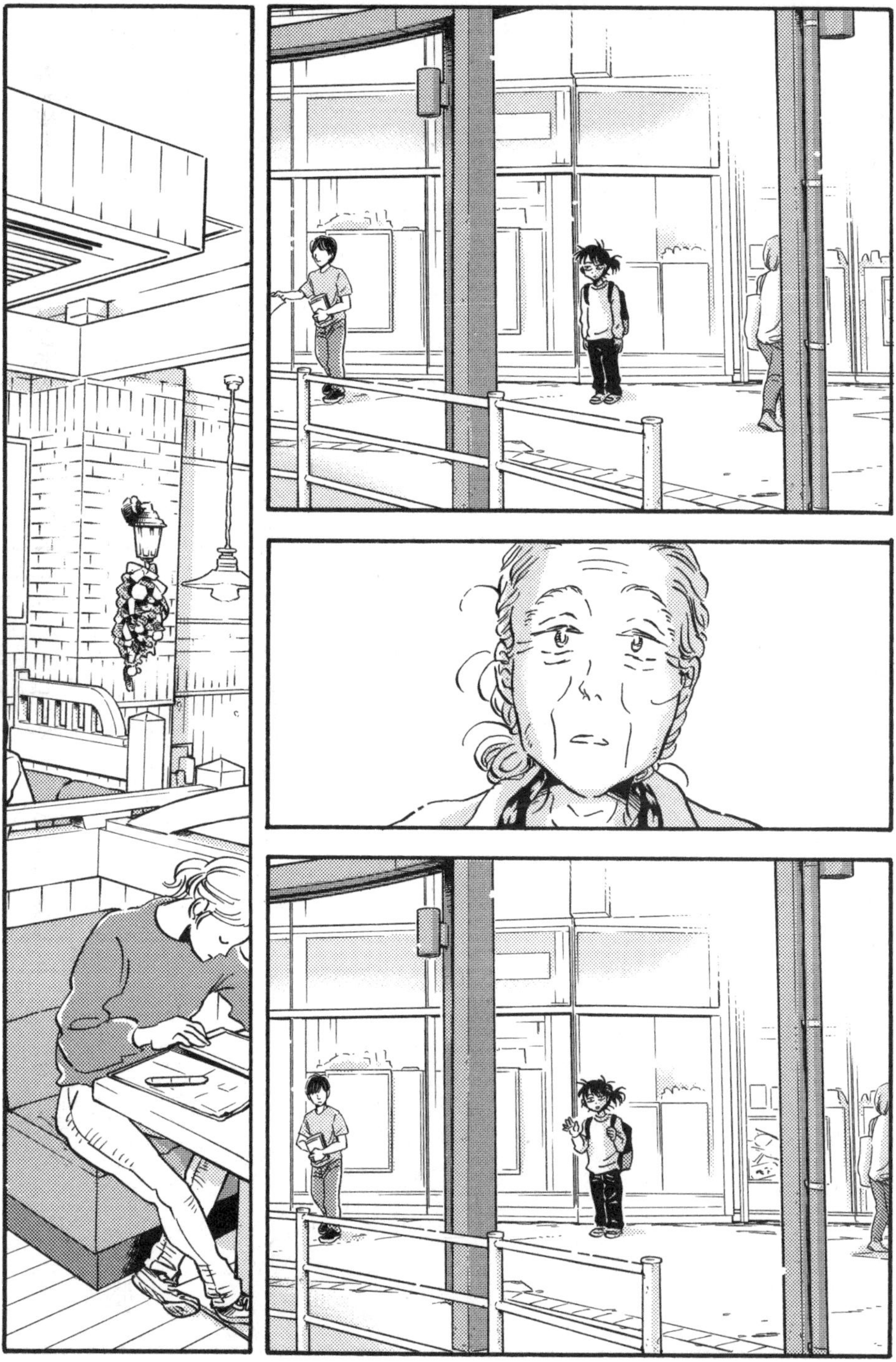

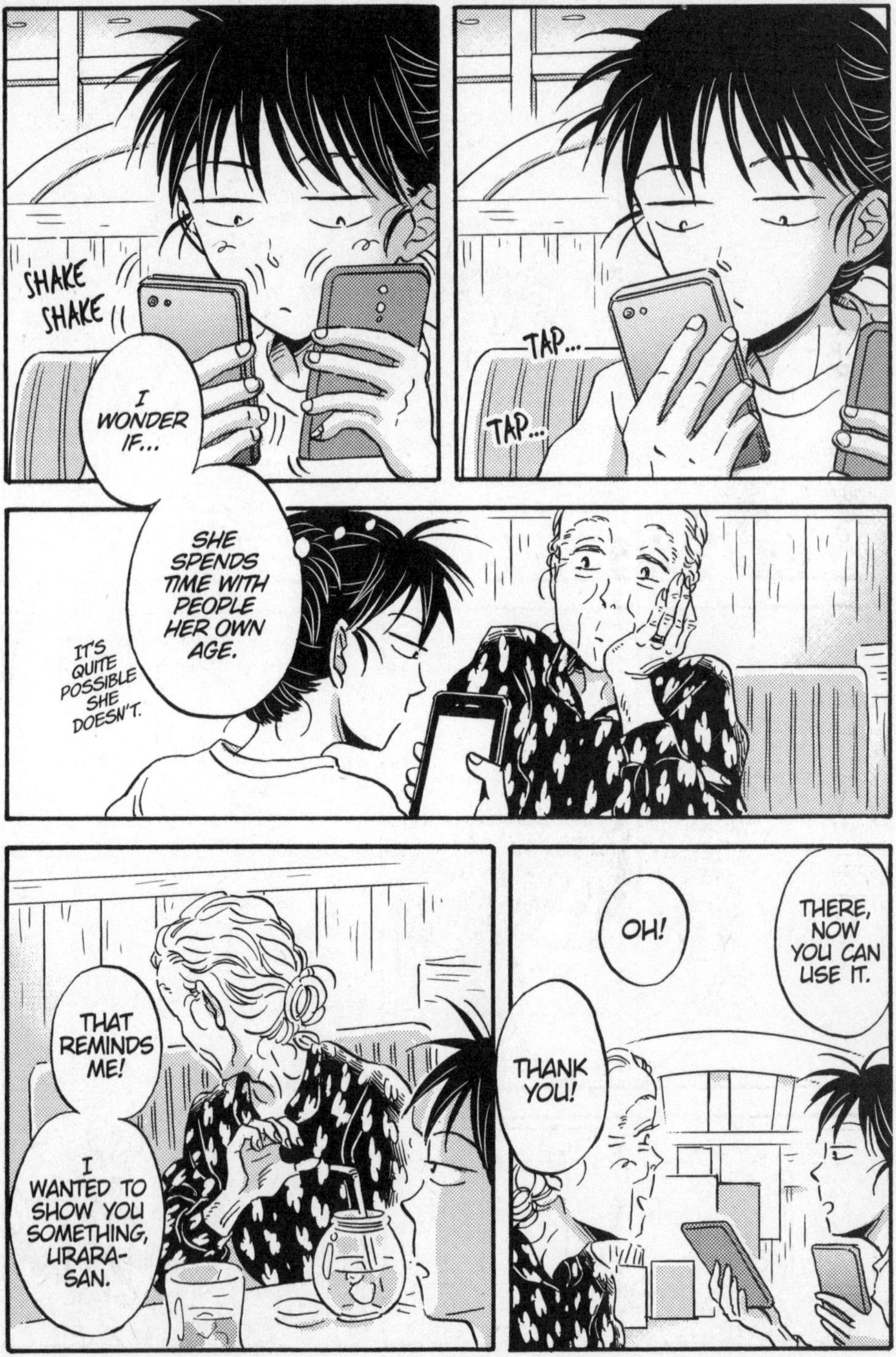
TAP... TAP...
SHAKE SHAKE
I WONDER IF...
SHE SPENDS TIME WITH PEOPLE HER OWN AGE.
IT'S QUITE POSSIBLE SHE DOESN'T.
THERE, NOW YOU CAN USE IT.
OH!
THANK YOU!
THAT REMINDS ME!
I WANTED TO SHOW YOU SOMETHING, URARA-SAN.

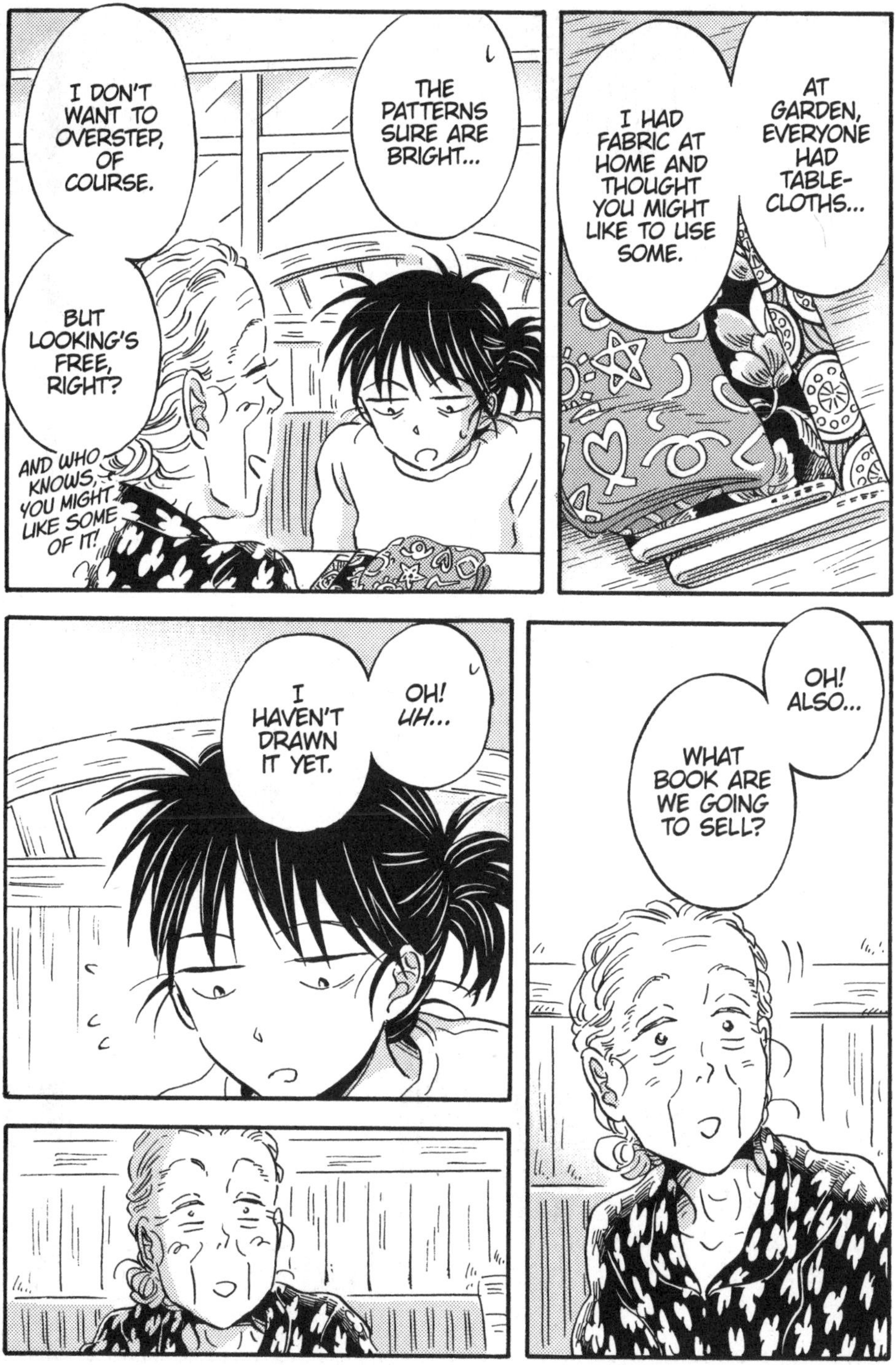
AT GARDEN, EVERYONE HAD TABLE-CLOTHS...
I HAD FABRIC AT HOME AND THOUGHT YOU MIGHT LIKE TO USE SOME.
THE PATTERNS SURE ARE BRIGHT...
I DON'T WANT TO OVERSTEP, OF COURSE.
BUT LOOKING'S FREE, RIGHT?
AND WHO KNOWS, YOU MIGHT LIKE SOME OF IT!
OH! ALSO...
WHAT BOOK ARE WE GOING TO SELL?
OH! UH...
I HAVEN'T DRAWN IT YET.

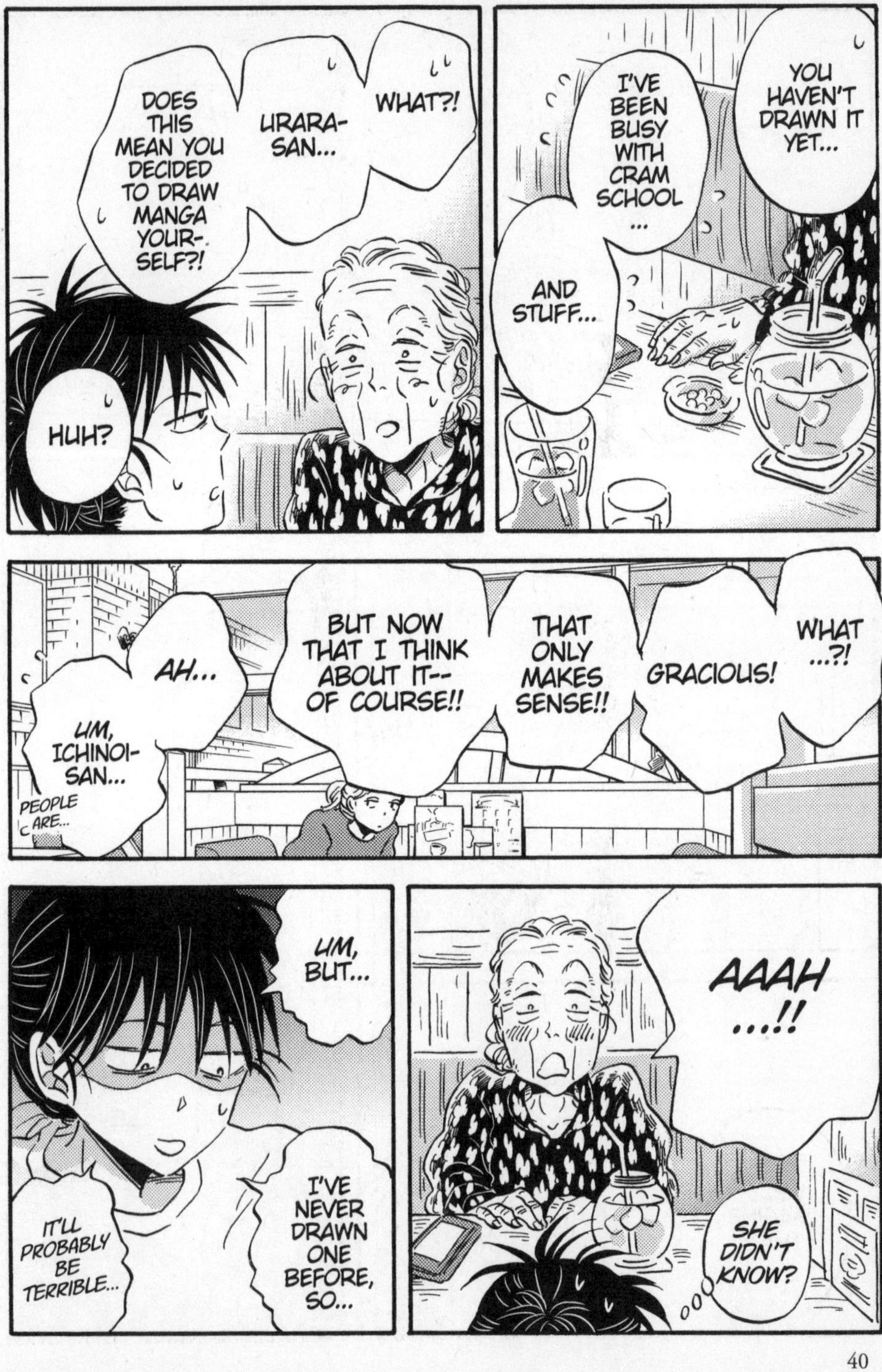
YOU HAVEN'T DRAWN IT YET...
I'VE BEEN BUSY WITH CRAM SCHOOL ...
AND STUFF...
WHAT?!
URARA-SAN...
DOES THIS MEAN YOU DECIDED TO DRAW MANGA YOURSELF?!
HUH?
WHAT ...?!
GRACIOUS!
THAT ONLY MAKES SENSE!!
BUT NOW THAT I THINK ABOUT IT-- OF COURSE!!
AH...
UM, ICHINOI-SAN...
PEOPLE ARE...
AAAH ...!!
SHE DIDN'T KNOW?
UM, BUT...
I'VE NEVER DRAWN ONE BEFORE, SO...
IT'LL PROBABLY BE TERRIBLE...

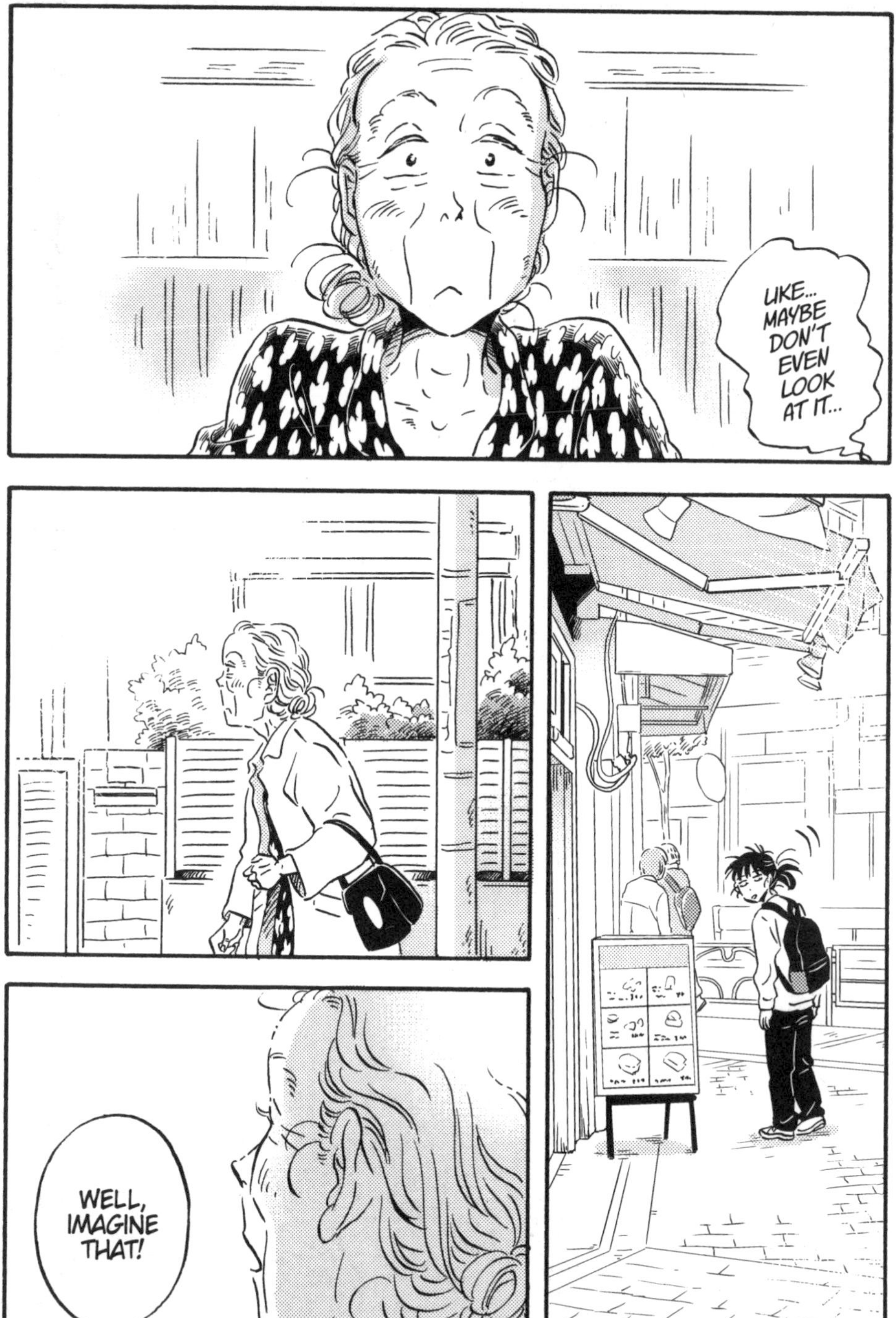
LIKE... MAYBE DON'T EVEN LOOK AT IT...
WELL, IMAGINE THAT!

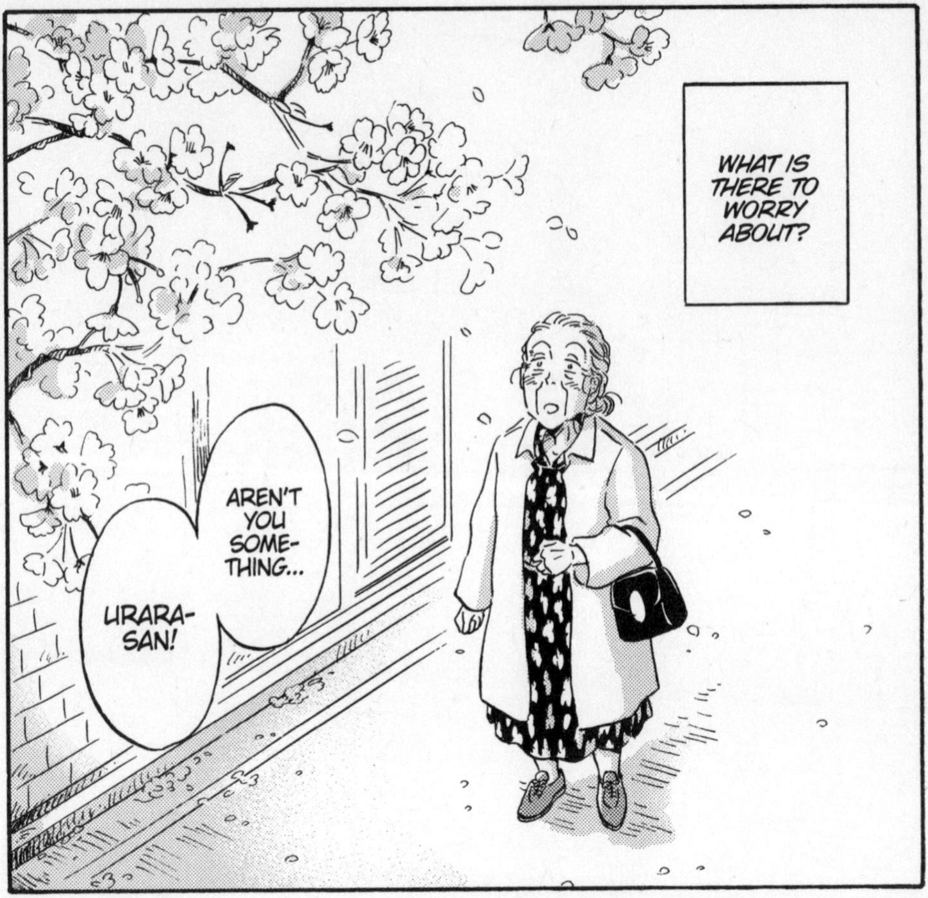
WHAT IS THERE TO WORRY ABOUT?
AREN'T YOU SOMETHING... URARA-SAN!

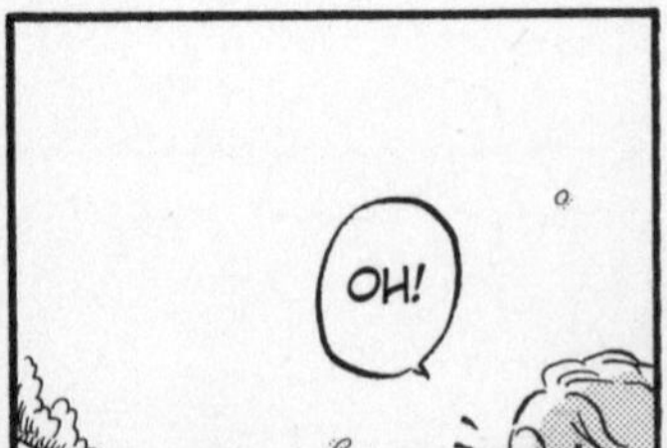
OH!

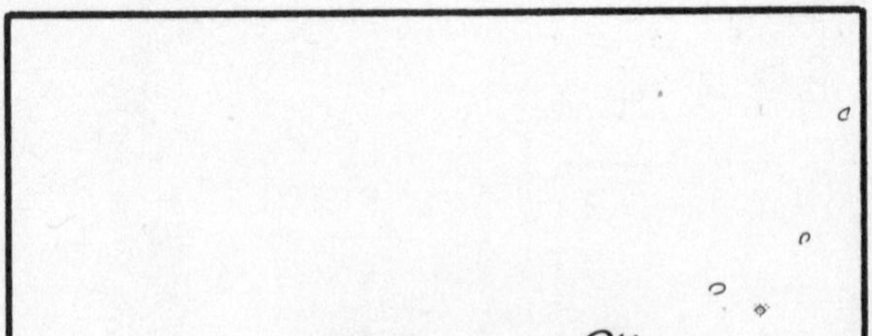
OH DEAR! YOU'RE SWEEPING UP AGAIN?!
IT'S FINE! YOU DON'T HAVE TO BOTHER!

Chapter 33/END

metamorphosis

Chapter 34

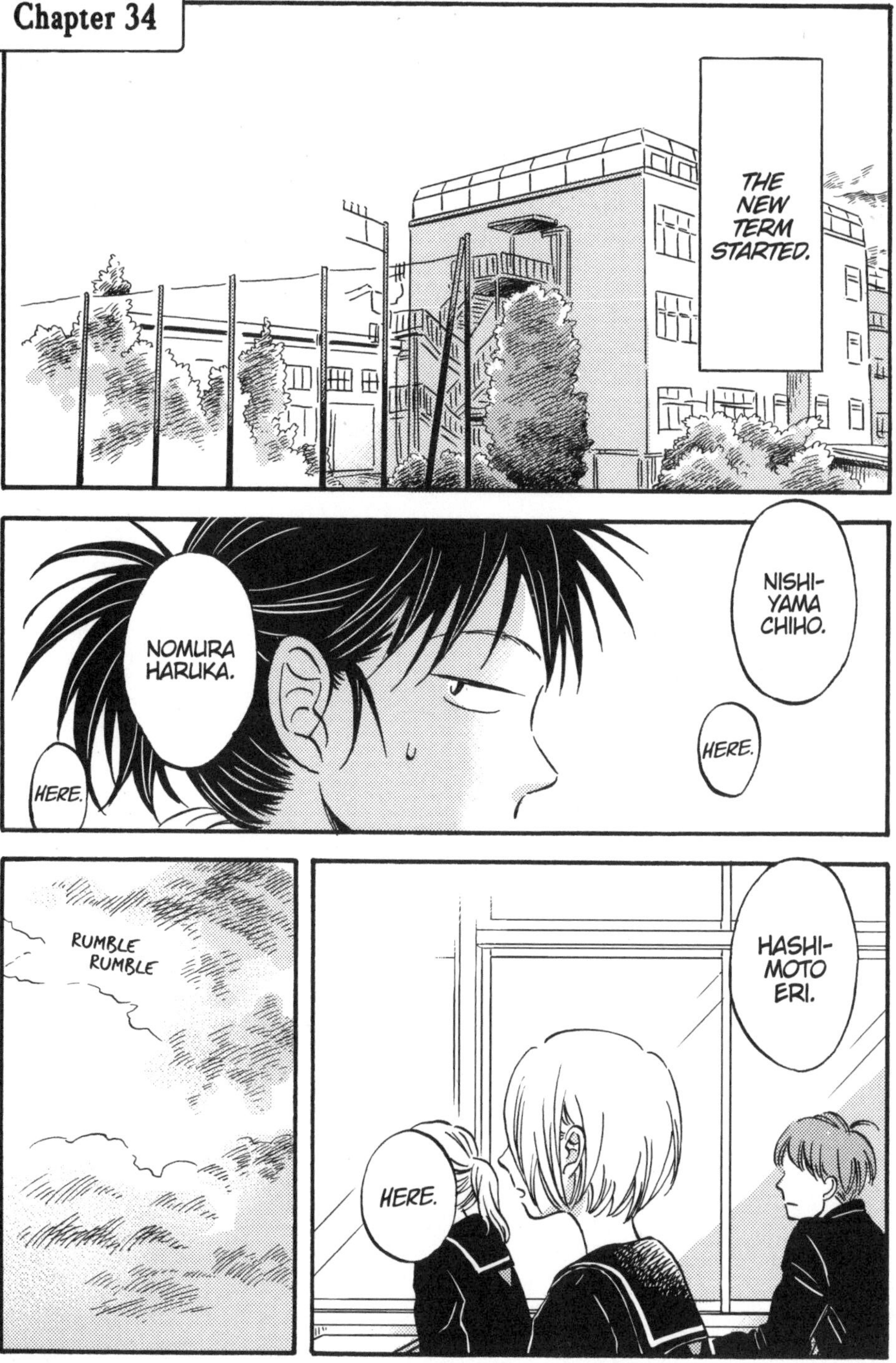

THE NEW TERM STARTED.
NISHI-YAMA CHIHO.
HERE.
NOMURA HARUKA.
HERE.
HASHI-MOTO ERI.
HERE.
RUMBLE RUMBLE

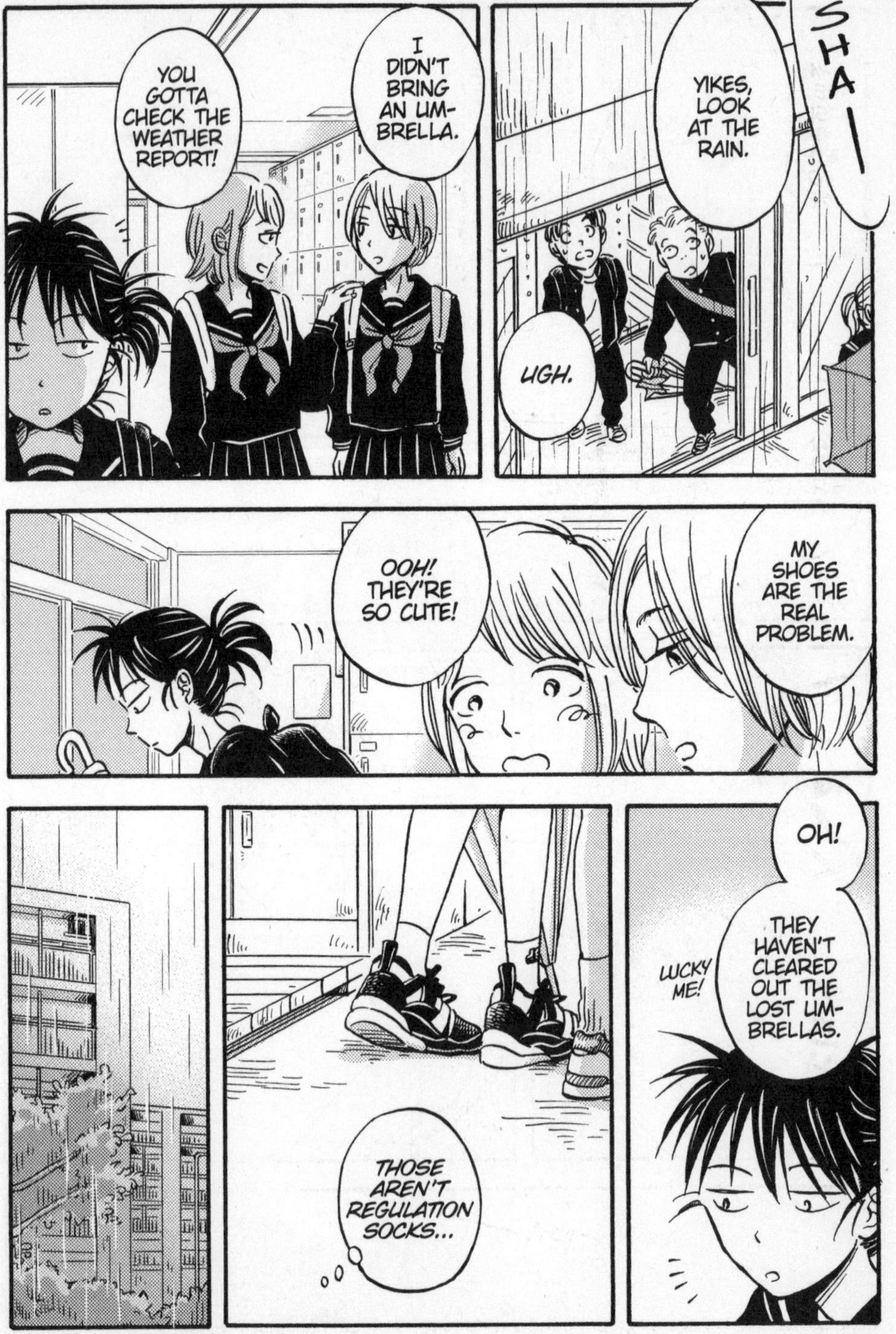
SHA
YIKES, LOOK AT THE RAIN.
UGH.
I DIDN'T BRING AN UM-BRELLA.
YOU GOTTA CHECK THE WEATHER REPORT!
MY SHOES ARE THE REAL PROBLEM.
OOH! THEY'RE SO CUTE!
OH!
THEY HAVEN'T CLEARED OUT THE LOST UM-BRELLAS.
LUCKY ME!
THOSE AREN'T REGULATION SOCKS...

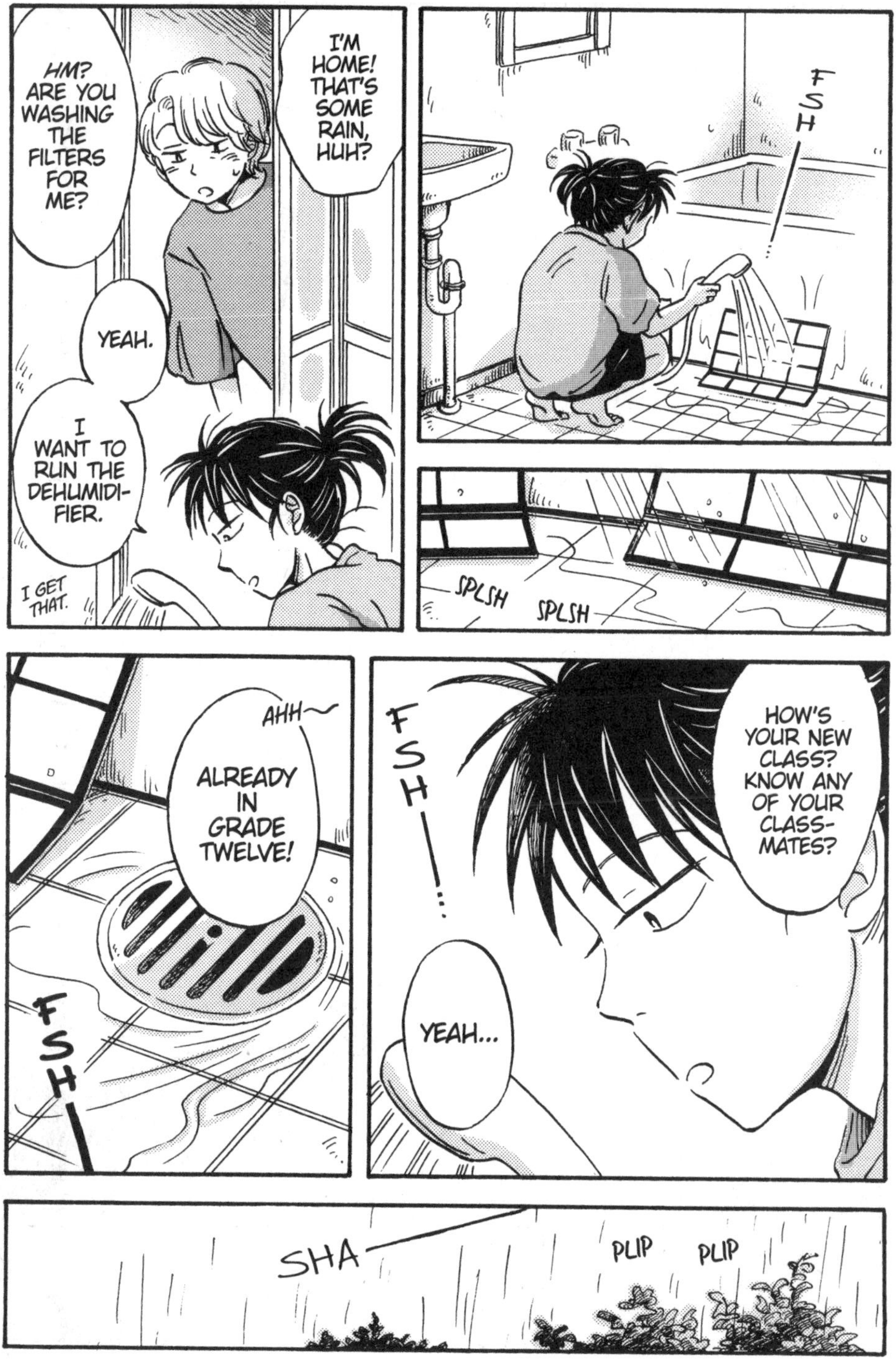
FSH
SPLSH
SPLSH
I'M HOME! THAT'S SOME RAIN, HUH?
HM? ARE YOU WASHING THE FILTERS FOR ME?
YEAH.
I WANT TO RUN THE DEHUMIDIFIER.
I GET THAT.
HOW'S YOUR NEW CLASS? KNOW ANY OF YOUR CLASSMATES?
FSH
YEAH...
AHH~
ALREADY IN GRADE TWELVE!
FSH
PLIP
PLIP
SHA

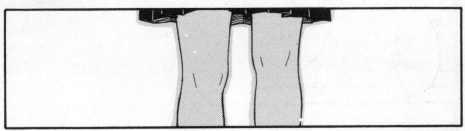

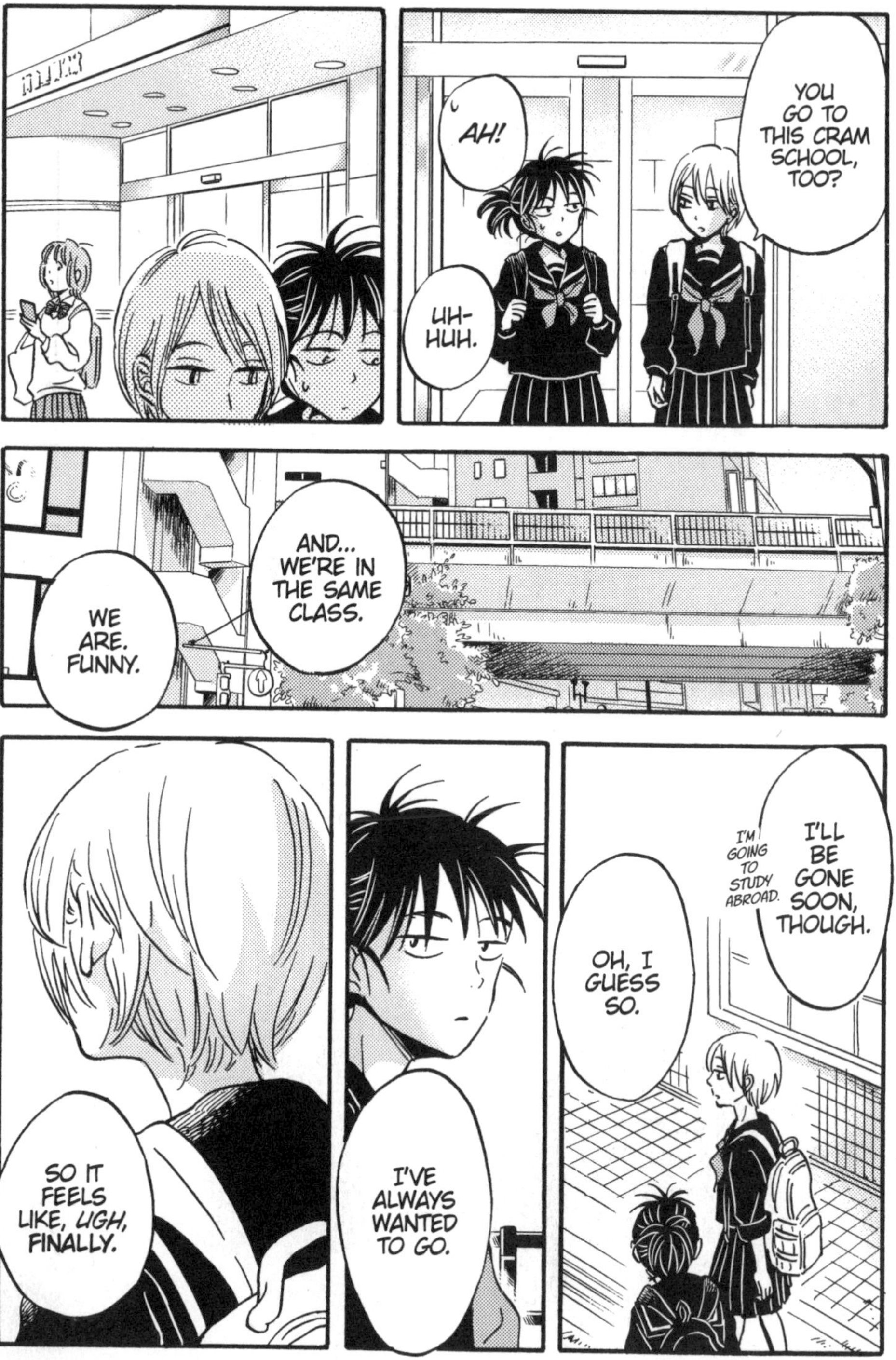
YOU GO TO THIS CRAM SCHOOL, TOO?
AH!
UH-HUH.
AND... WE'RE IN THE SAME CLASS.
WE ARE. FUNNY.
I'LL BE GONE SOON, THOUGH.
I'M GOING TO STUDY ABROAD.
OH, I GUESS SO.
I'VE ALWAYS WANTED TO GO.
SO IT FEELS LIKE, *UGH*, FINALLY.

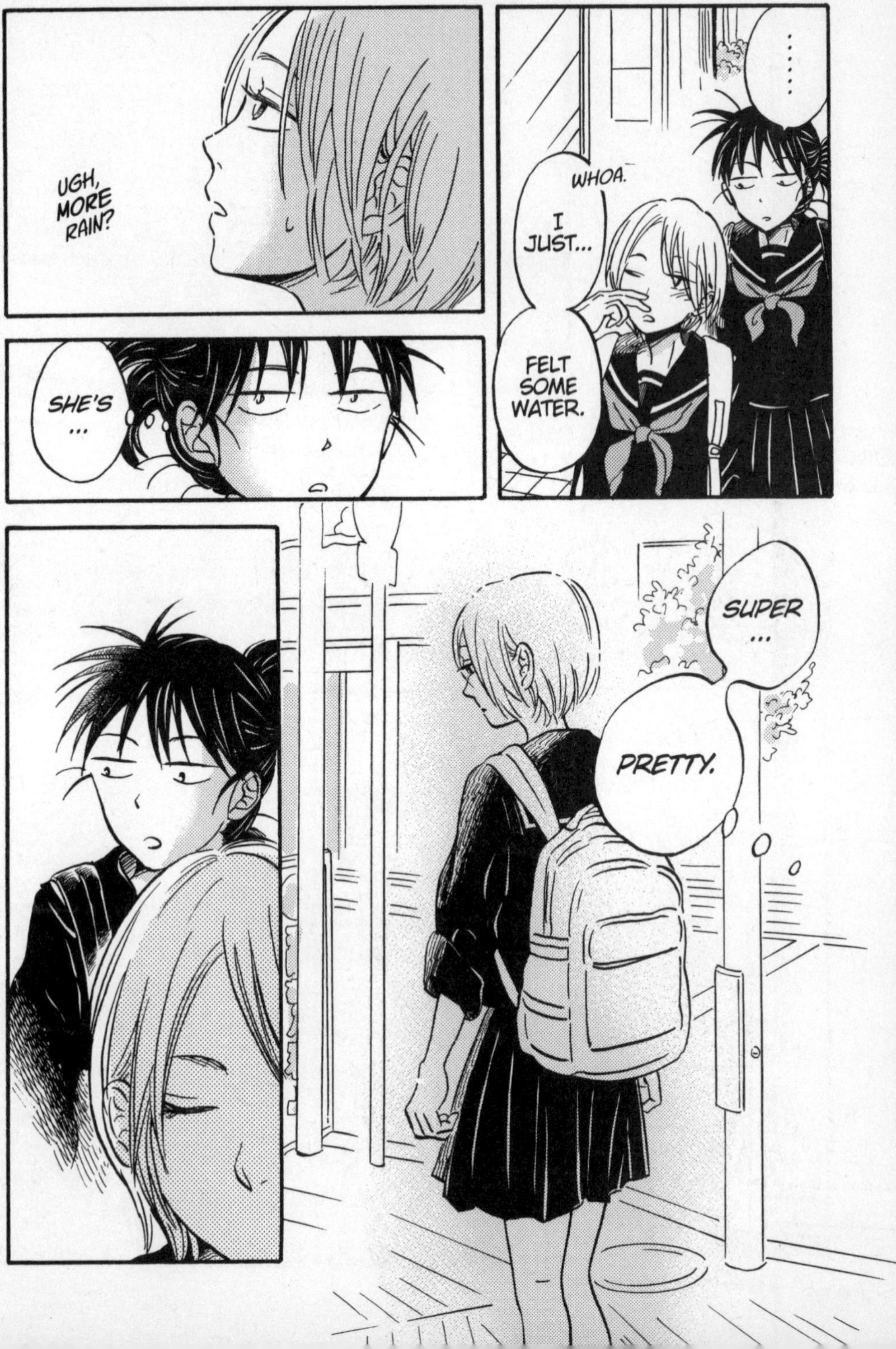
......
WHOA.
I JUST...
FELT SOME WATER.
UGH, MORE RAIN?
SHE'S ...
SUPER ...
PRETTY.

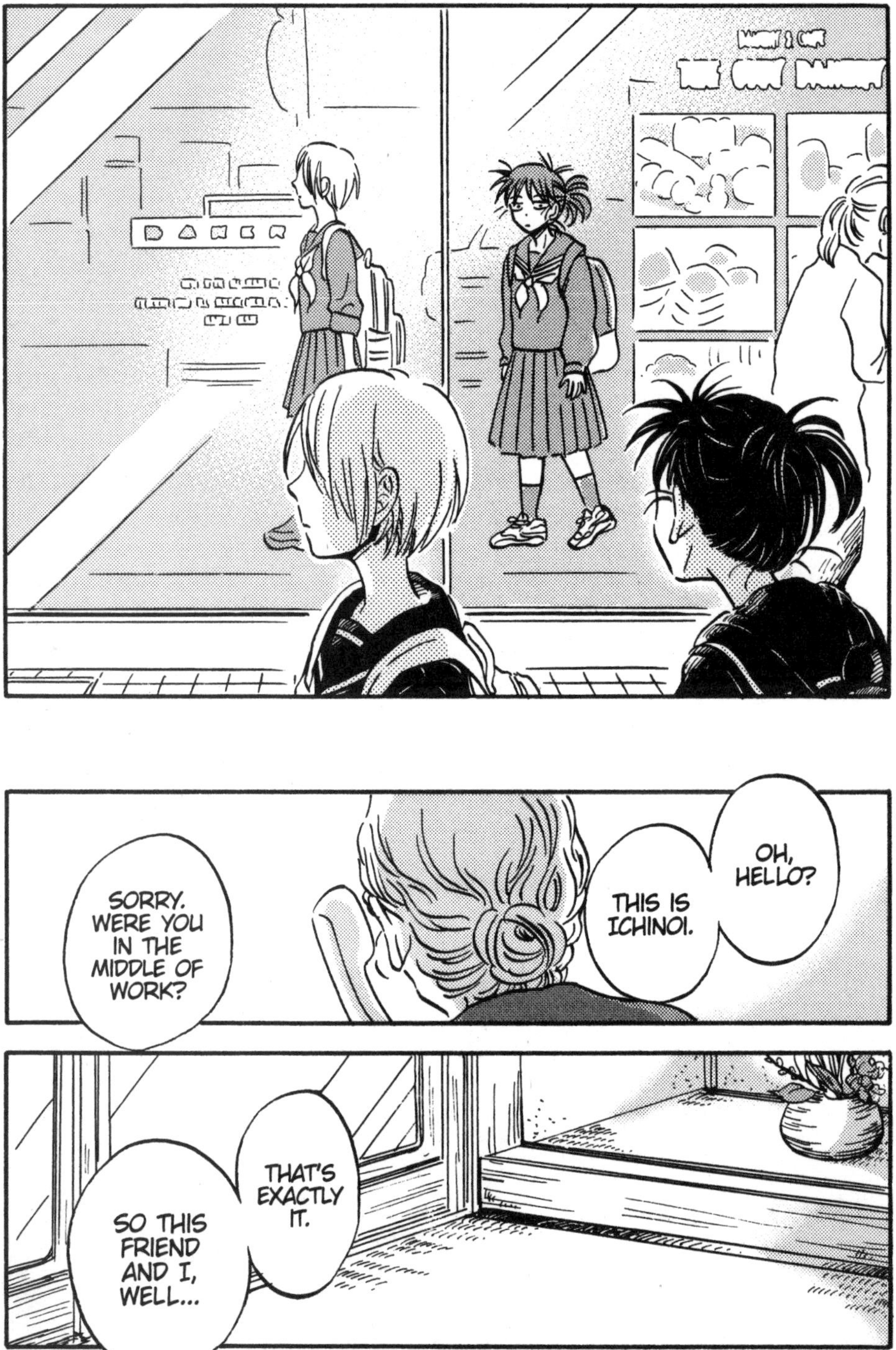
OH, HELLO?
THIS IS ICHINOI.
SORRY. WERE YOU IN THE MIDDLE OF WORK?
THAT'S EXACTLY IT.
SO THIS FRIEND AND I, WELL...

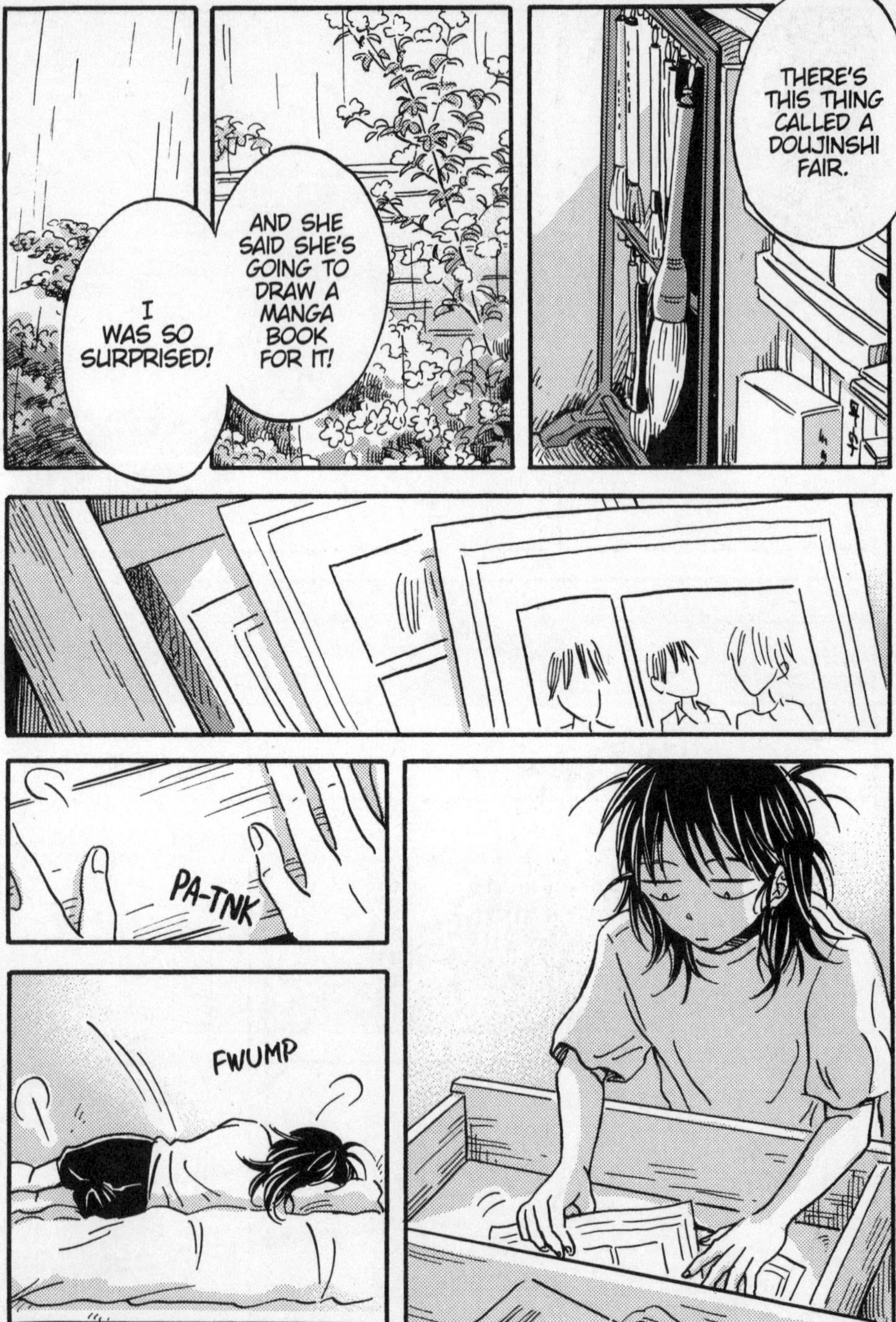
THERE'S THIS THING CALLED A DOUJINSHI FAIR.
AND SHE SAID SHE'S GOING TO DRAW A MANGA BOOK FOR IT!
I WAS SO SURPRISED!
PA-TNK
FWUMP

YOU'RE NOT GOING TO DRAW?

I'M TIRED.

VWRRR

UH-UH.

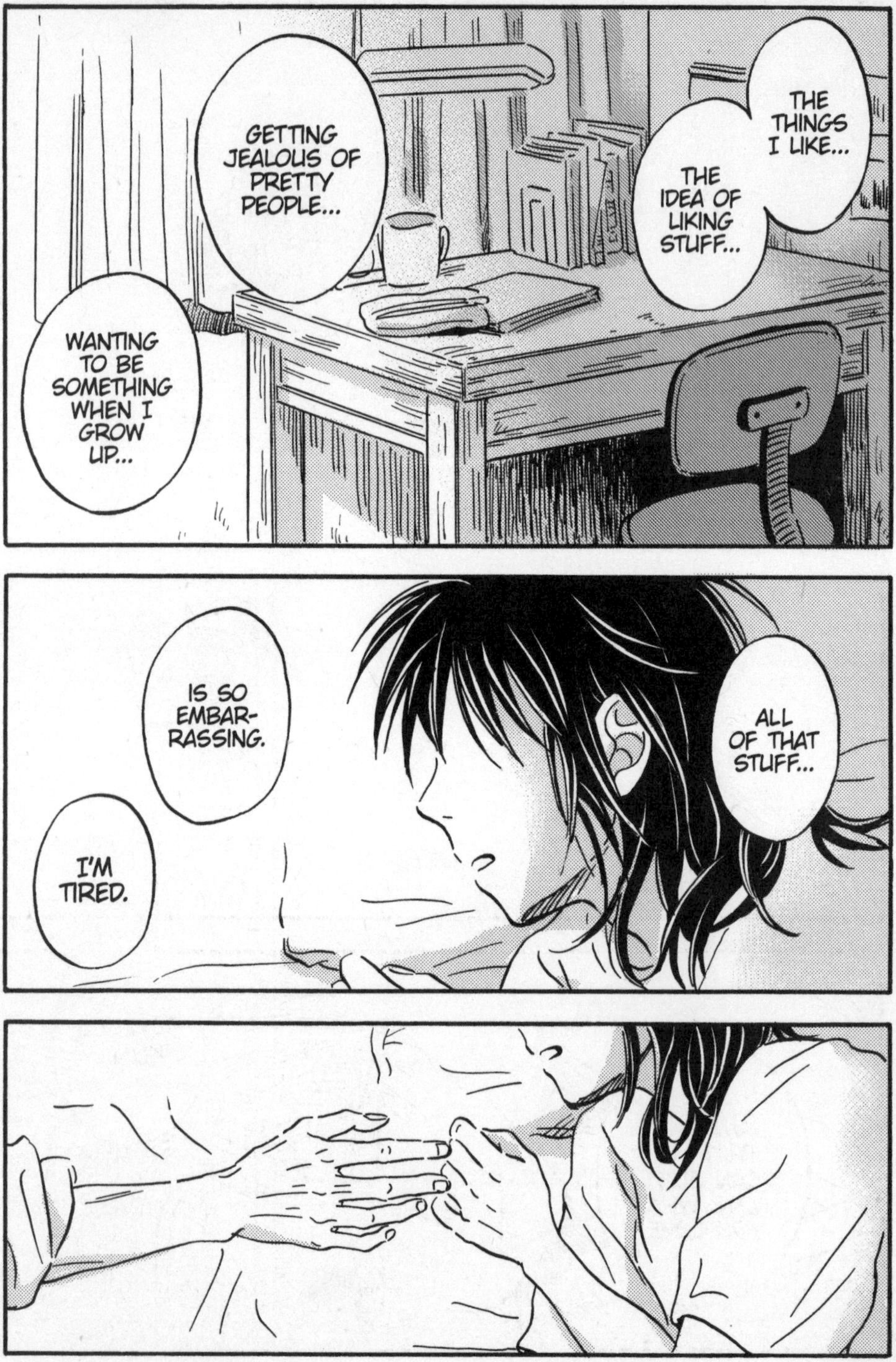
THE THINGS I LIKE...
THE IDEA OF LIKING STUFF...
GETTING JEALOUS OF PRETTY PEOPLE...
WANTING TO BE SOMETHING WHEN I GROW UP...
ALL OF THAT STUFF...
IS SO EMBARRASSING.
I'M TIRED.

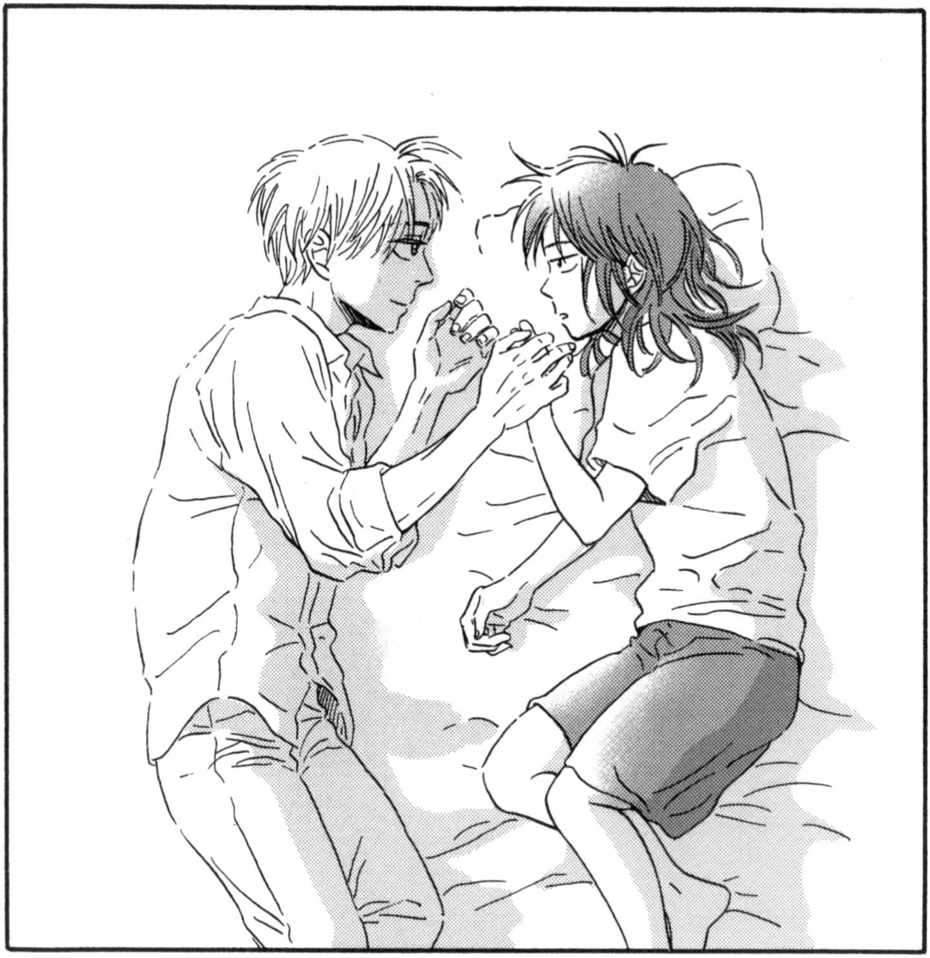

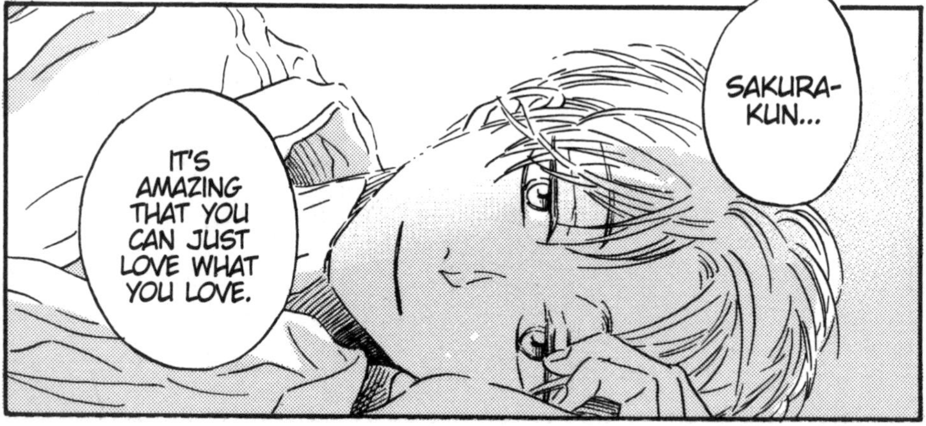
SAKURA-KUN...
IT'S AMAZING THAT YOU CAN JUST LOVE WHAT YOU LOVE.

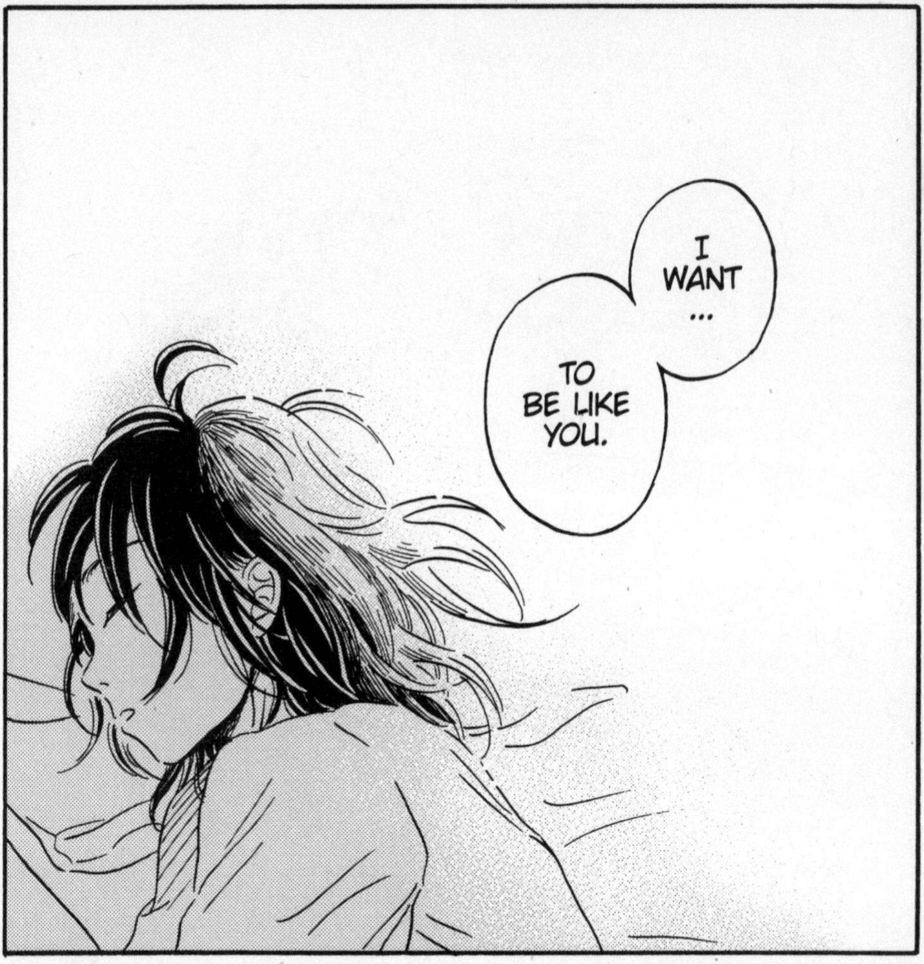
I WANT ...
TO BE LIKE YOU.
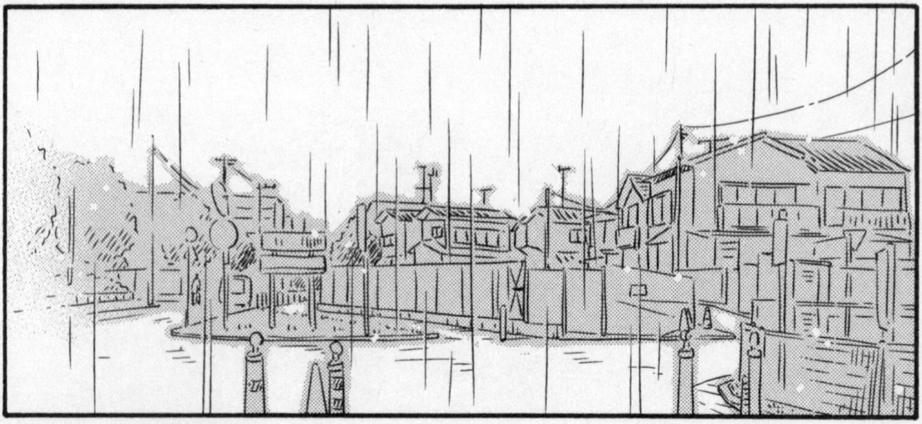

Chapter 34/END

metamorphosis

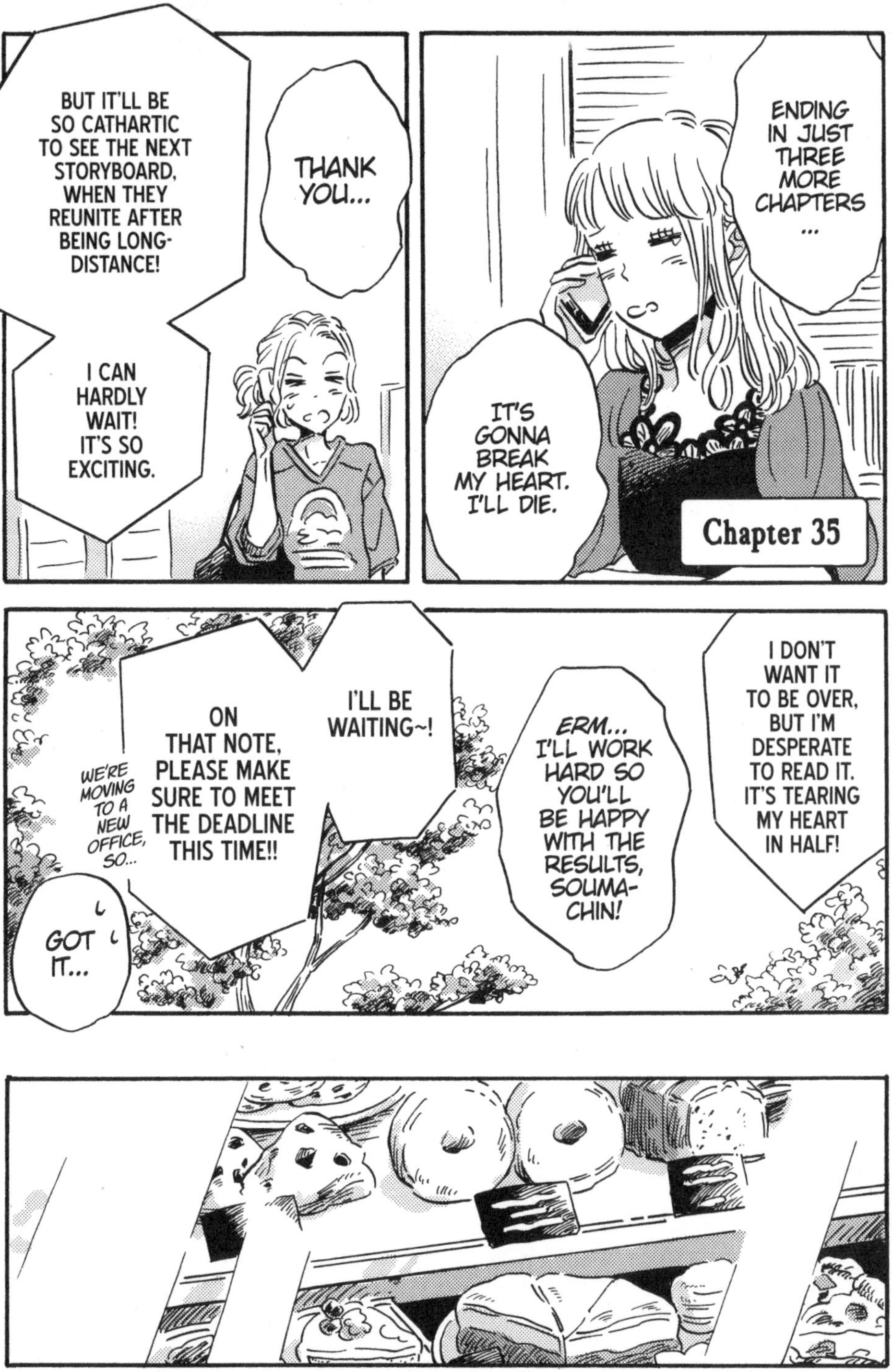
ENDING IN JUST THREE MORE CHAPTERS...
IT'S GONNA BREAK MY HEART. I'LL DIE.
Chapter 35
THANK YOU...
BUT IT'LL BE SO CATHARTIC TO SEE THE NEXT STORYBOARD, WHEN THEY REUNITE AFTER BEING LONG-DISTANCE!
I CAN HARDLY WAIT! IT'S SO EXCITING.
I DON'T WANT IT TO BE OVER, BUT I'M DESPERATE TO READ IT. IT'S TEARING MY HEART IN HALF!
ERM... I'LL WORK HARD SO YOU'LL BE HAPPY WITH THE RESULTS, SOUMA-CHIN!
I'LL BE WAITING~!
ON THAT NOTE, PLEASE MAKE SURE TO MEET THE DEADLINE THIS TIME!!
WE'RE MOVING TO A NEW OFFICE, SO...
GOT IT...

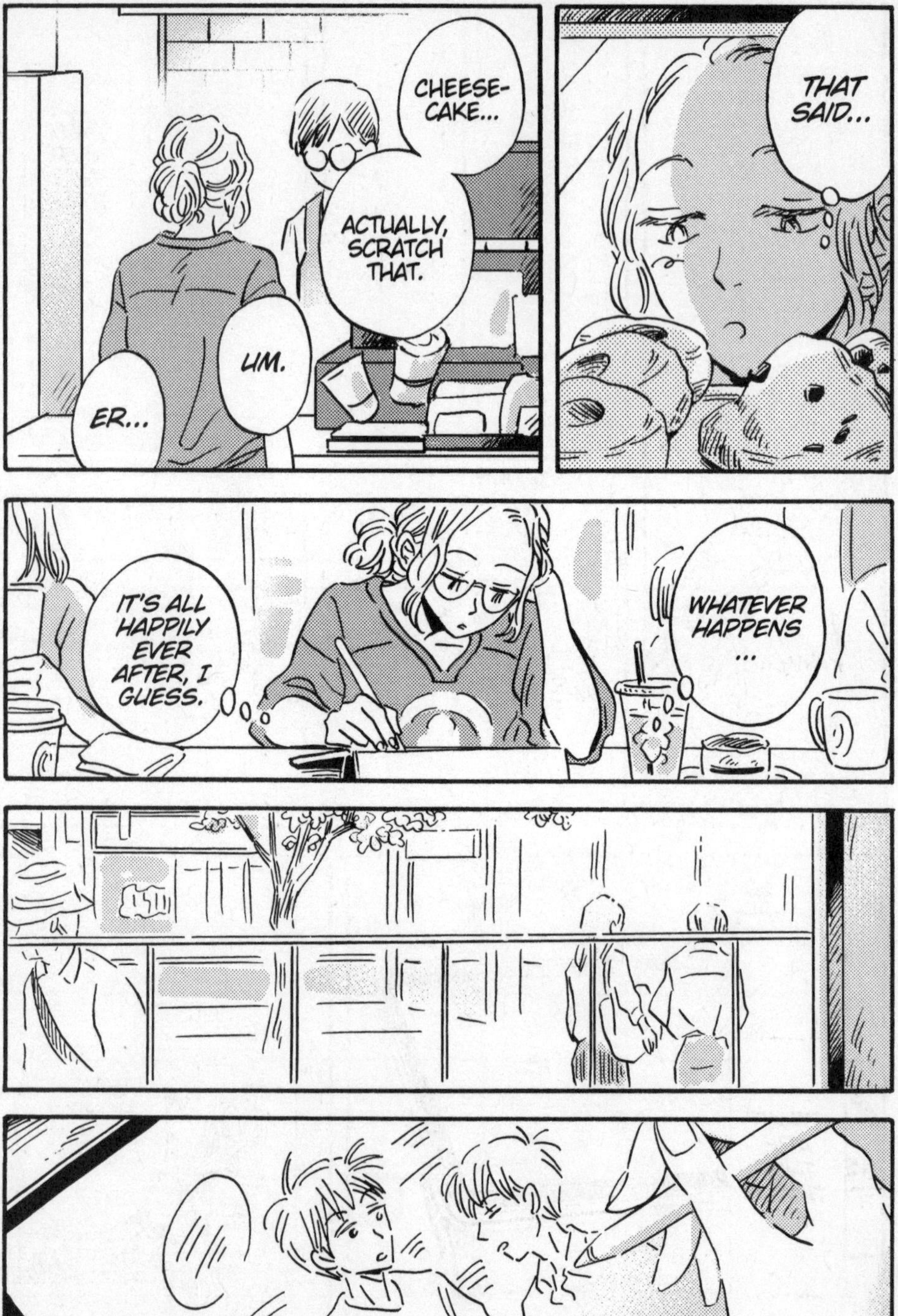
THAT SAID...
CHEESE-CAKE...
ACTUALLY, SCRATCH THAT.
UM.
ER...
WHATEVER HAPPENS ...
IT'S ALL HAPPILY EVER AFTER, I GUESS.

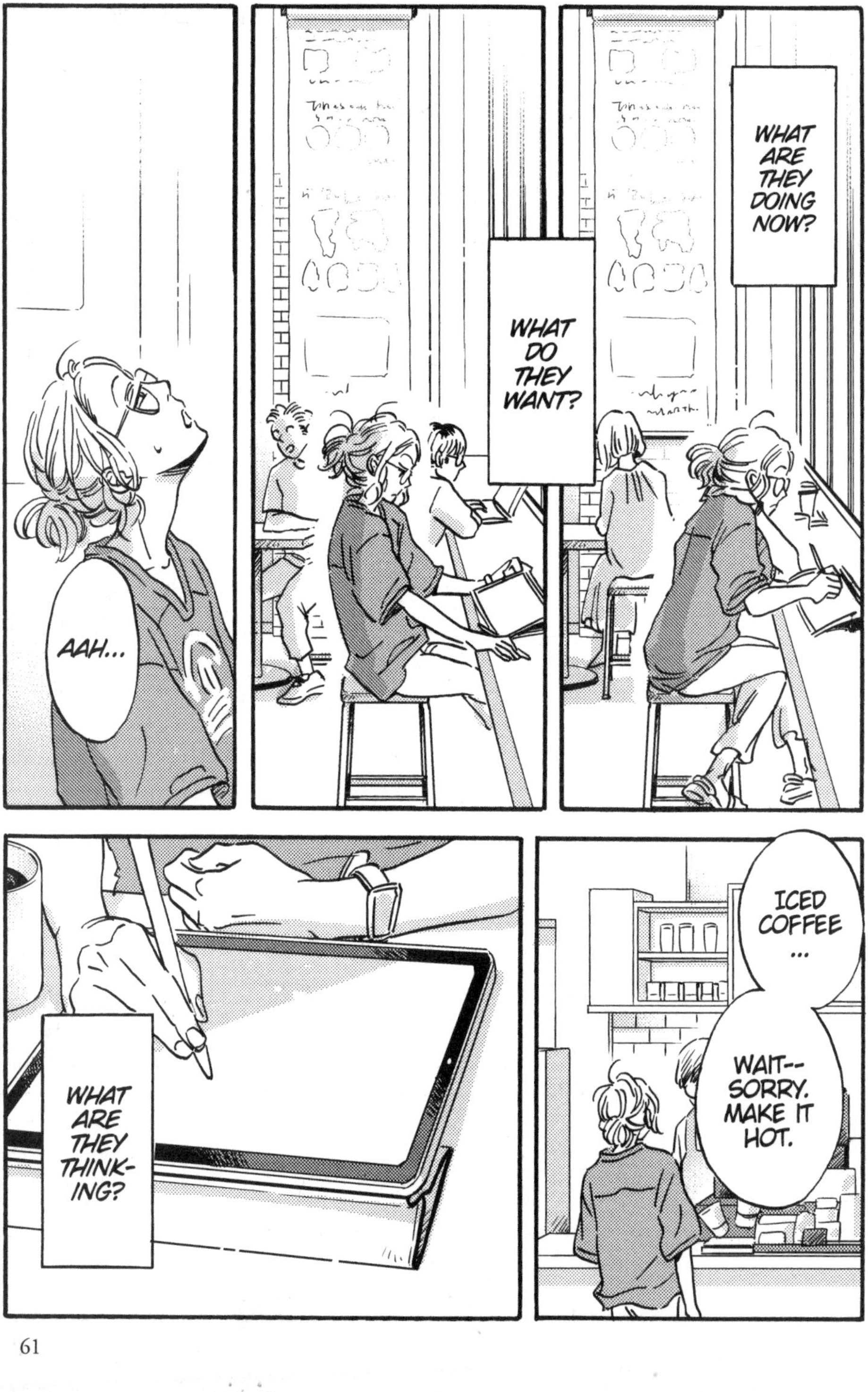
WHAT ARE THEY DOING NOW?
WHAT DO THEY WANT?
AAH...
ICED COFFEE ...
WAIT-- SORRY. MAKE IT HOT.
WHAT ARE THEY THINKING?

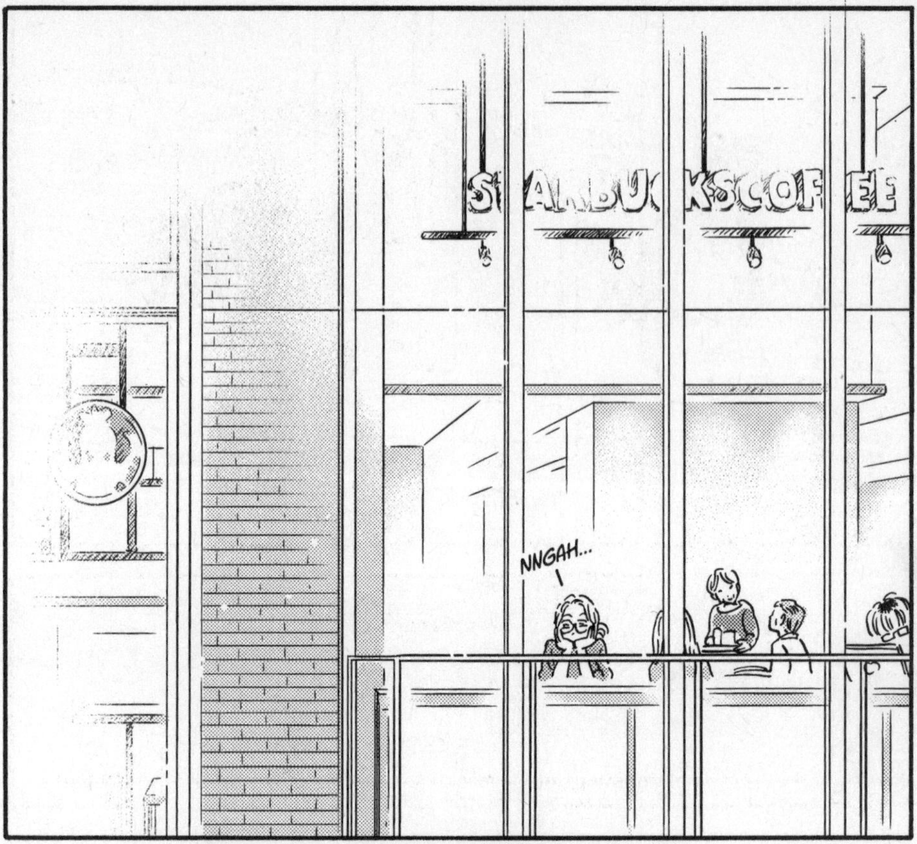
NNGAH...

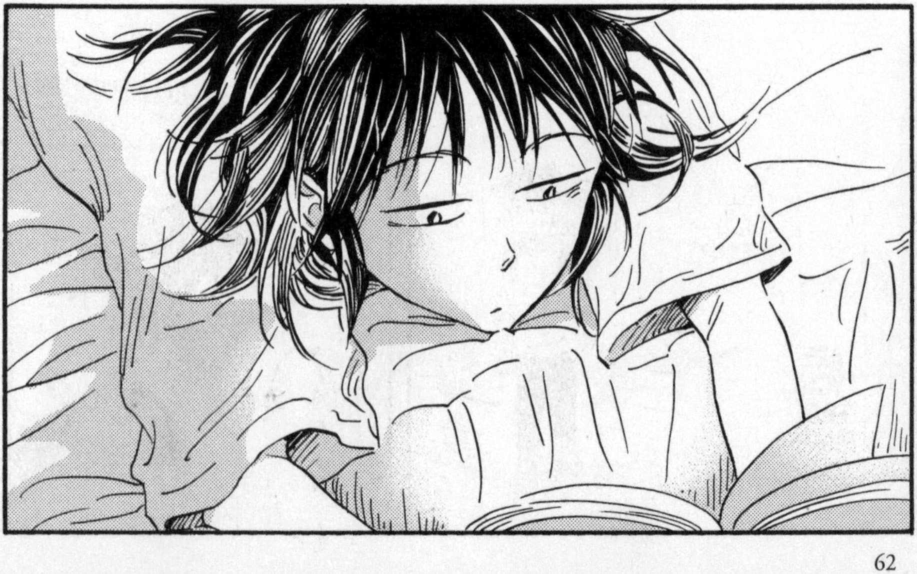

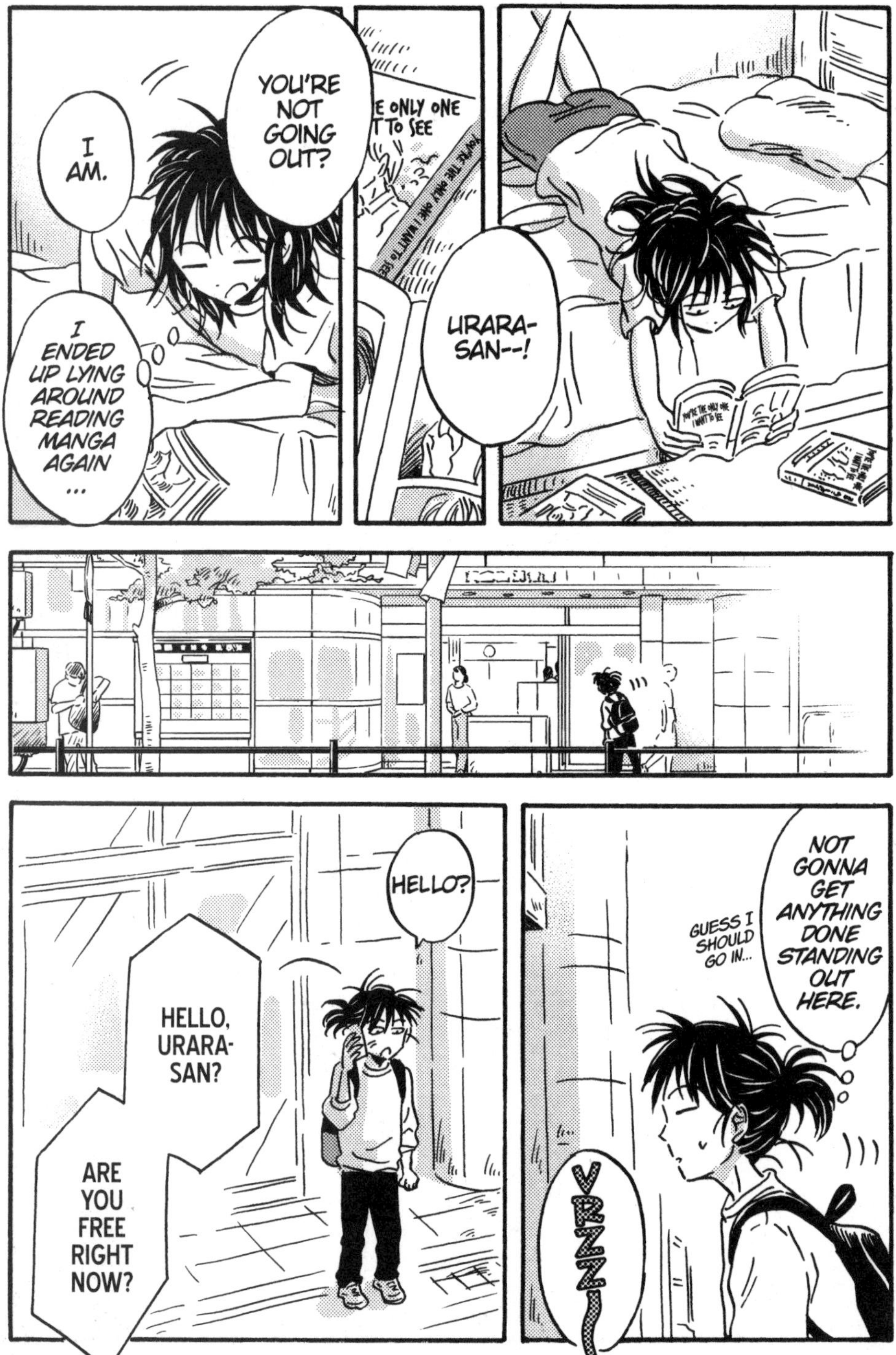
URARA-SAN--!
YOU'RE THE ONLY ONE I WANT TO SEE
YOU'RE NOT GOING OUT?
I AM.
I ENDED UP LYING AROUND READING MANGA AGAIN ...
NOT GONNA GET ANYTHING DONE STANDING OUT HERE.
GUESS I SHOULD GO IN...
VRZZ
HELLO?
HELLO, URARA-SAN?
ARE YOU FREE RIGHT NOW?

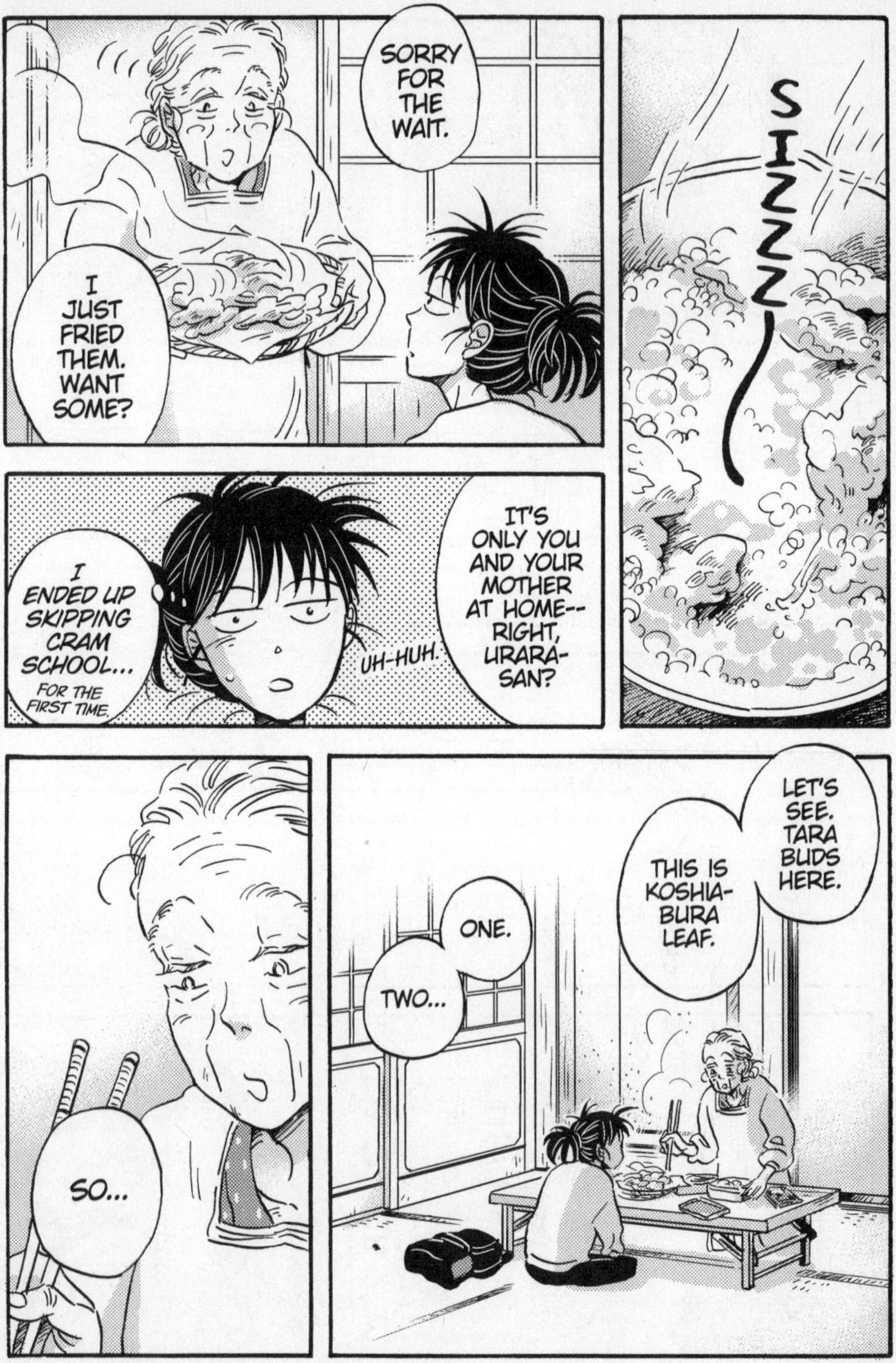
SIZZZ
SORRY FOR THE WAIT.
I JUST FRIED THEM. WANT SOME?
IT'S ONLY YOU AND YOUR MOTHER AT HOME-- RIGHT, URARA-SAN?
UH-HUH.
I ENDED UP SKIPPING CRAM SCHOOL... FOR THE FIRST TIME.
LET'S SEE. TARA BUDS HERE.
THIS IS KOSHIA-BURA LEAF.
ONE.
TWO...
SO...

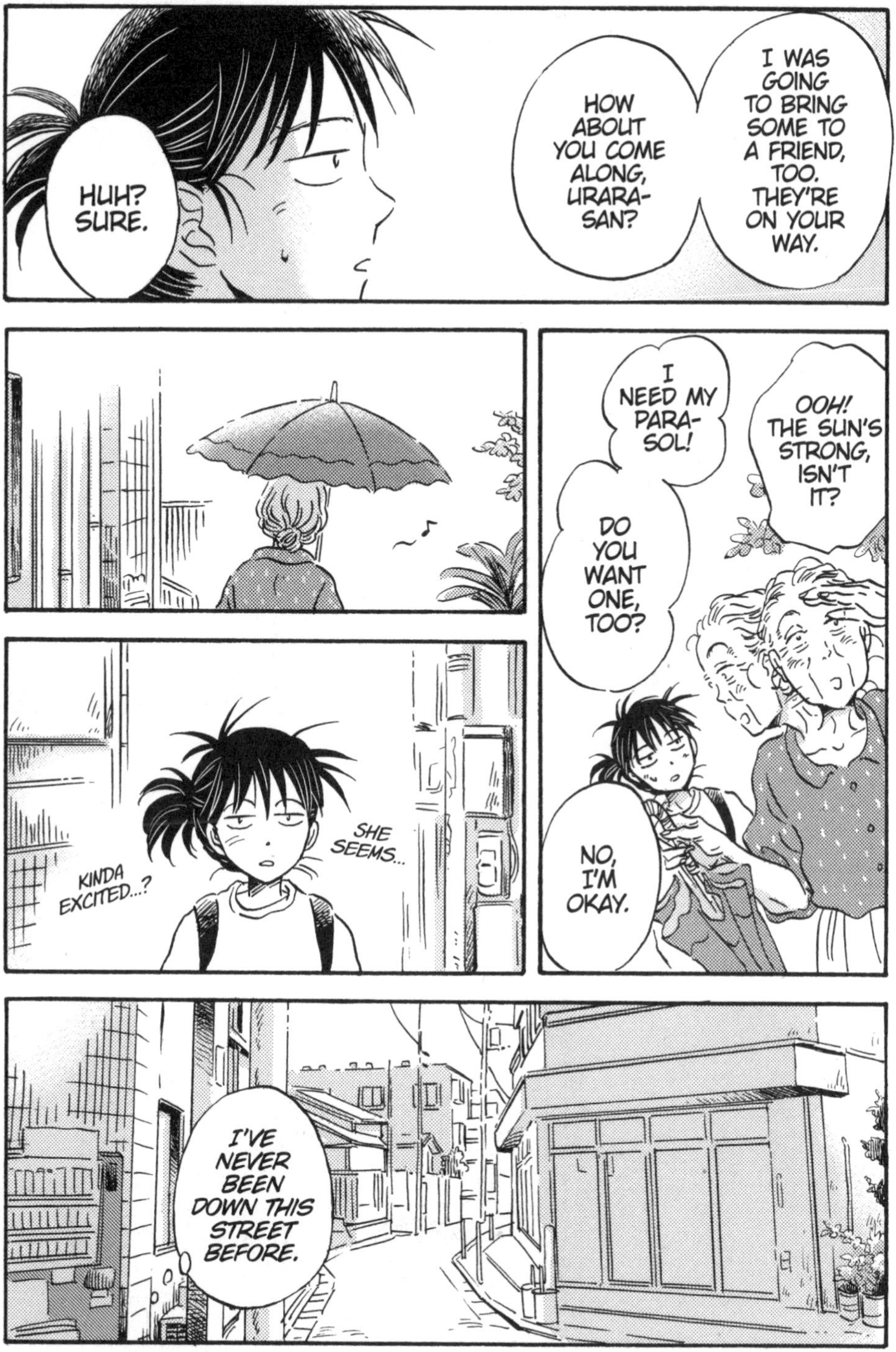
I WAS GOING TO BRING SOME TO A FRIEND, TOO. THEY'RE ON YOUR WAY.
HOW ABOUT YOU COME ALONG, URARA-SAN?
HUH? SURE.
OOH! THE SUN'S STRONG, ISN'T IT?
I NEED MY PARA-SOL!
DO YOU WANT ONE, TOO?
NO, I'M OKAY.
SHE SEEMS...
KINDA EXCITED...?
I'VE NEVER BEEN DOWN THIS STREET BEFORE.

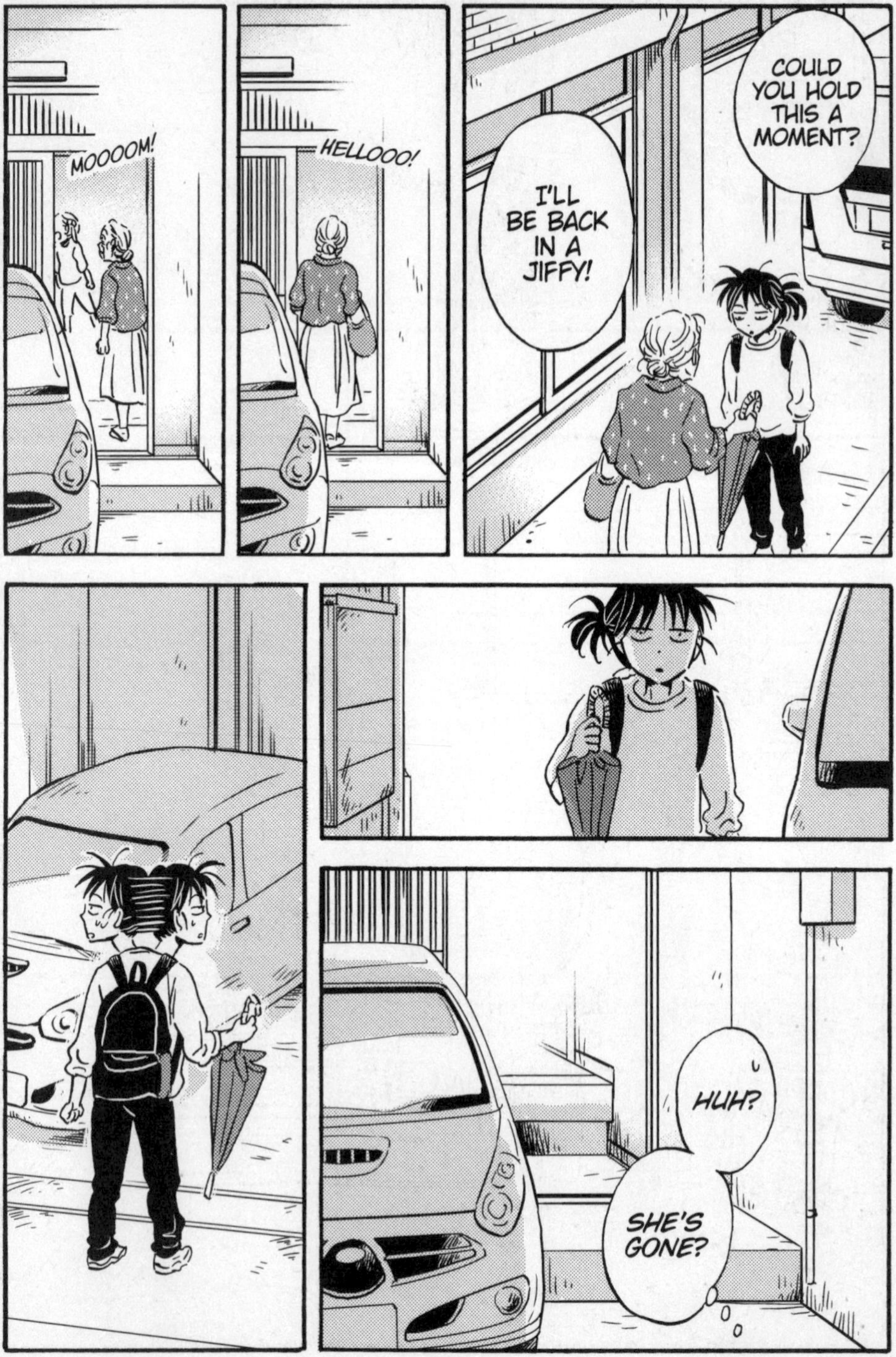
COULD YOU HOLD THIS A MOMENT?
I'LL BE BACK IN A JIFFY!
HELLOOO!
MOOOOM!
HUH?
SHE'S GONE?

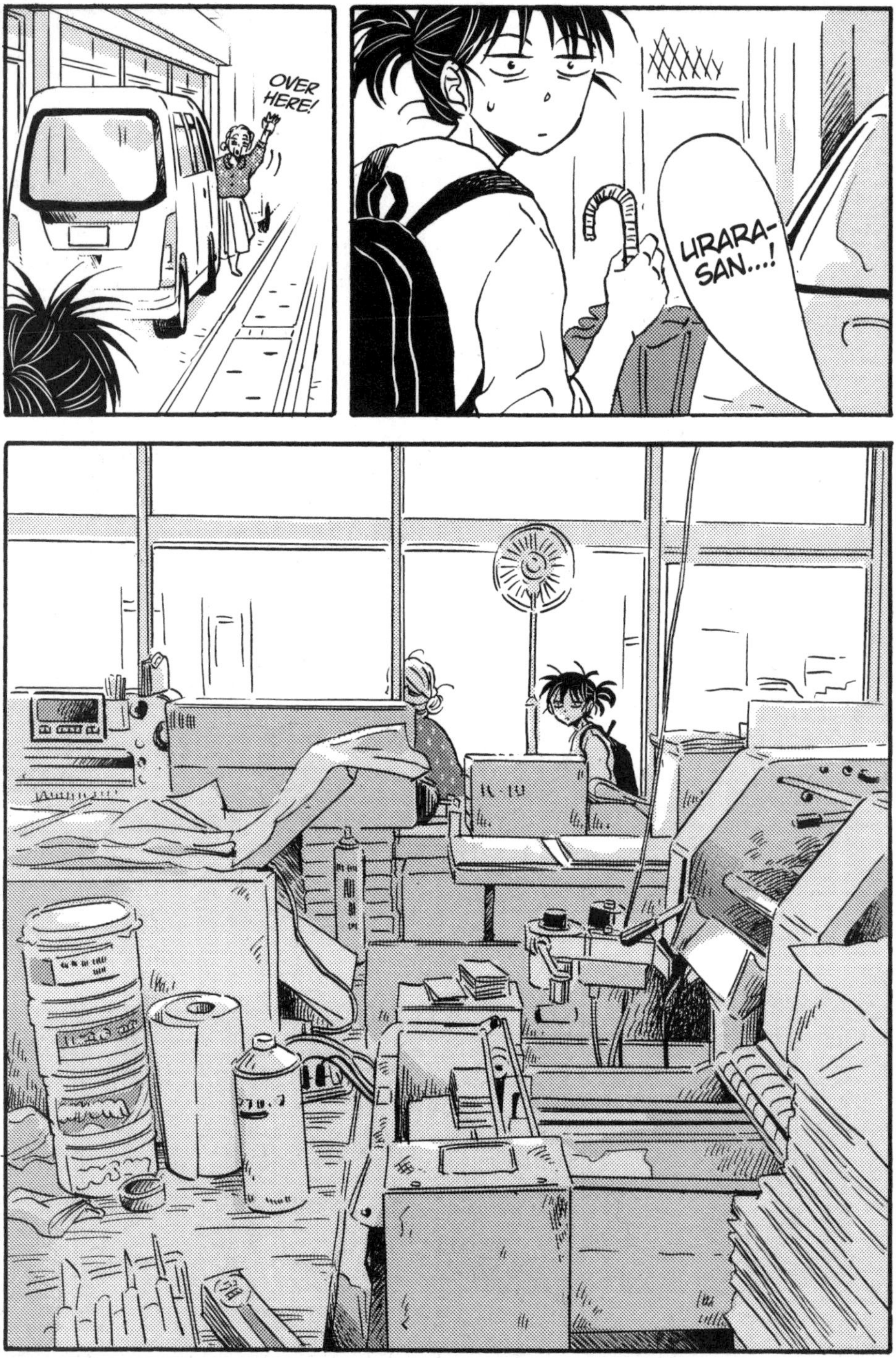
URARA-SAN...!
OVER HERE!

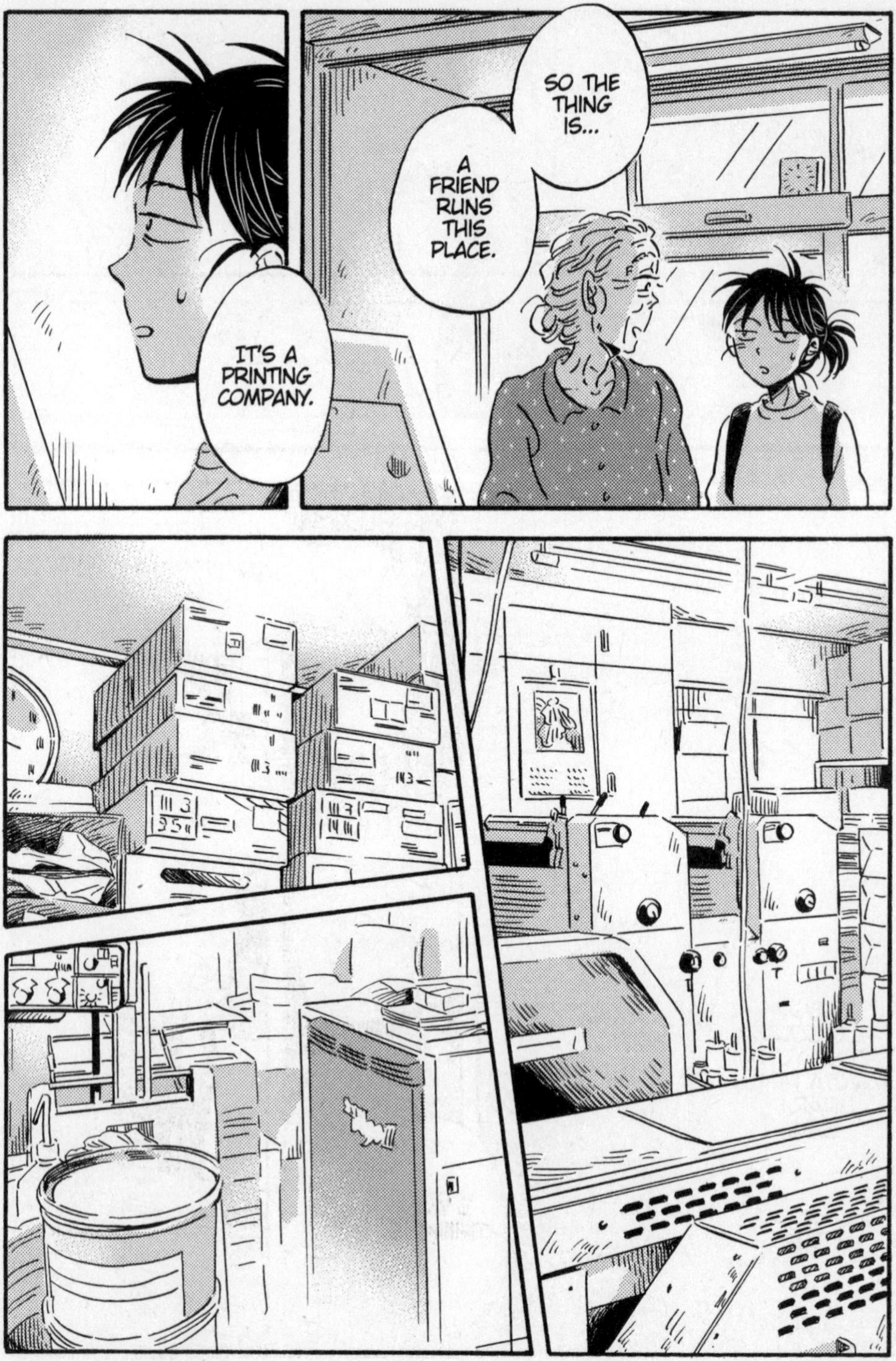
SO THE THING IS...
A FRIEND RUNS THIS PLACE.
IT'S A PRINTING COMPANY.

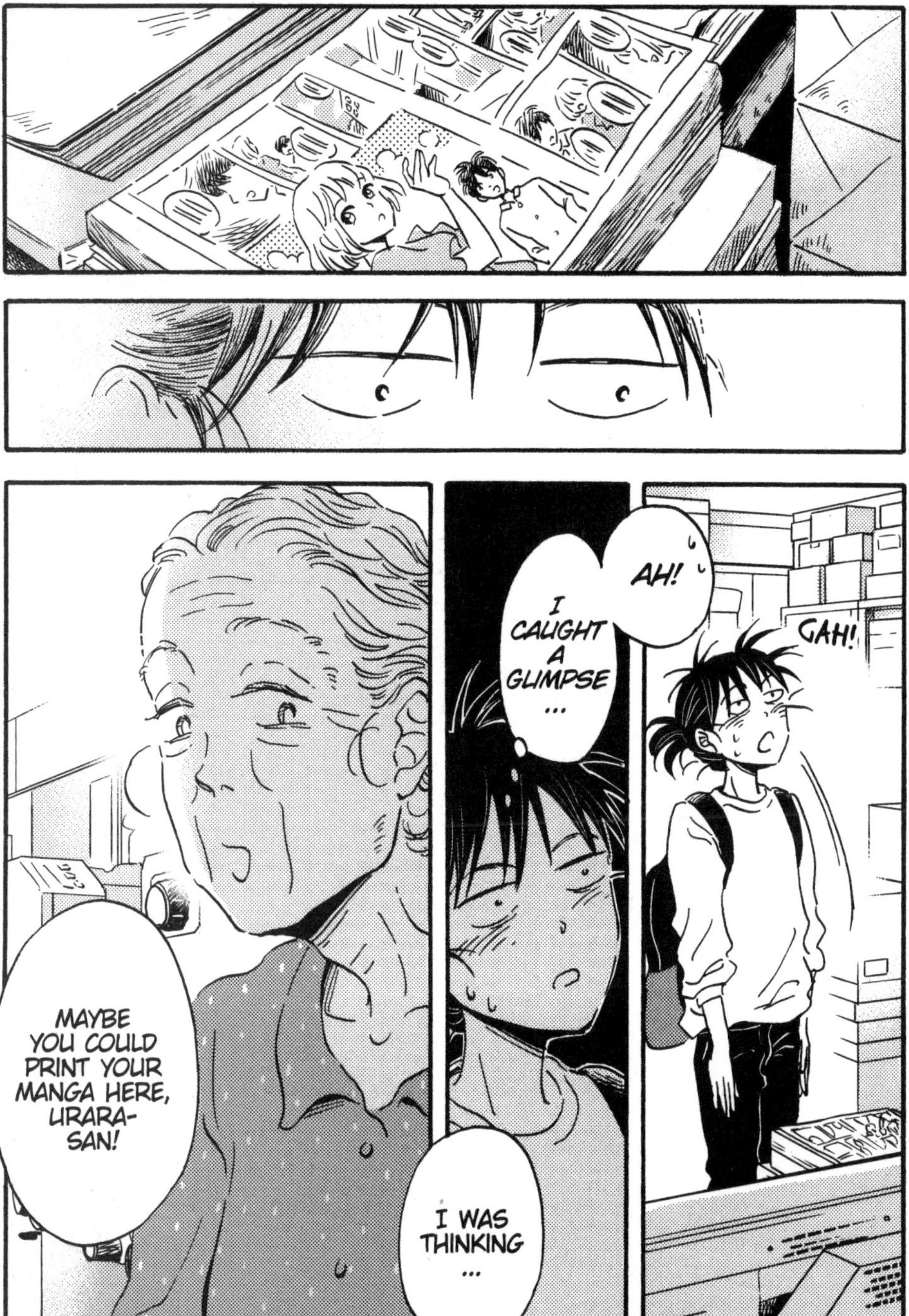
GAH!
AH!
I CAUGHT A GLIMPSE ...
I WAS THINKING ...
MAYBE YOU COULD PRINT YOUR MANGA HERE, URARA-SAN!

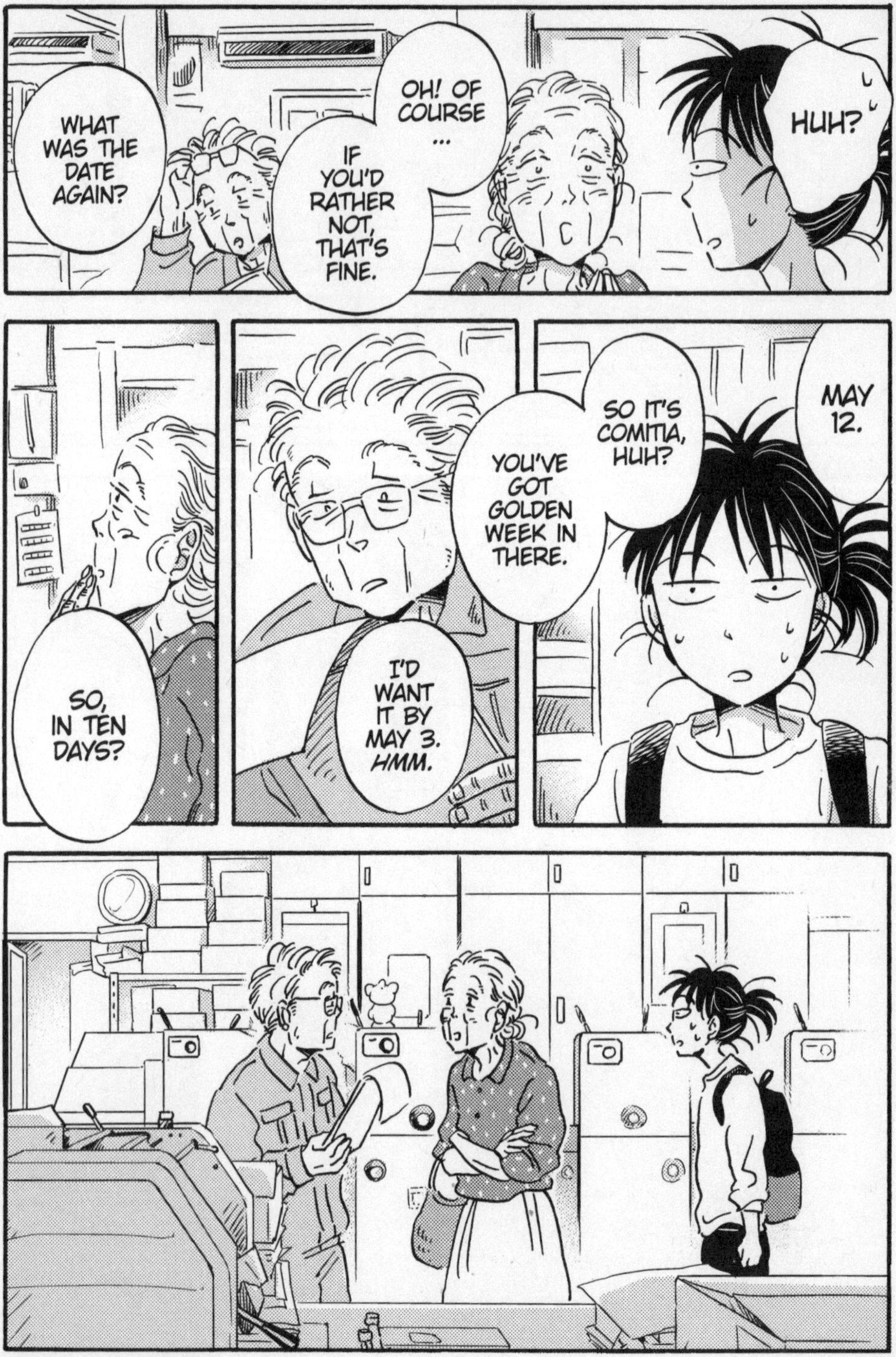
HUH?
OH! OF COURSE ...
IF YOU'D RATHER NOT, THAT'S FINE.
WHAT WAS THE DATE AGAIN?
MAY 12.
SO IT'S COMITIA, HUH?
YOU'VE GOT GOLDEN WEEK IN THERE.
I'D WANT IT BY MAY 3. *HMM.*
SO, IN TEN DAYS?

Chapter 35/END

metamorphosis

Chapter 36

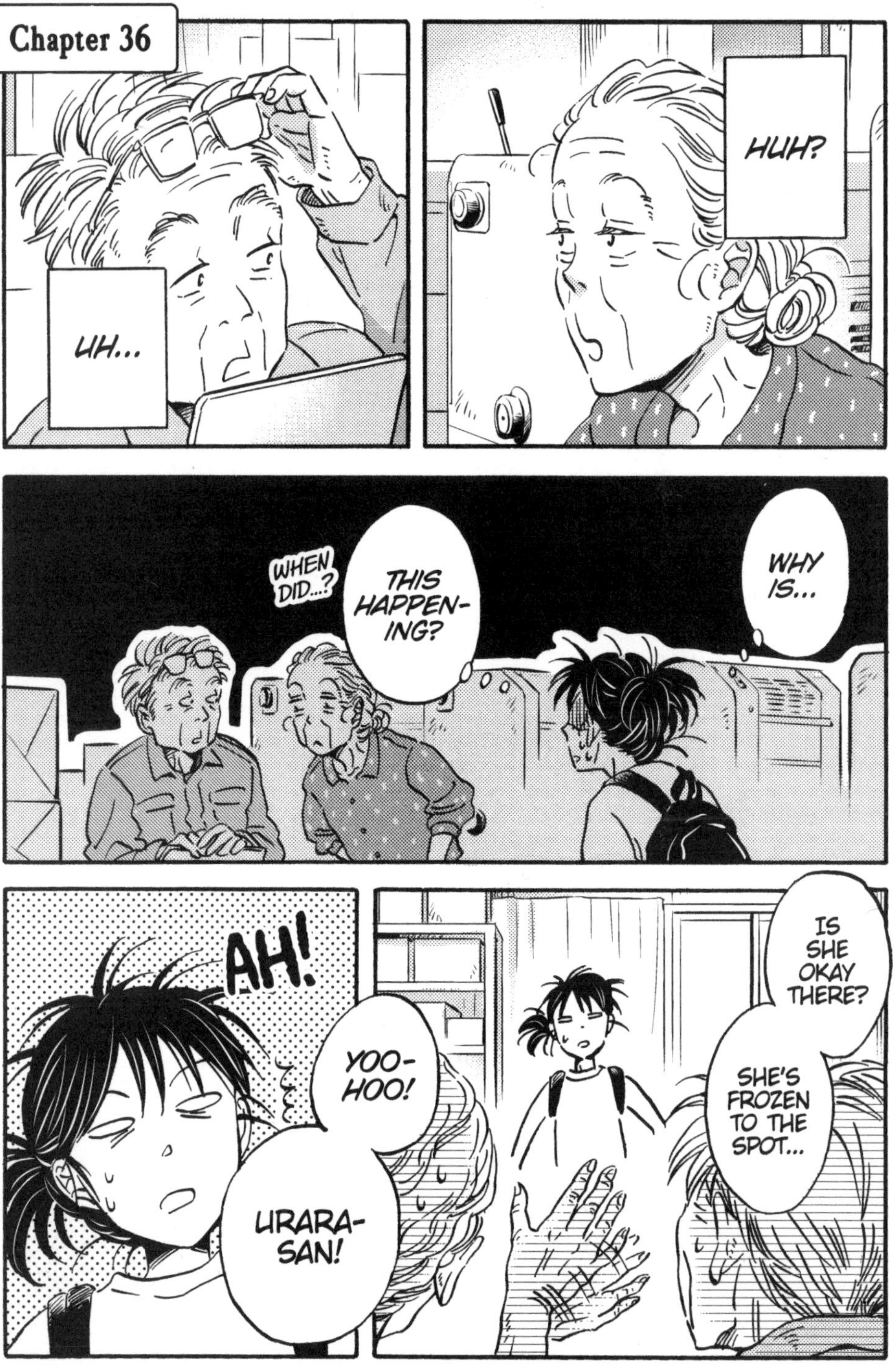
HUH?
UH...
WHY IS...
THIS HAPPENING?
WHEN DID...?
IS SHE OKAY THERE?
SHE'S FROZEN TO THE SPOT...
YOO-HOO!
URARA-SAN!
AH!

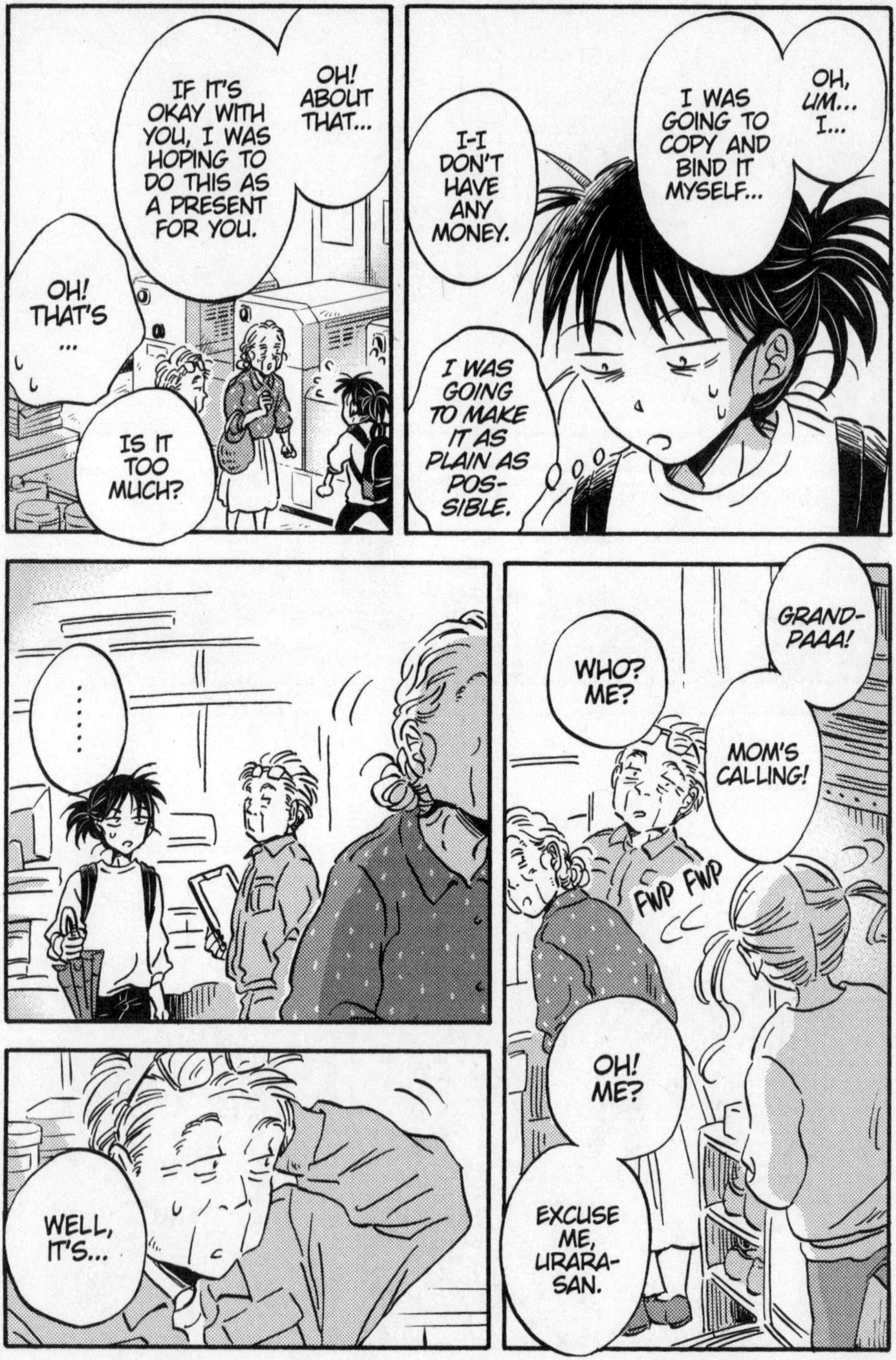
OH, UM... I...
I WAS GOING TO COPY AND BIND IT MYSELF...
I-I DON'T HAVE ANY MONEY.
I WAS GOING TO MAKE IT AS PLAIN AS POS-SIBLE.
OH! ABOUT THAT...
IF IT'S OKAY WITH YOU, I WAS HOPING TO DO THIS AS A PRESENT FOR YOU.
OH! THAT'S ...
IS IT TOO MUCH?
GRAND-PAAA!
WHO? ME?
MOM'S CALLING!
FWP FWP
OH! ME?
EXCUSE ME, URARA-SAN.
......
WELL, IT'S...

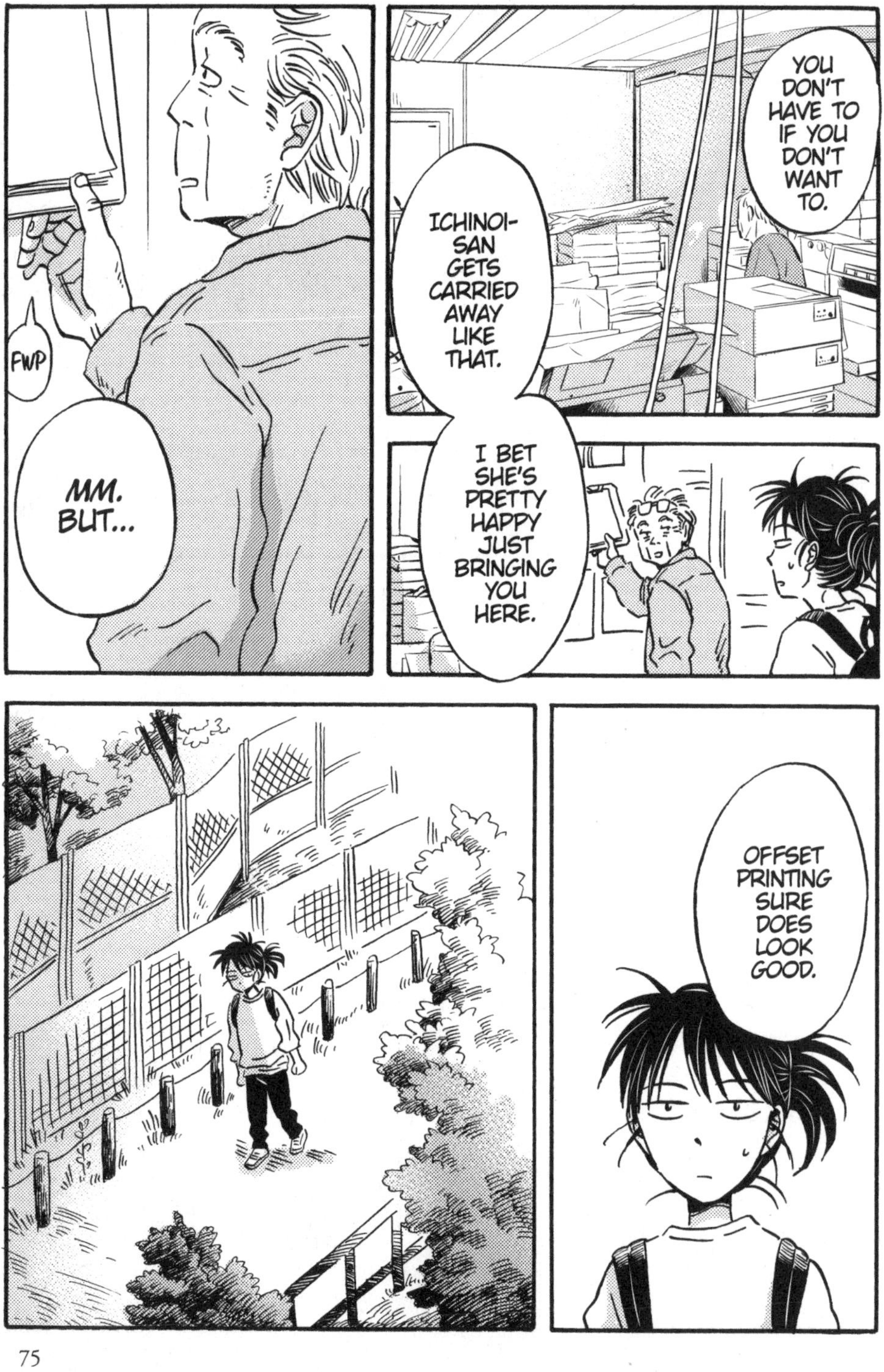

YOU DON'T HAVE TO IF YOU DON'T WANT TO.
ICHINOI-SAN GETS CARRIED AWAY LIKE THAT.
I BET SHE'S PRETTY HAPPY JUST BRINGING YOU HERE.
FWP
MM. BUT...
OFFSET PRINTING SURE DOES LOOK GOOD.

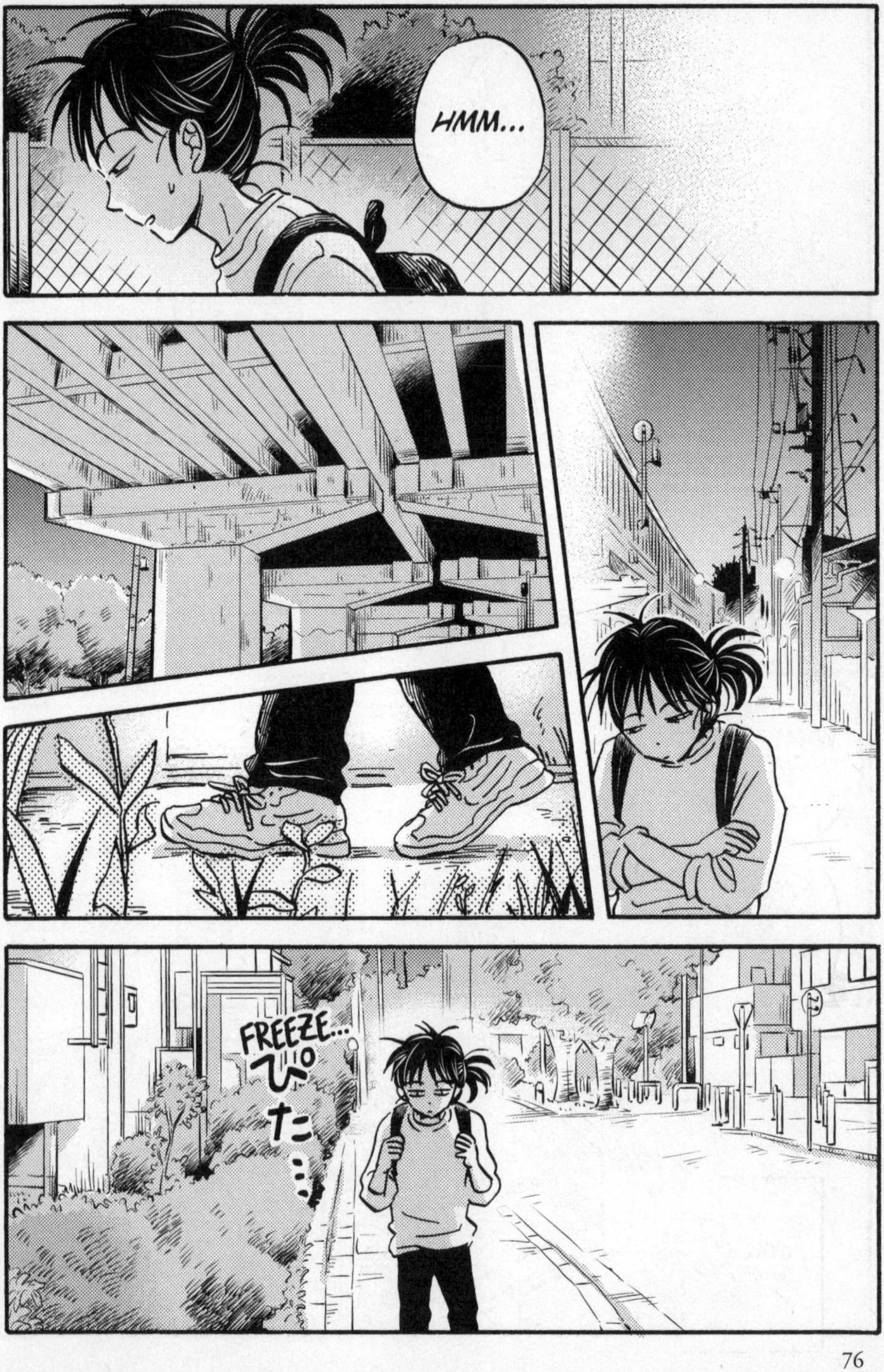
HMM...
FREEZE...
ぴた...

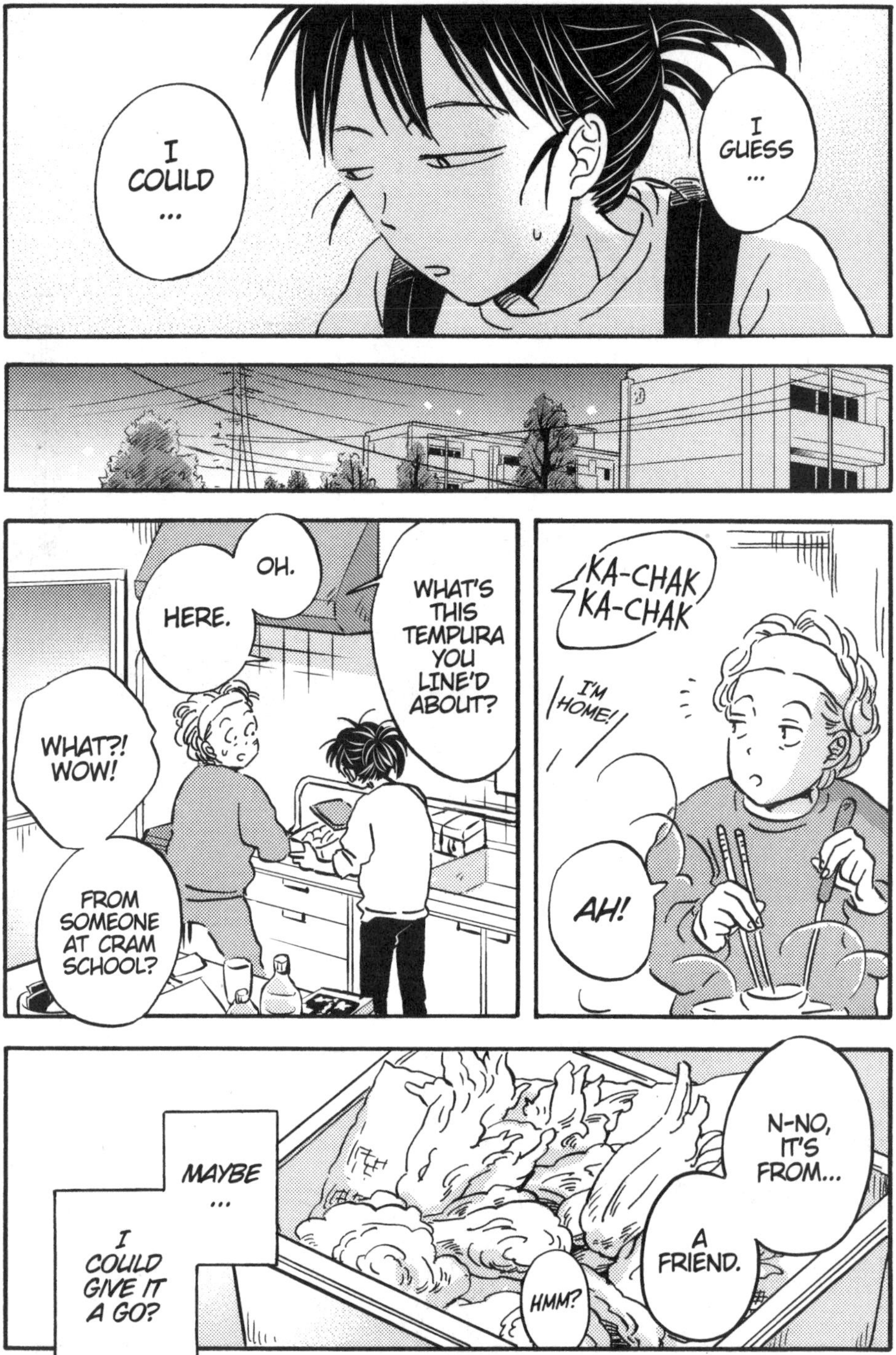
I GUESS ...
I COULD ...
KA-CHAK KA-CHAK
I'M HOME!
AH!
WHAT'S THIS TEMPURA YOU LINE'D ABOUT?
OH.
HERE.
WHAT?! WOW!
FROM SOMEONE AT CRAM SCHOOL?
N-NO, IT'S FROM...
A FRIEND.
HMM?
MAYBE ...
I COULD GIVE IT A GO?

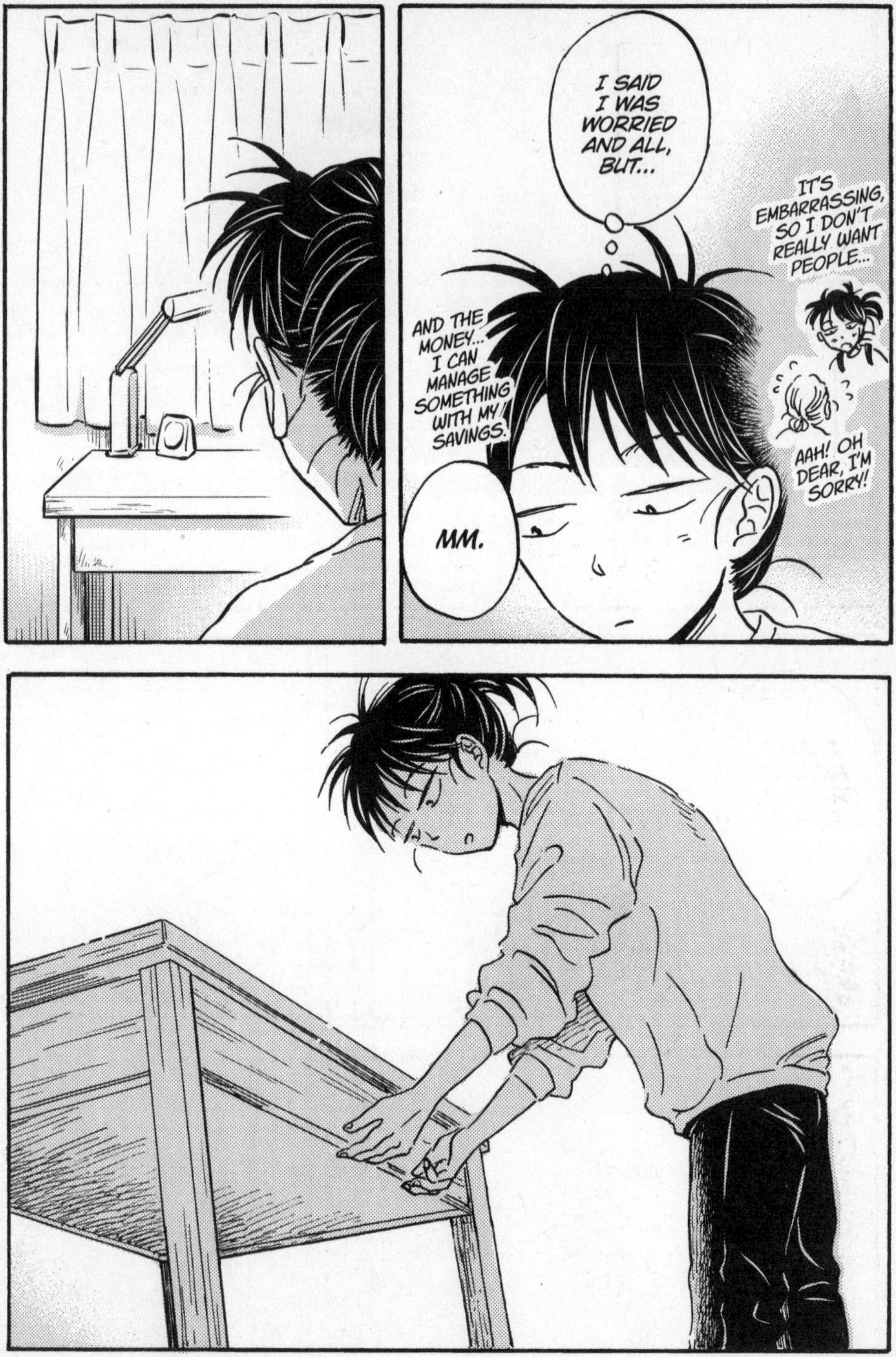

I SAID I WAS WORRIED AND ALL, BUT...
IT'S EMBARRASSING, SO I DON'T REALLY WANT PEOPLE...
AAH! OH DEAR, I'M SORRY!
AND THE MONEY... I CAN MANAGE SOMETHING WITH MY SAVINGS.
MM.

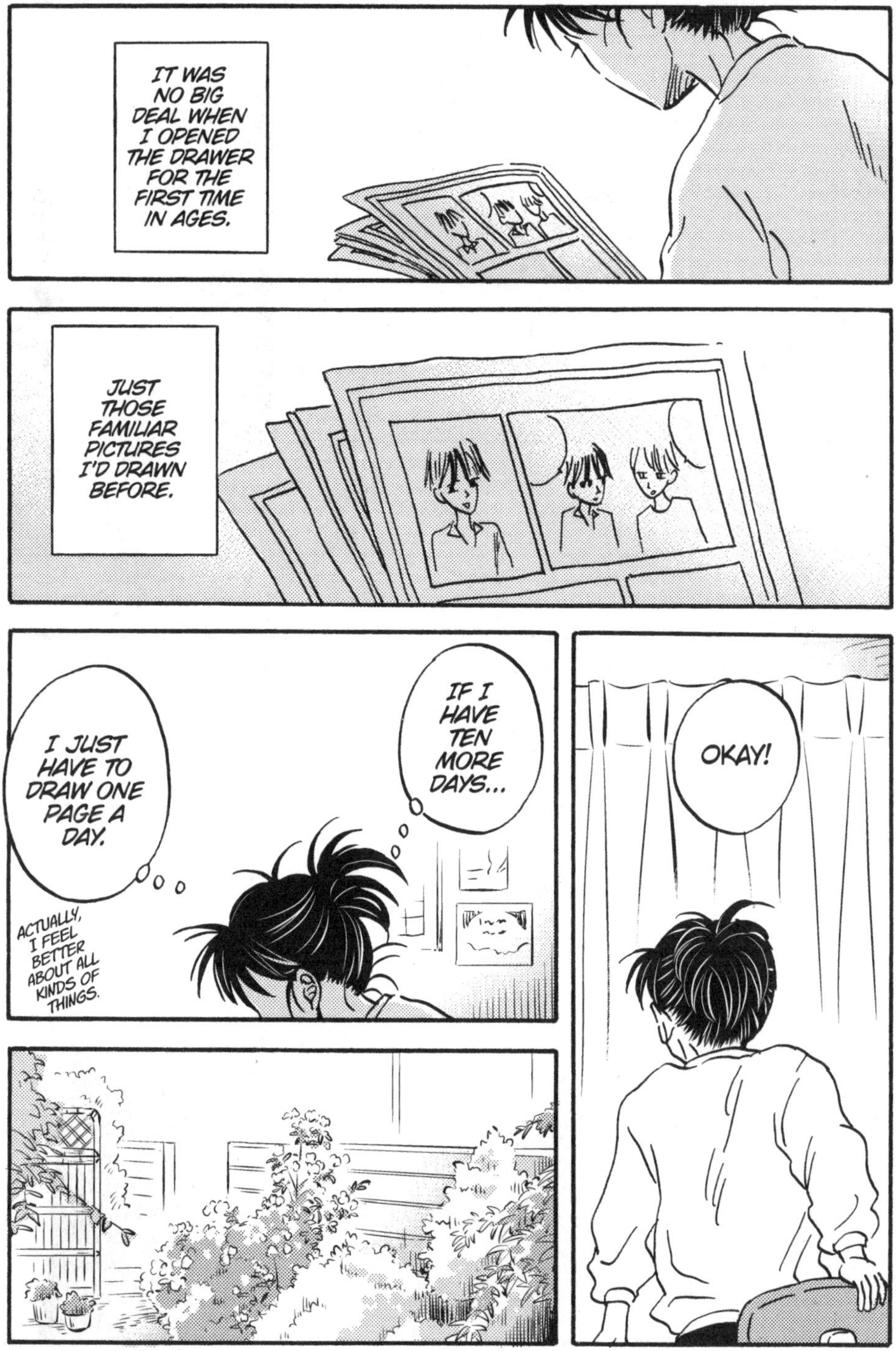
IT WAS NO BIG DEAL WHEN I OPENED THE DRAWER FOR THE FIRST TIME IN AGES.
JUST THOSE FAMILIAR PICTURES I'D DRAWN BEFORE.
OKAY!
IF I HAVE TEN MORE DAYS...
I JUST HAVE TO DRAW ONE PAGE A DAY.
ACTUALLY, I FEEL BETTER ABOUT ALL KINDS OF THINGS.

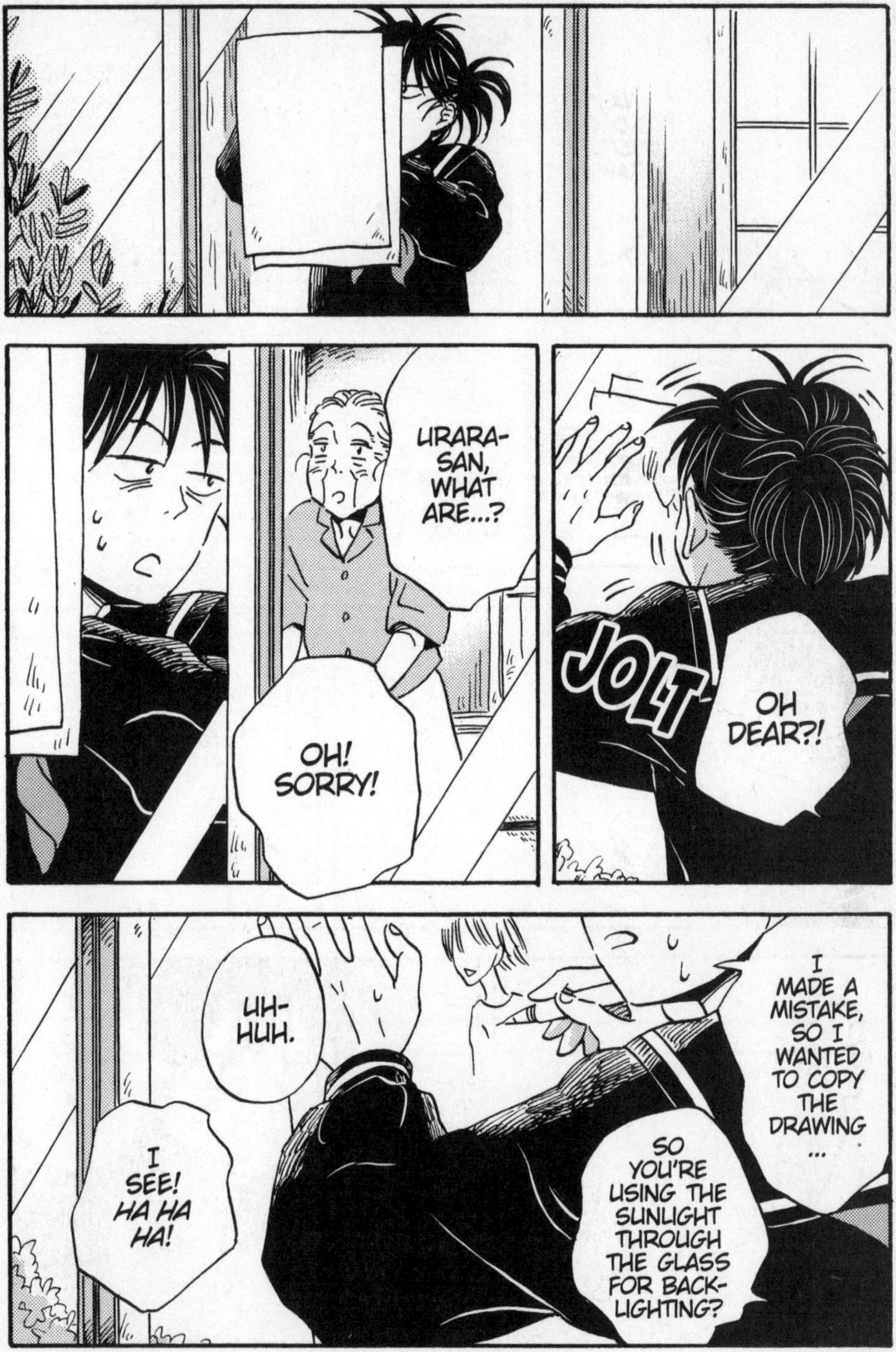
JOLT
OH DEAR?!
URARA-SAN, WHAT ARE...?
OH! SORRY!
I MADE A MISTAKE, SO I WANTED TO COPY THE DRAWING ...
SO YOU'RE USING THE SUNLIGHT THROUGH THE GLASS FOR BACK-LIGHTING?
UH-HUH.
I SEE! HA HA HA!

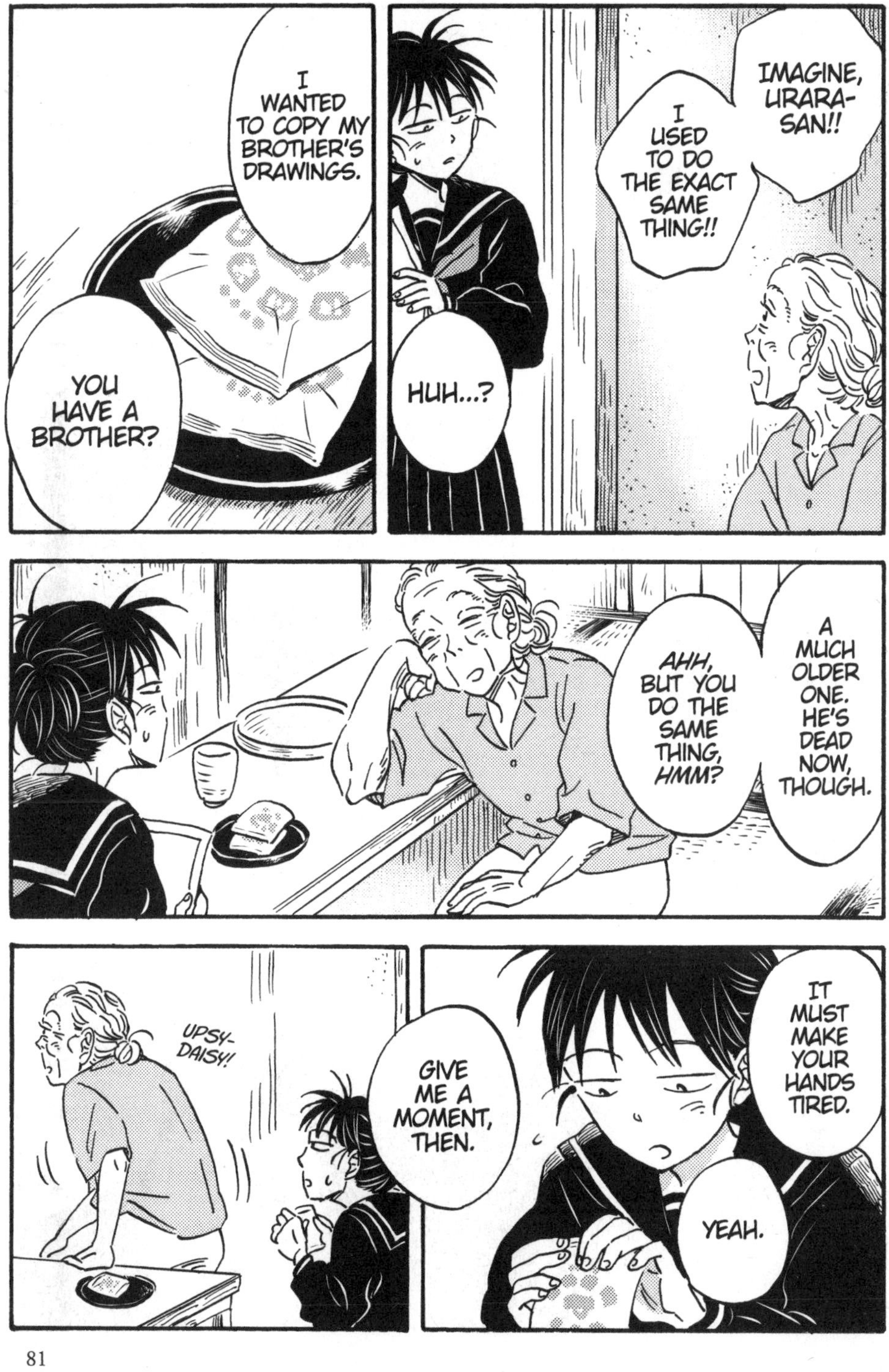
IMAGINE, URARA-SAN!!
I USED TO DO THE EXACT SAME THING!!
HUH...?
I WANTED TO COPY MY BROTHER'S DRAWINGS.
YOU HAVE A BROTHER?
A MUCH OLDER ONE. HE'S DEAD NOW, THOUGH.
AHH, BUT YOU DO THE SAME THING, *HMM?*
IT MUST MAKE YOUR HANDS TIRED.
YEAH.
GIVE ME A MOMENT, THEN.
UPSY-DAISY!

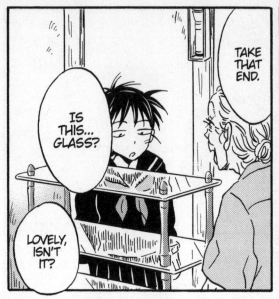

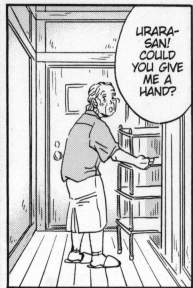

URARA-SAN! COULD YOU GIVE ME A HAND?
TAKE THAT END.
IS THIS... GLASS?
LOVELY, ISN'T IT?
IT COMES APART TIDILY.
TWIST THAT BIT ON THE TOP.

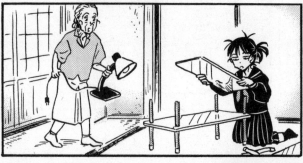

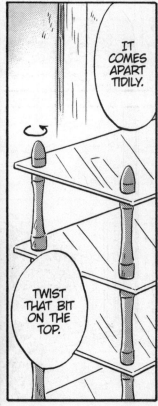

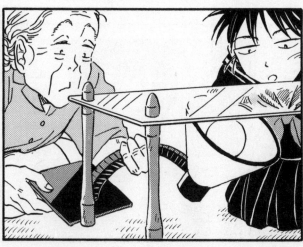

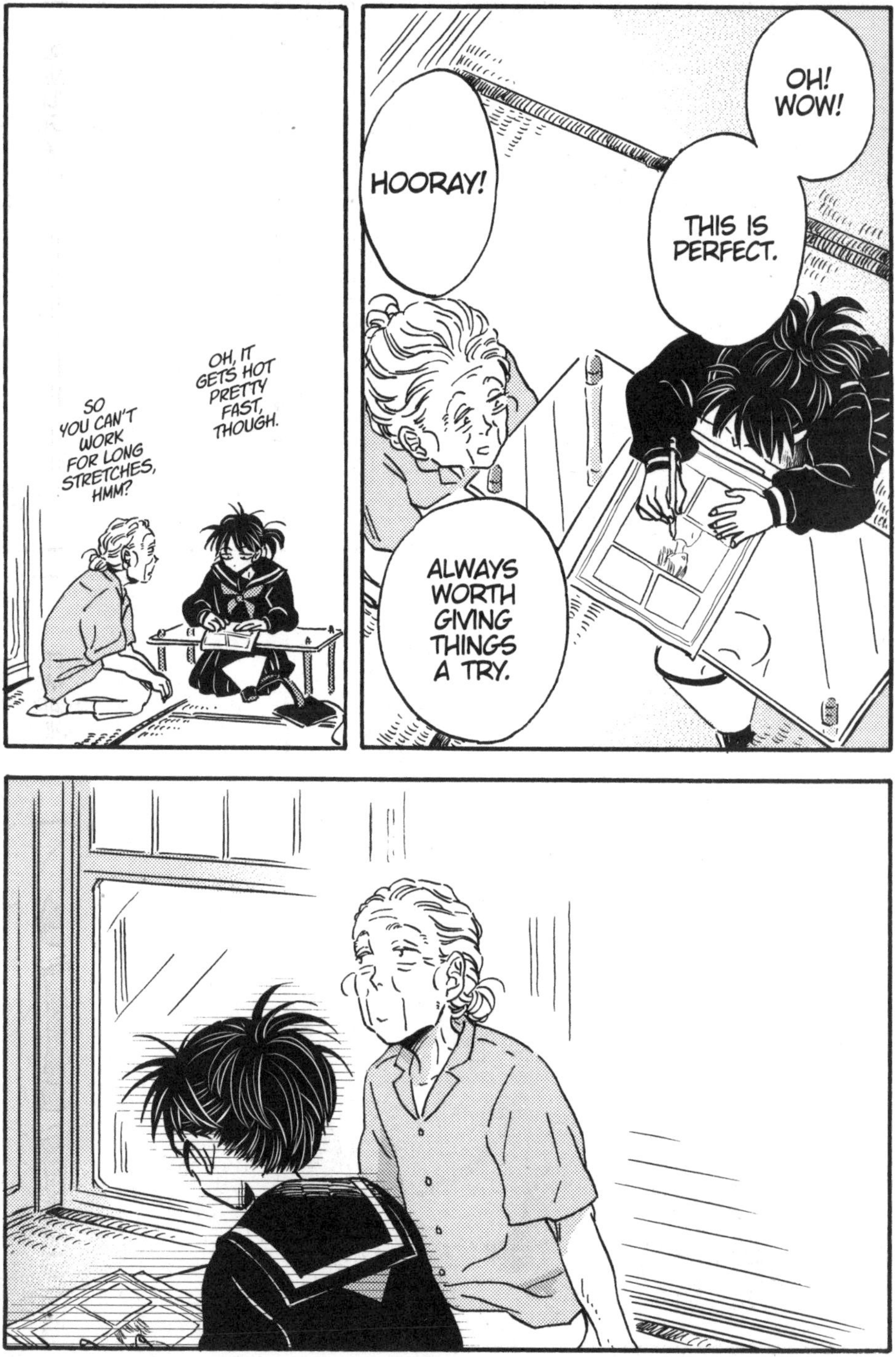
OH! WOW!
THIS IS PERFECT.
HOORAY!
ALWAYS WORTH GIVING THINGS A TRY.
OH, IT GETS HOT PRETTY FAST, THOUGH.
SO YOU CAN'T WORK FOR LONG STRETCHES, HMM?

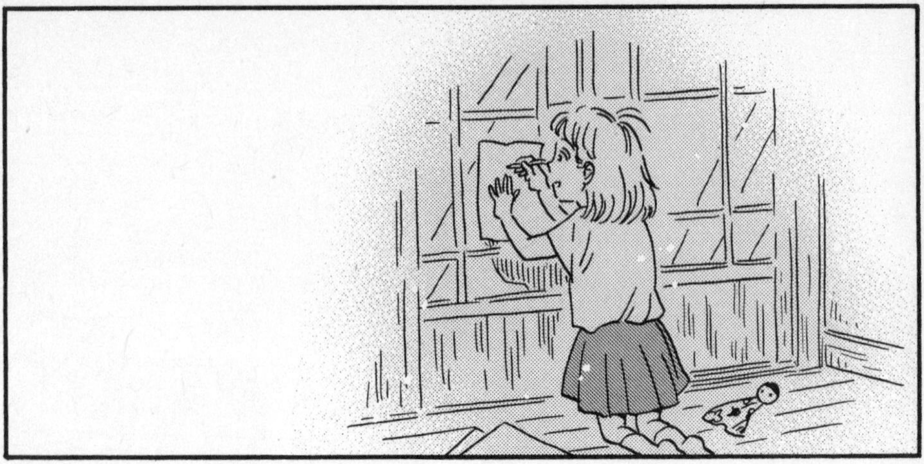

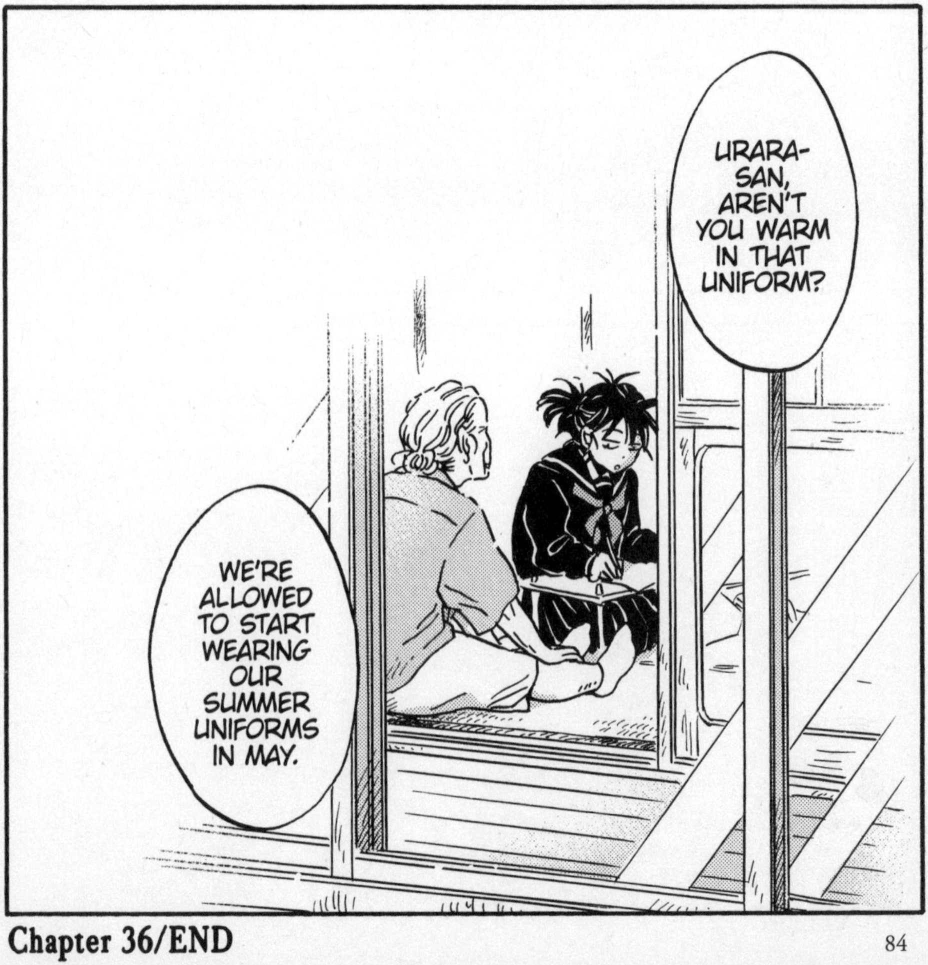
URARA-SAN, AREN'T YOU WARM IN THAT UNIFORM?
WE'RE ALLOWED TO START WEARING OUR SUMMER UNIFORMS IN MAY.

Chapter 36/END

metamorphosis

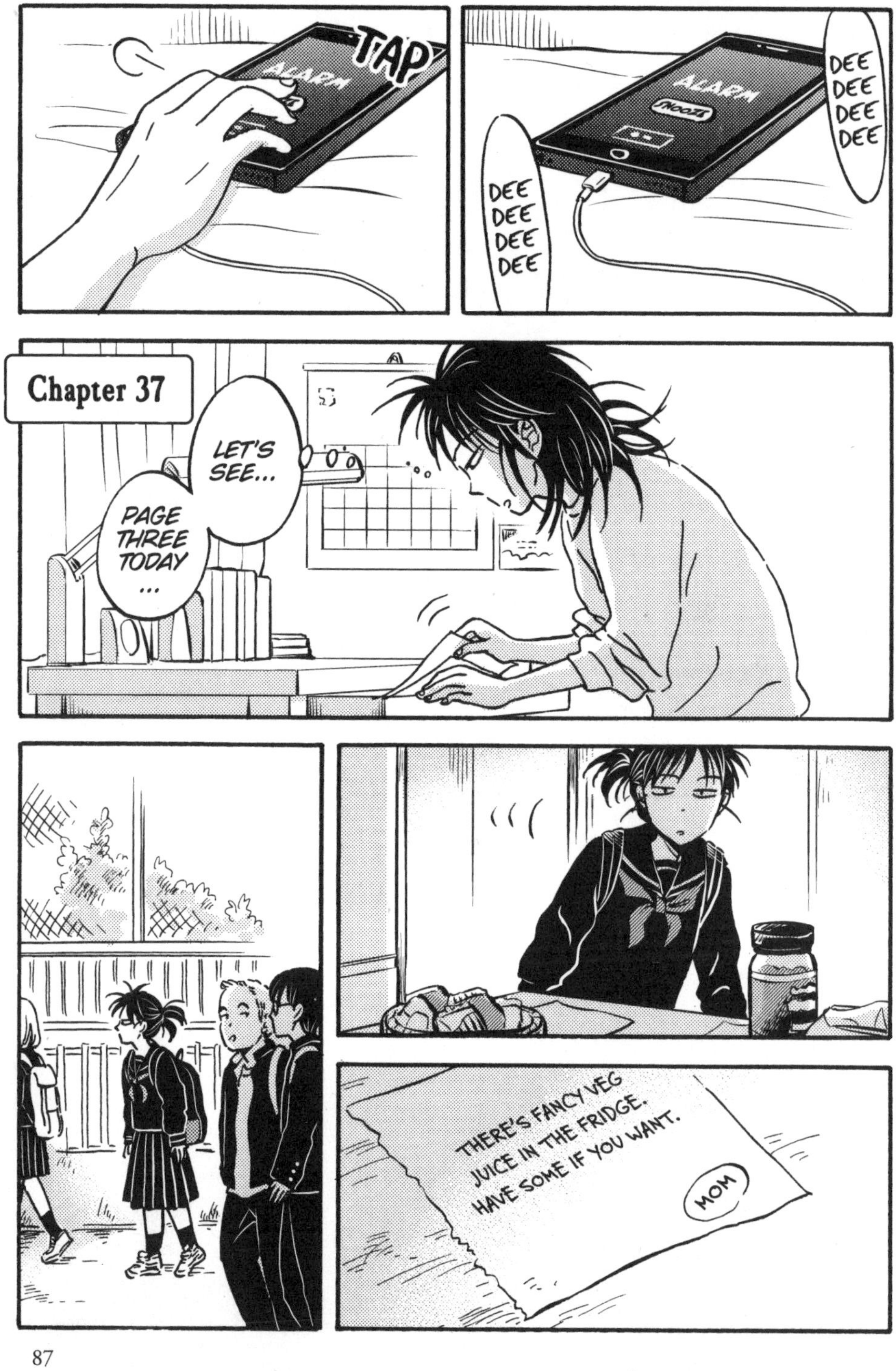
DEE DEE DEE DEE
ALARM
SNOOZE
DEE DEE DEE DEE
TAP
ALARM
Chapter 37
LET'S SEE...
PAGE THREE TODAY ...
THERE'S FANCY VEG JUICE IN THE FRIDGE. HAVE SOME IF YOU WANT.
MOM

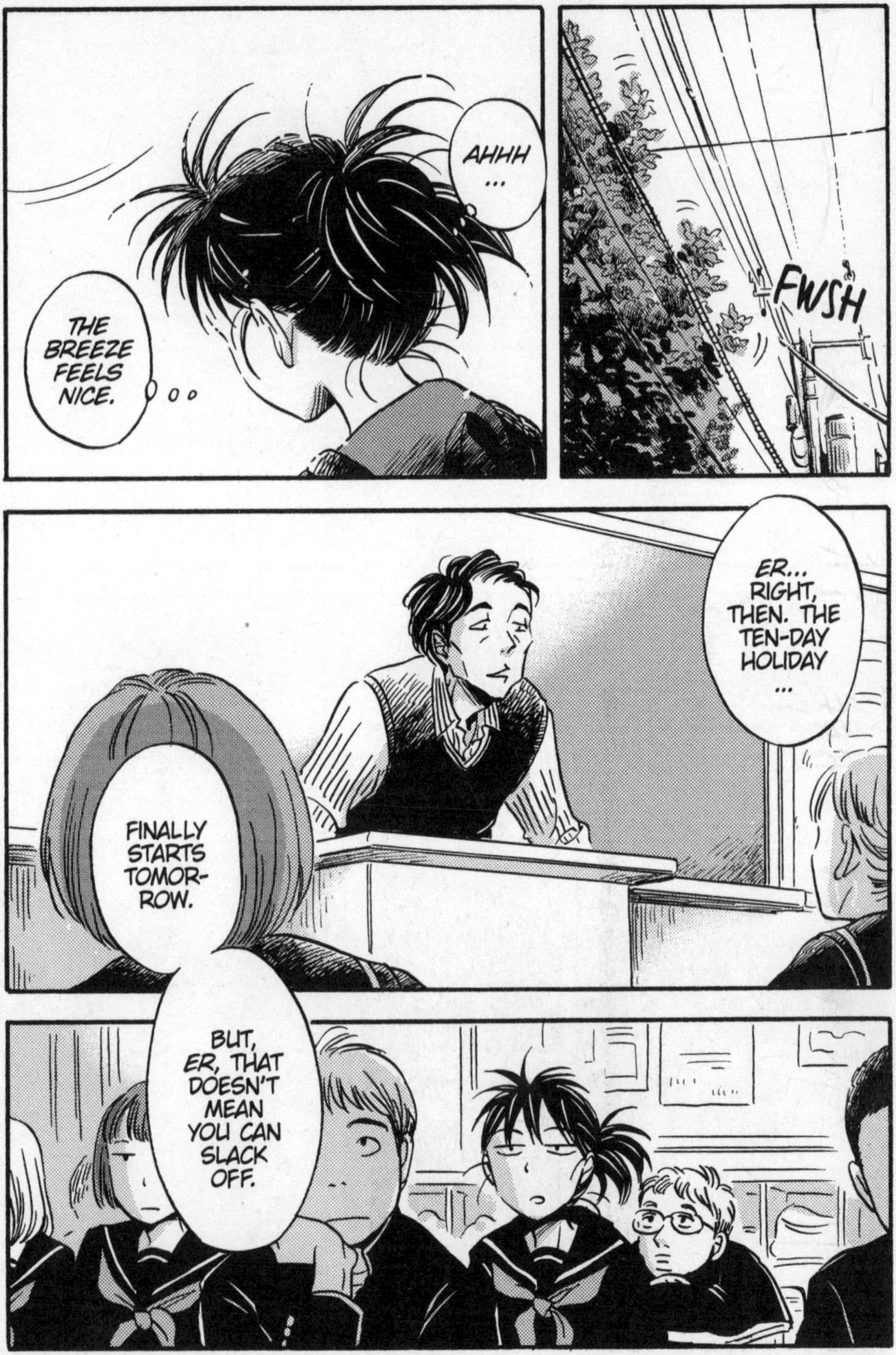
FWSH
AHHH ...
THE BREEZE FEELS NICE.
ER... RIGHT, THEN. THE TEN-DAY HOLIDAY ...
FINALLY STARTS TOMORROW.
BUT, ER, THAT DOESN'T MEAN YOU CAN SLACK OFF.

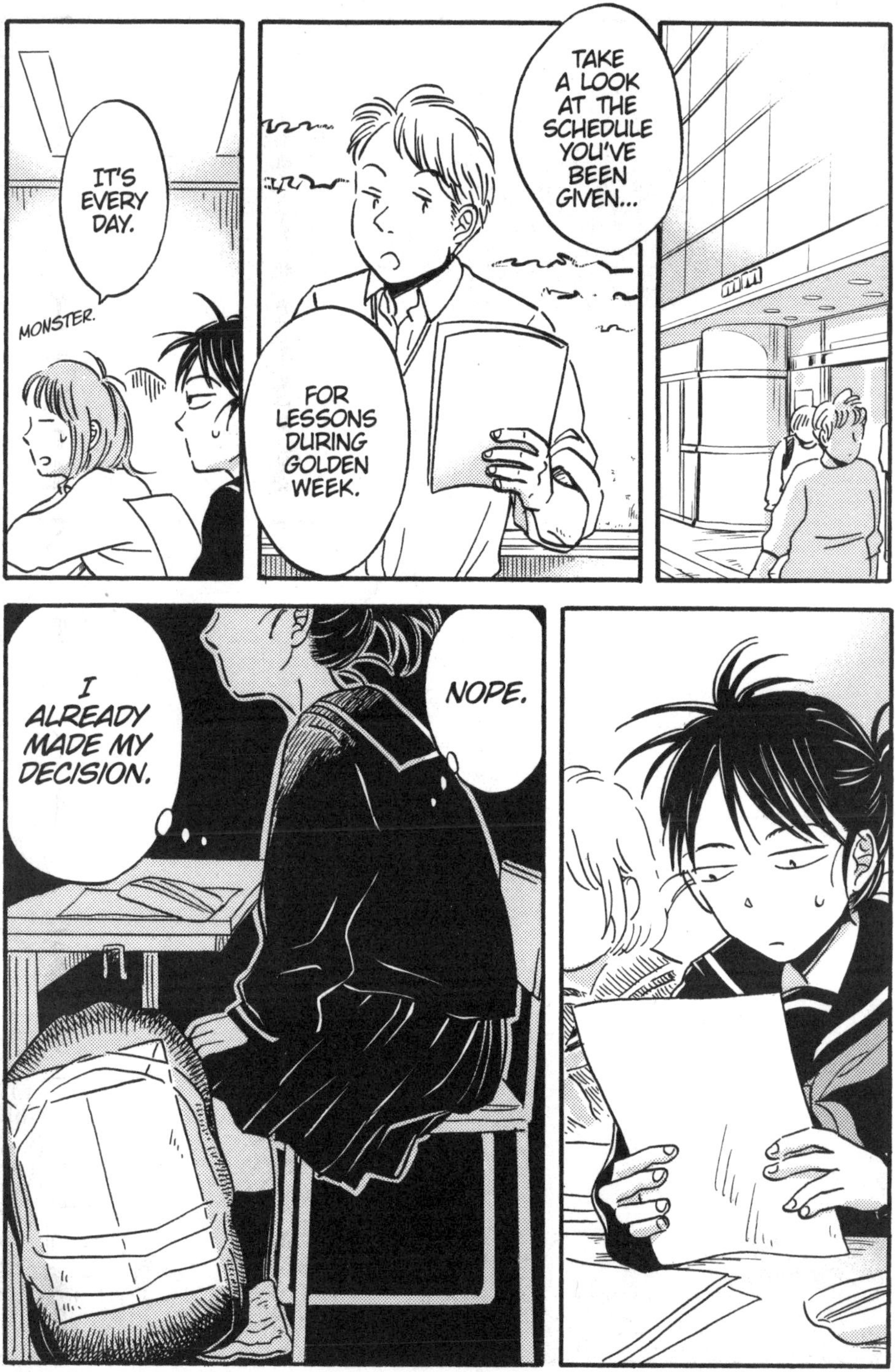
TAKE A LOOK AT THE SCHEDULE YOU'VE BEEN GIVEN...
FOR LESSONS DURING GOLDEN WEEK.
IT'S EVERY DAY.
MONSTER.
NOPE.
I ALREADY MADE MY DECISION.

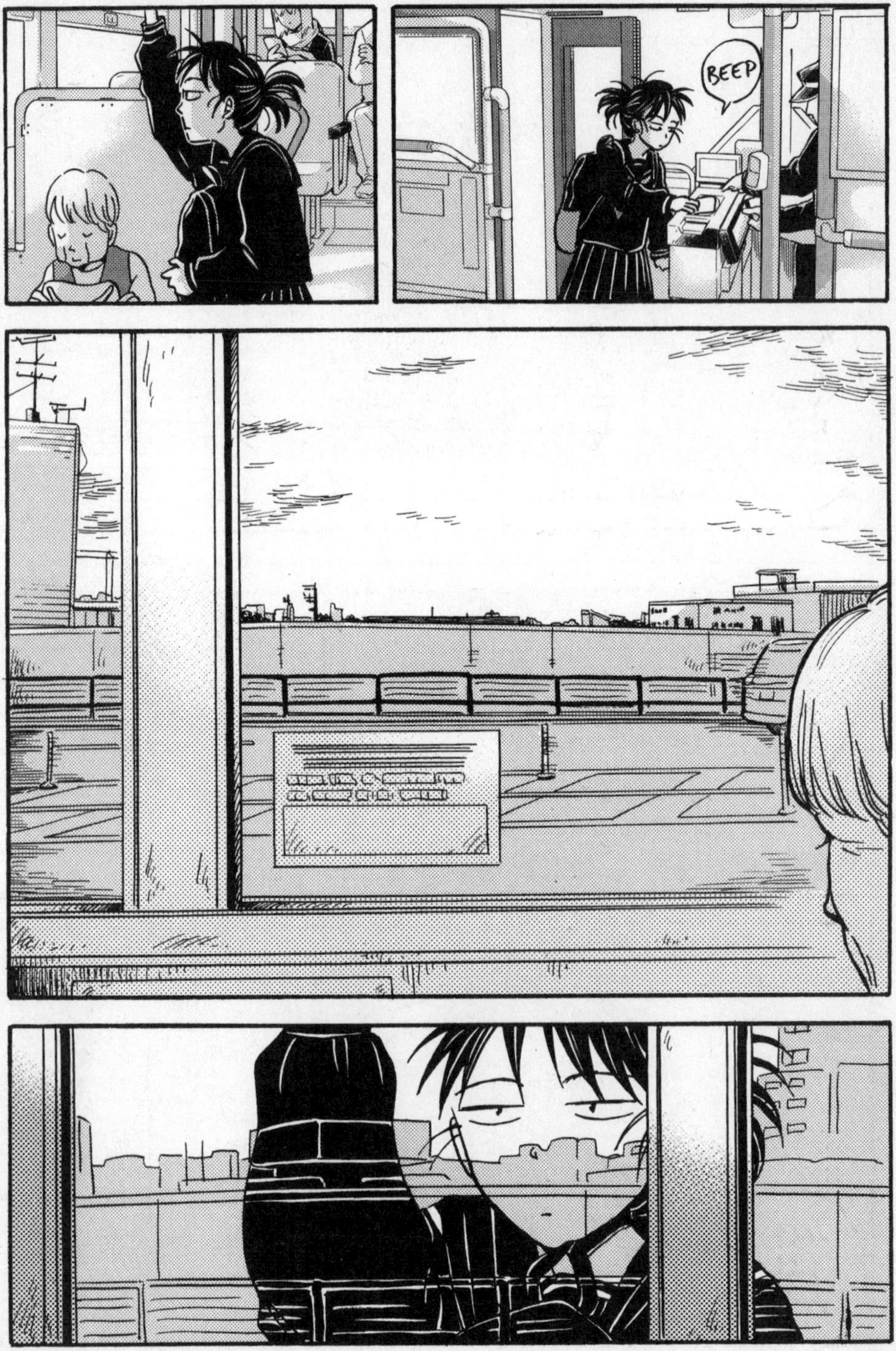
BEEP

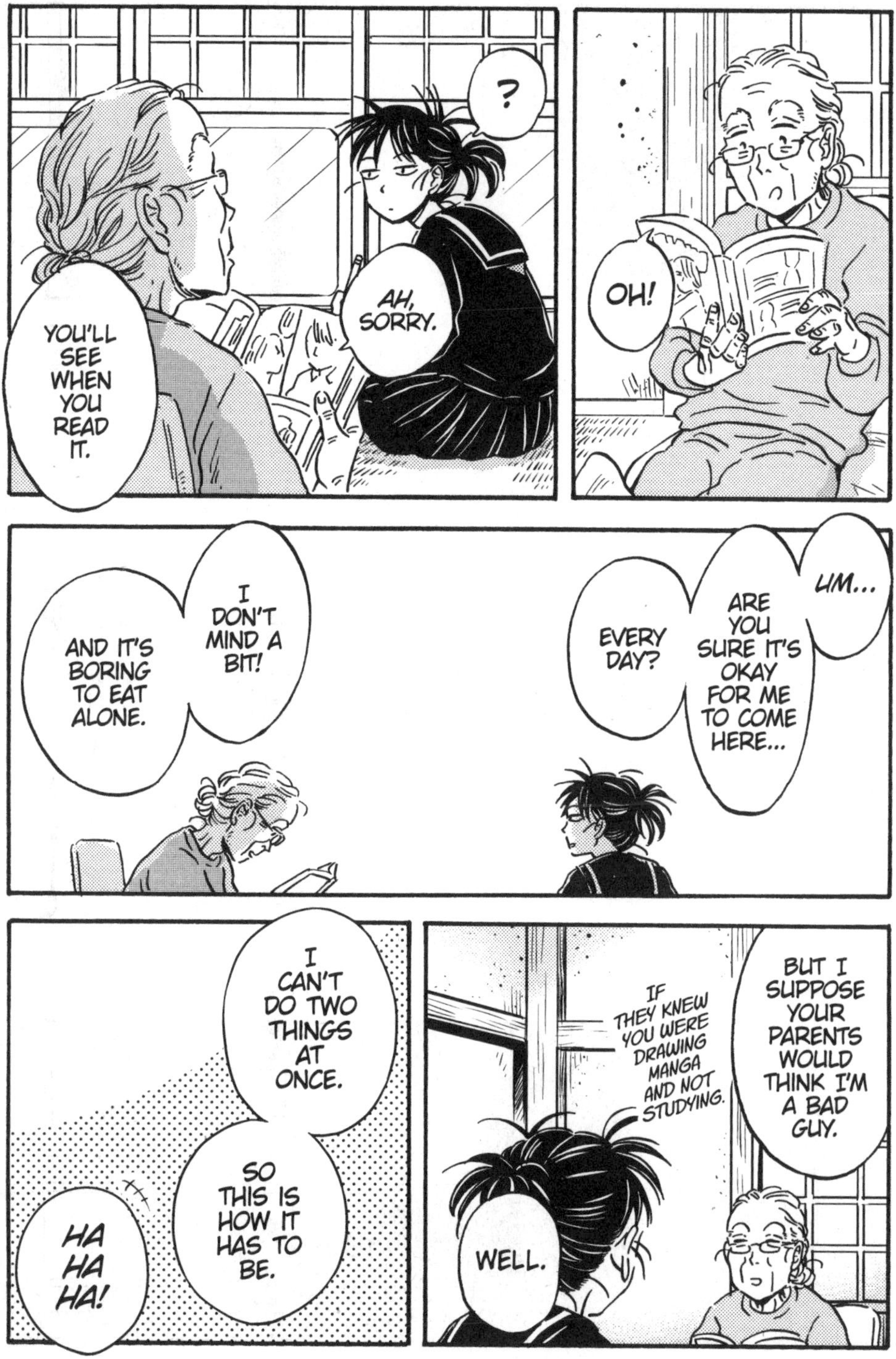
OH!
?
AH, SORRY.
YOU'LL SEE WHEN YOU READ IT.
UM...
ARE YOU SURE IT'S OKAY FOR ME TO COME HERE...
EVERY DAY?
I DON'T MIND A BIT!
AND IT'S BORING TO EAT ALONE.
BUT I SUPPOSE YOUR PARENTS WOULD THINK I'M A BAD GUY.
IF THEY KNEW YOU WERE DRAWING MANGA AND NOT STUDYING.
WELL.
I CAN'T DO TWO THINGS AT ONCE.
SO THIS IS HOW IT HAS TO BE.
HA HA HA!

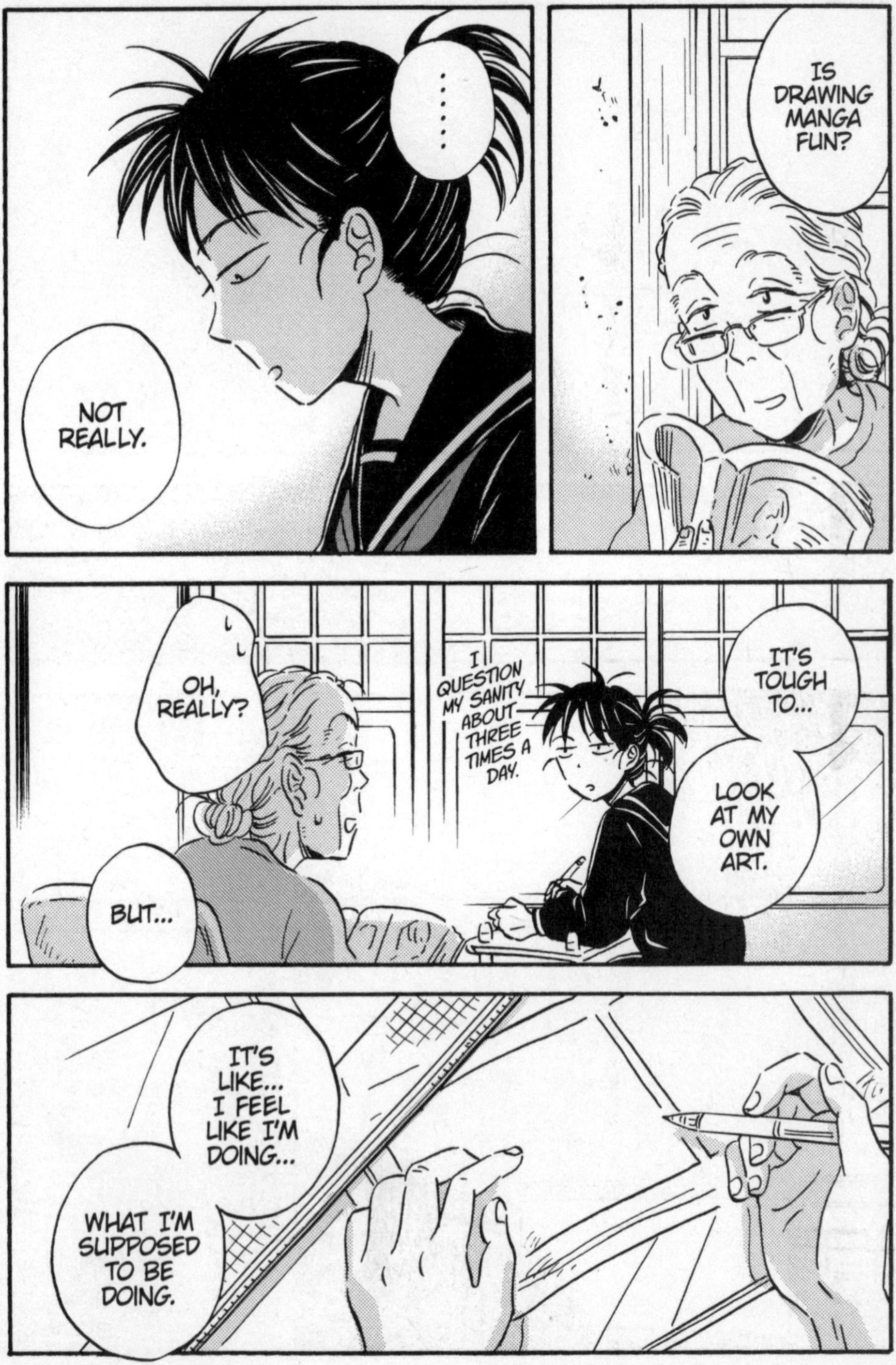
IS DRAWING MANGA FUN?
......
NOT REALLY.
IT'S TOUGH TO...
LOOK AT MY OWN ART.
I QUESTION MY SANITY ABOUT THREE TIMES A DAY.
OH, REALLY?
BUT...
IT'S LIKE... I FEEL LIKE I'M DOING...
WHAT I'M SUPPOSED TO BE DOING.

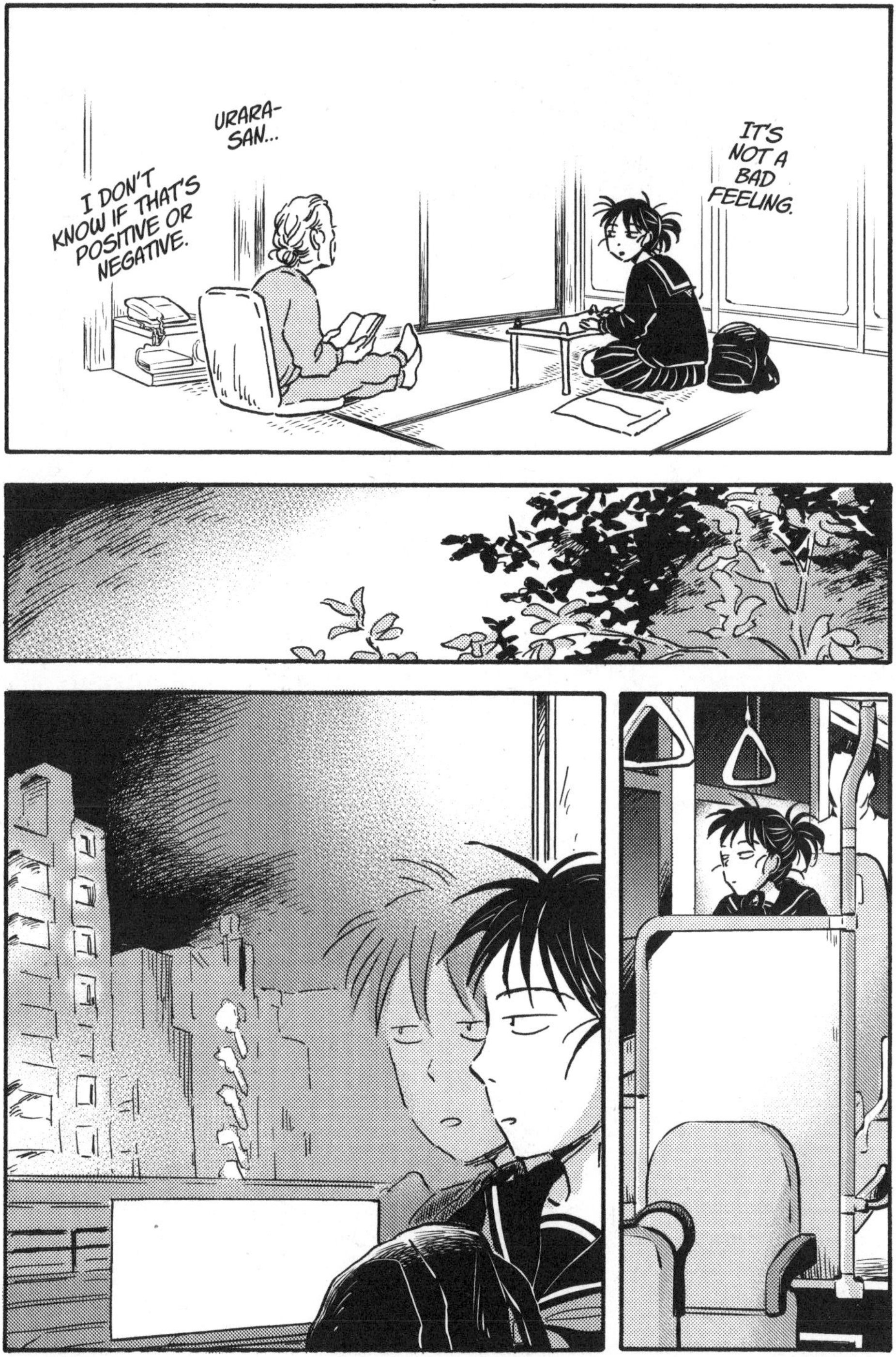
IT'S NOT A BAD FEELING.
URARA-SAN...
I DON'T KNOW IF THAT'S POSITIVE OR NEGATIVE.

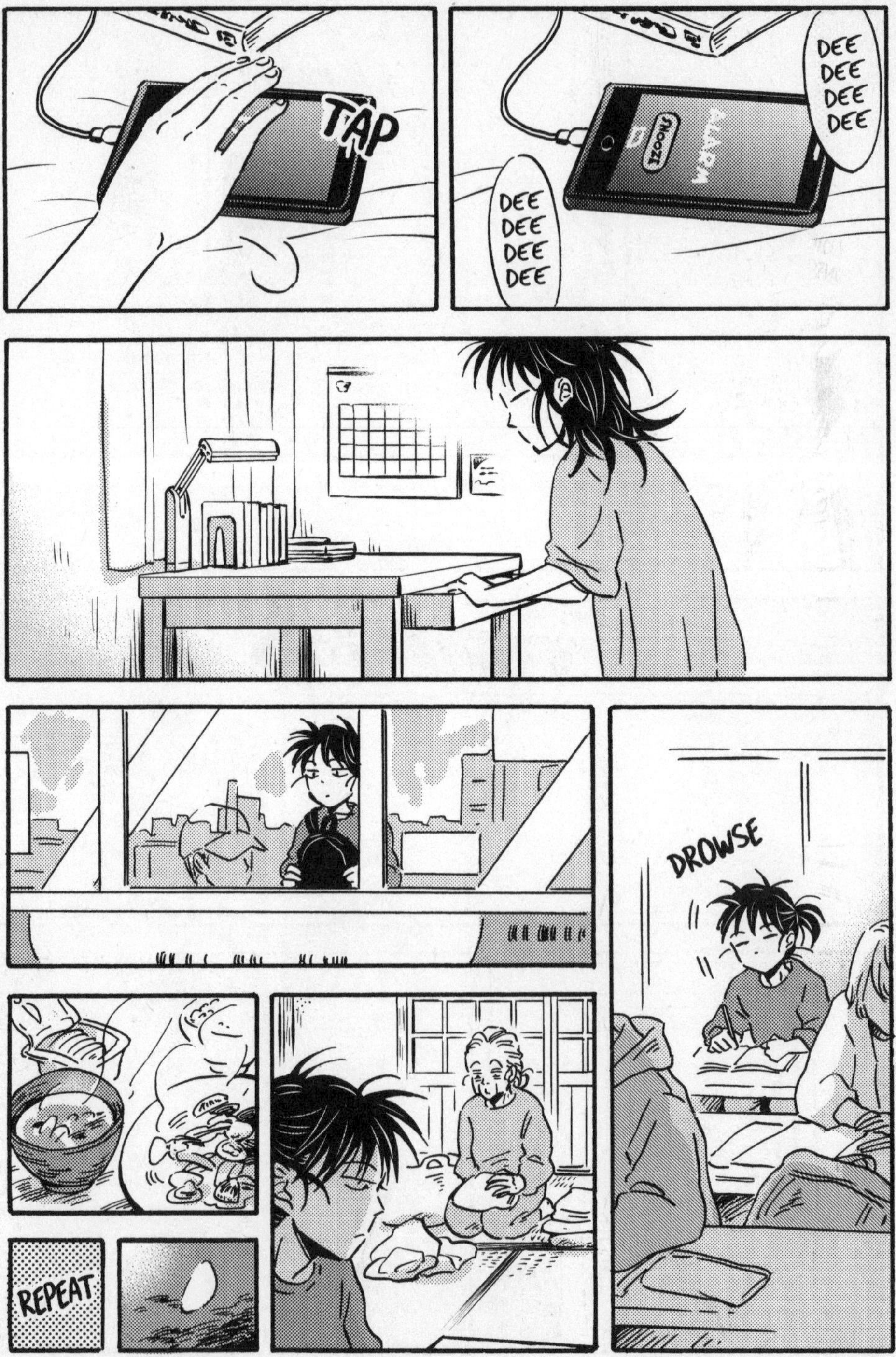
DEE
DEE
DEE
DEE
ALARM
SNOOZE
DEE
DEE
DEE
DEE
TAP
DROWSE
REPEAT

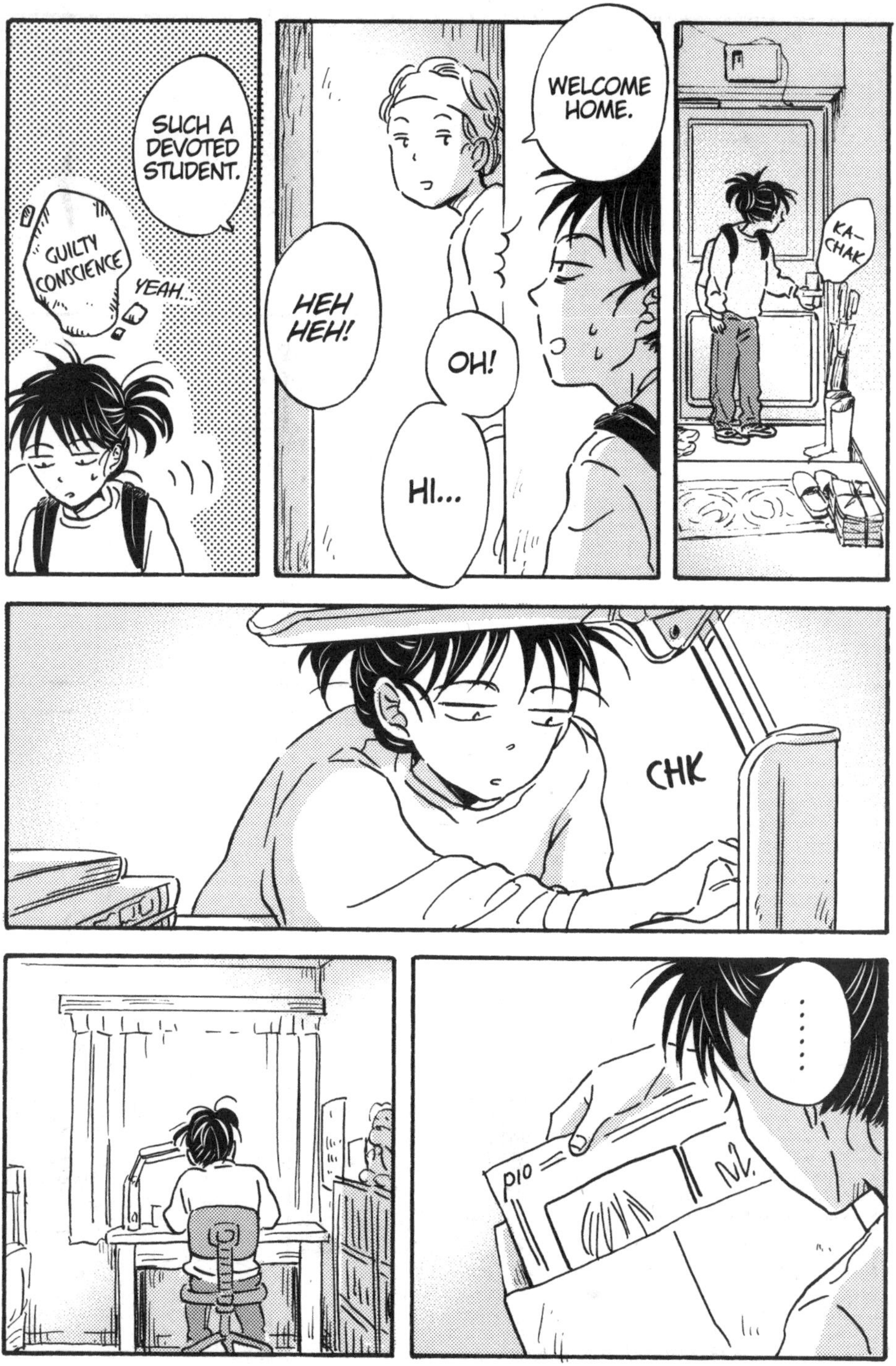
KA-CHAK
WELCOME HOME.
OH!
HI...
HEH HEH!
SUCH A DEVOTED STUDENT.
GUILTY CONSCIENCE
YEAH...
CHK
......

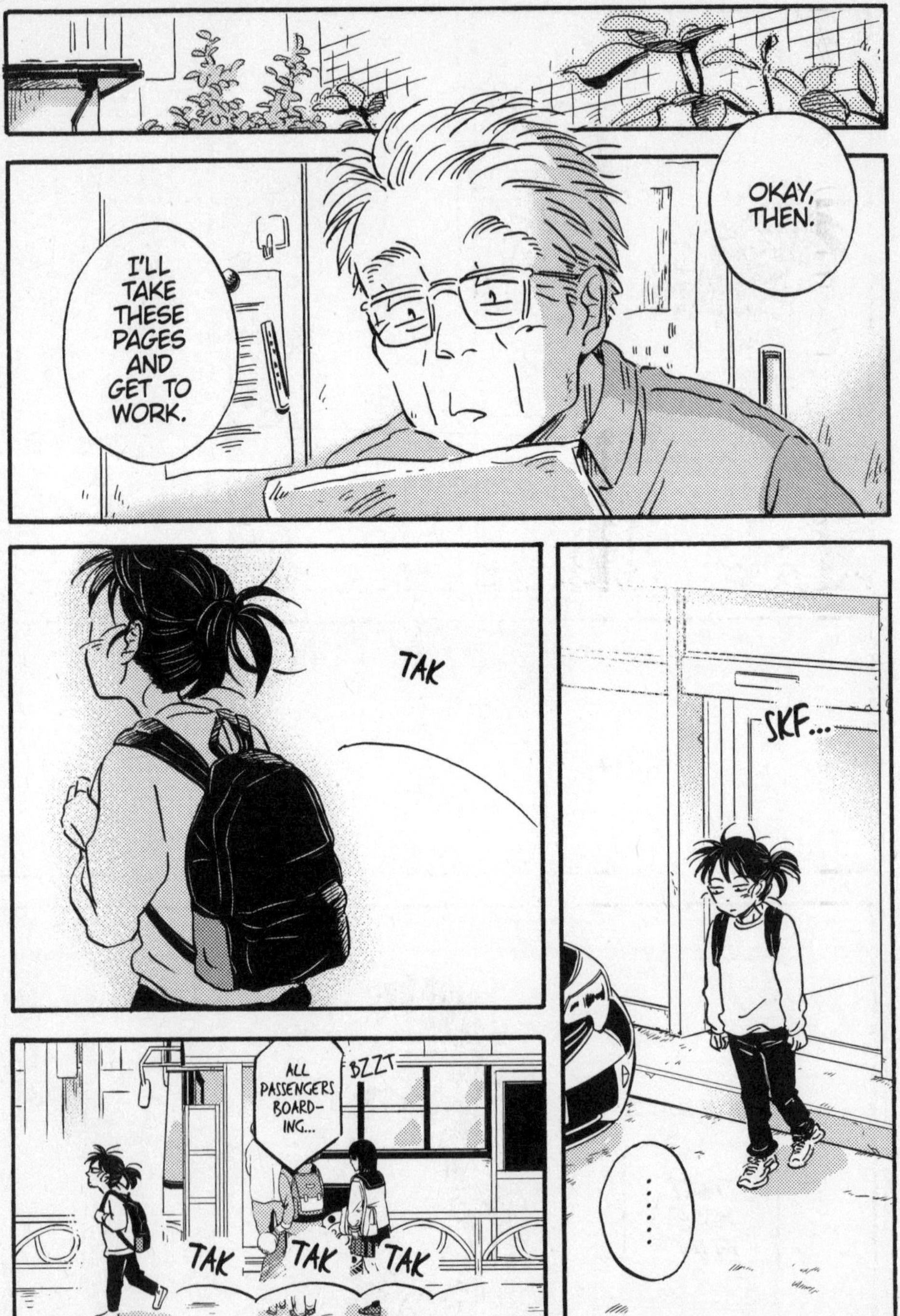

OKAY, THEN.
I'LL TAKE THESE PAGES AND GET TO WORK.
SKF...
......
TAK
BZZT
ALL PASSENGERS BOARD-ING...
TAK TAK TAK

"IS DRAWING MANGA FUN?"

"NOT...

"REALLY."

HAAH...

THAT WAS FUN.

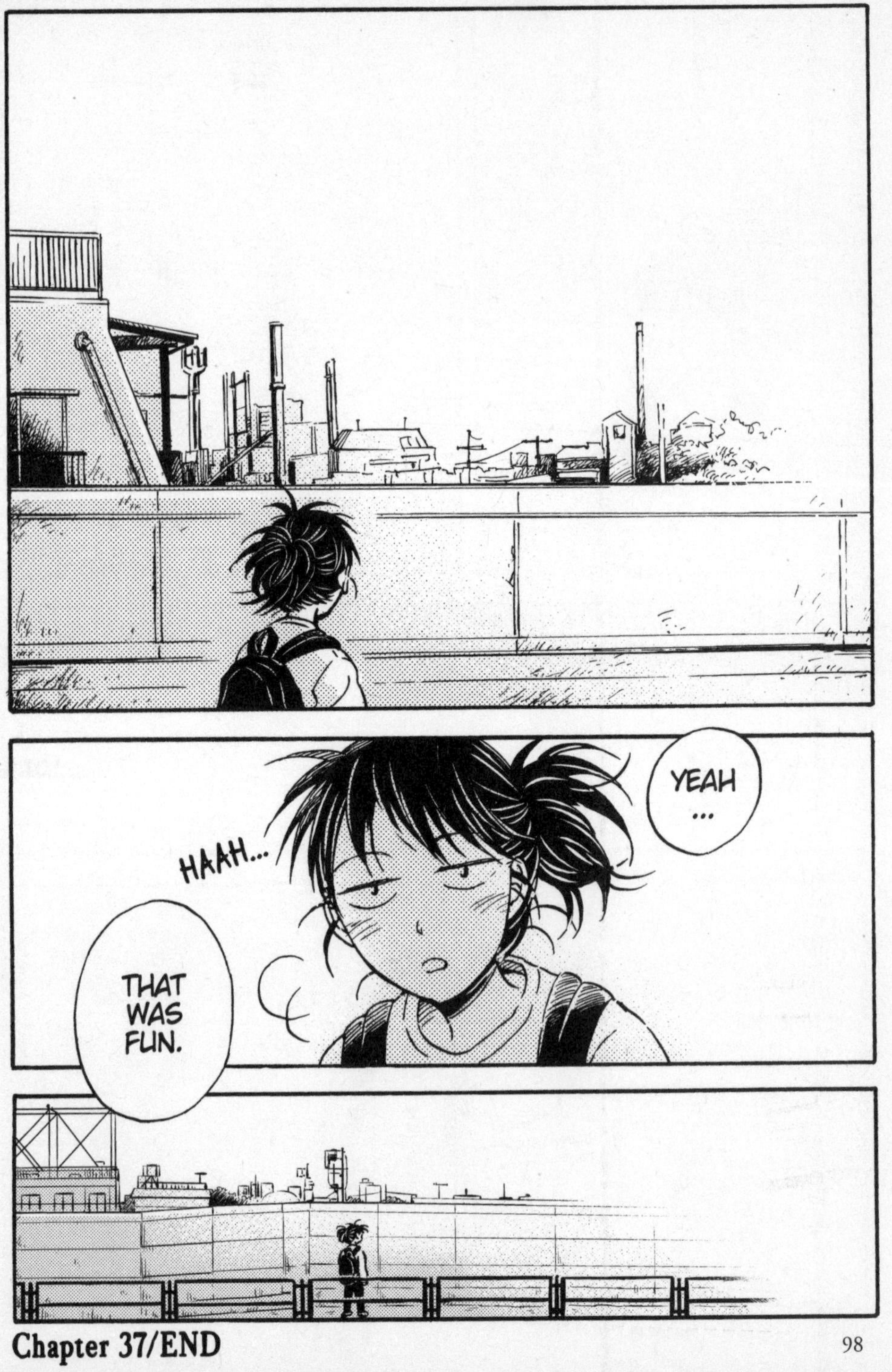
YEAH ...
HAAH...
THAT WAS FUN.

Chapter 37/END

metamorphosis

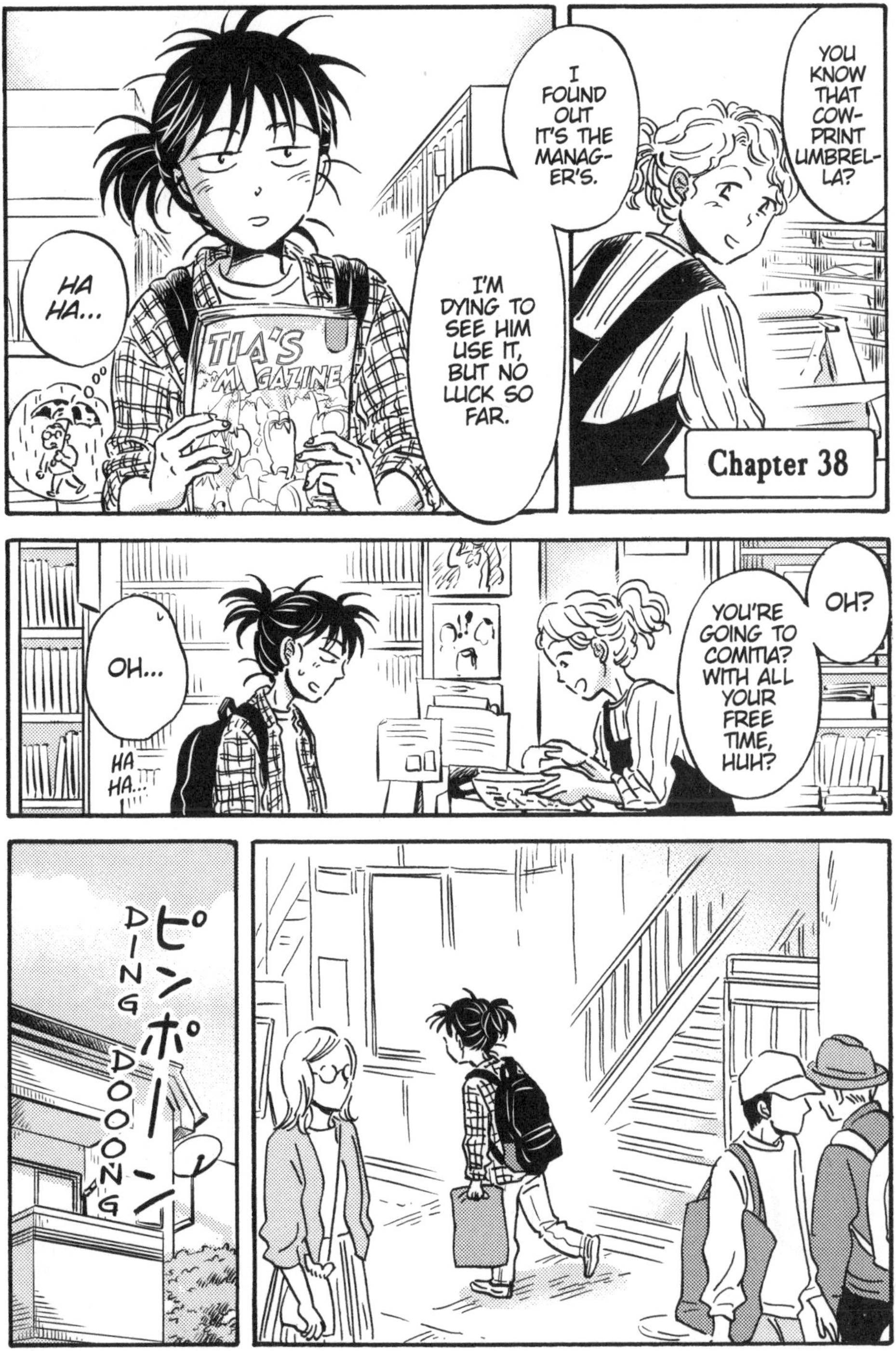
YOU KNOW THAT COW-PRINT UMBREL-LA?
Chapter 38
I FOUND OUT IT'S THE MANAG-ER'S.
I'M DYING TO SEE HIM USE IT, BUT NO LUCK SO FAR.
HA HA...
OH?
YOU'RE GOING TO COMITIA? WITH ALL YOUR FREE TIME, HUH?
OH...
HA HA...
ピンポーン
DING DOOOONG

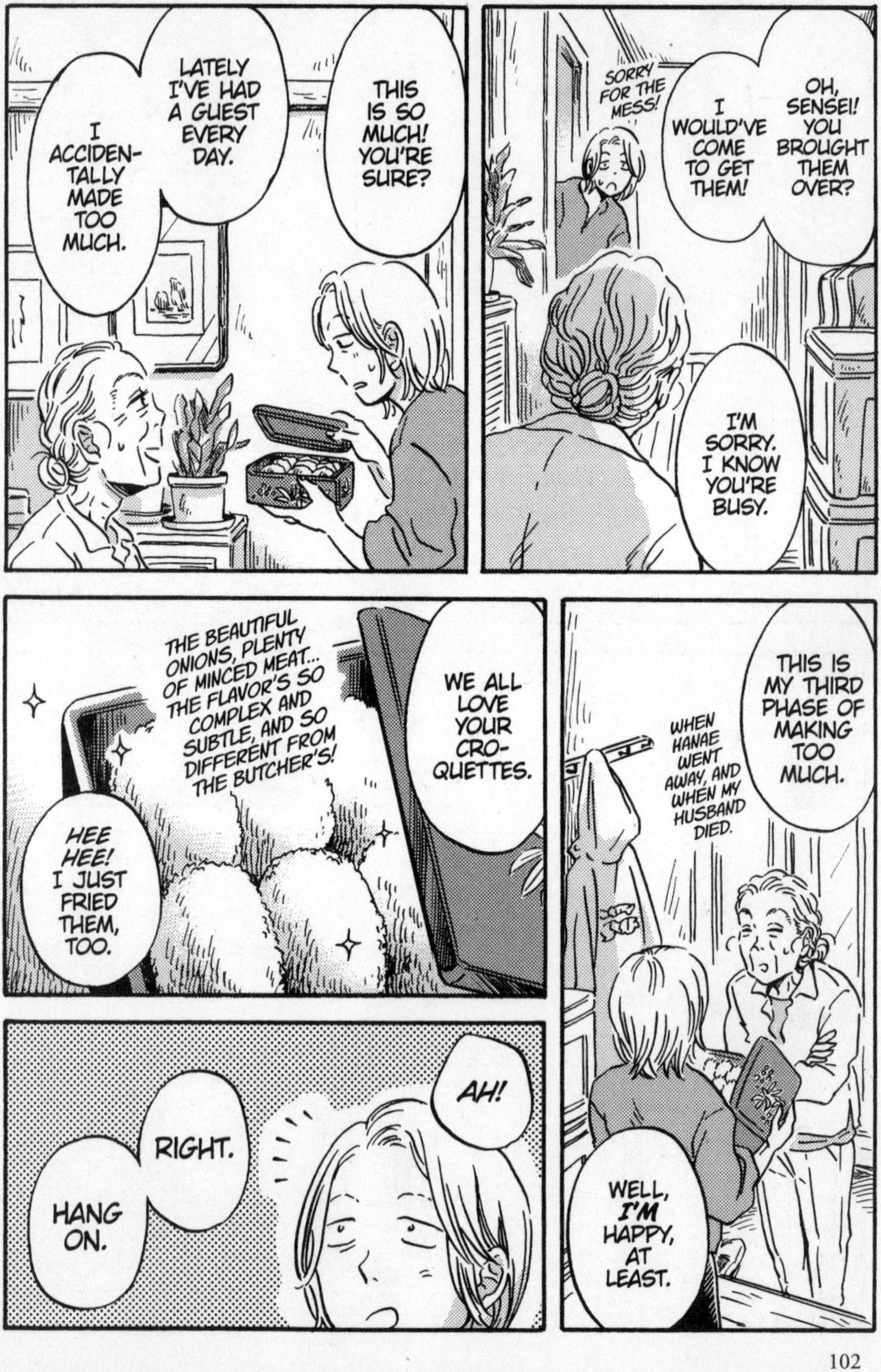
OH, SENSEI! YOU BROUGHT THEM OVER?
I WOULD'VE COME TO GET THEM!
SORRY FOR THE MESS!
I'M SORRY. I KNOW YOU'RE BUSY.
THIS IS SO MUCH! YOU'RE SURE?
LATELY I'VE HAD A GUEST EVERY DAY.
I ACCIDENTALLY MADE TOO MUCH.
THIS IS MY THIRD PHASE OF MAKING TOO MUCH.
WHEN HANAE WENT AWAY, AND WHEN MY HUSBAND DIED.
WELL, *I'M* HAPPY, AT LEAST.
WE ALL LOVE YOUR CROQUETTES.
THE BEAUTIFUL ONIONS, PLENTY OF MINCED MEAT... THE FLAVOR'S SO COMPLEX AND SUBTLE, AND SO DIFFERENT FROM THE BUTCHER'S!
HEE HEE! I JUST FRIED THEM, TOO.
AH!
RIGHT.
HANG ON.

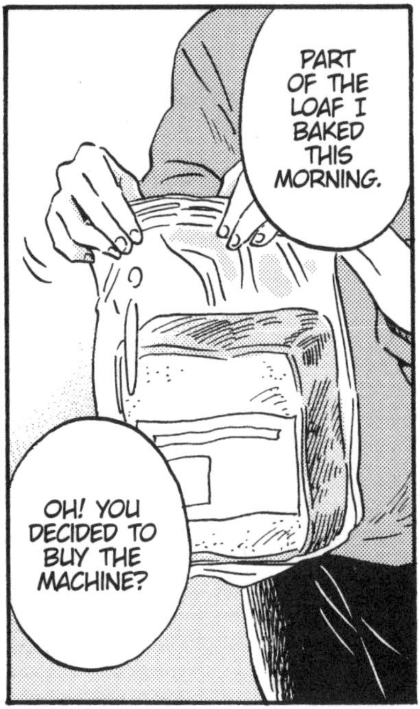
PART OF THE LOAF I BAKED THIS MORNING.
OH! YOU DECIDED TO BUY THE MACHINE?

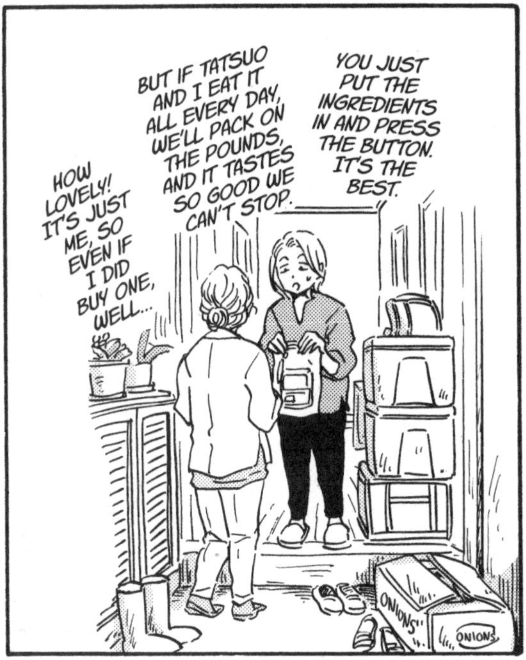
YOU JUST PUT THE INGREDIENTS IN AND PRESS THE BUTTON. IT'S THE BEST.
BUT IF TATSUO AND I EAT IT ALL EVERY DAY, WE'LL PACK ON THE POUNDS, AND IT TASTES SO GOOD WE CAN'T STOP.
HOW LOVELY! IT'S JUST ME, SO EVEN IF I DID BUY ONE, WELL...
ONIONS
ONIONS

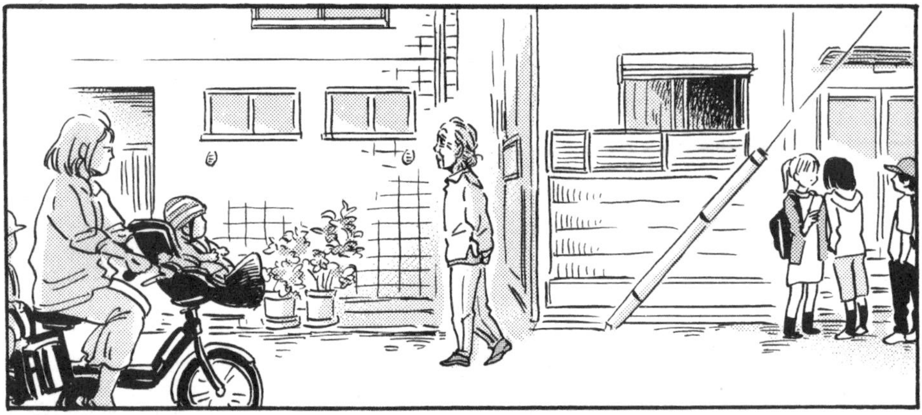

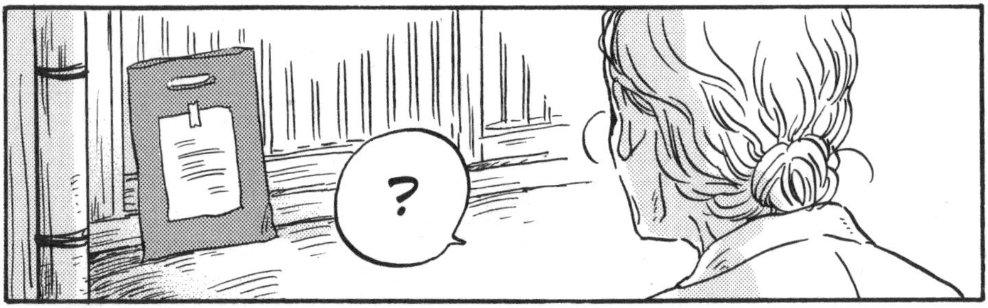
?

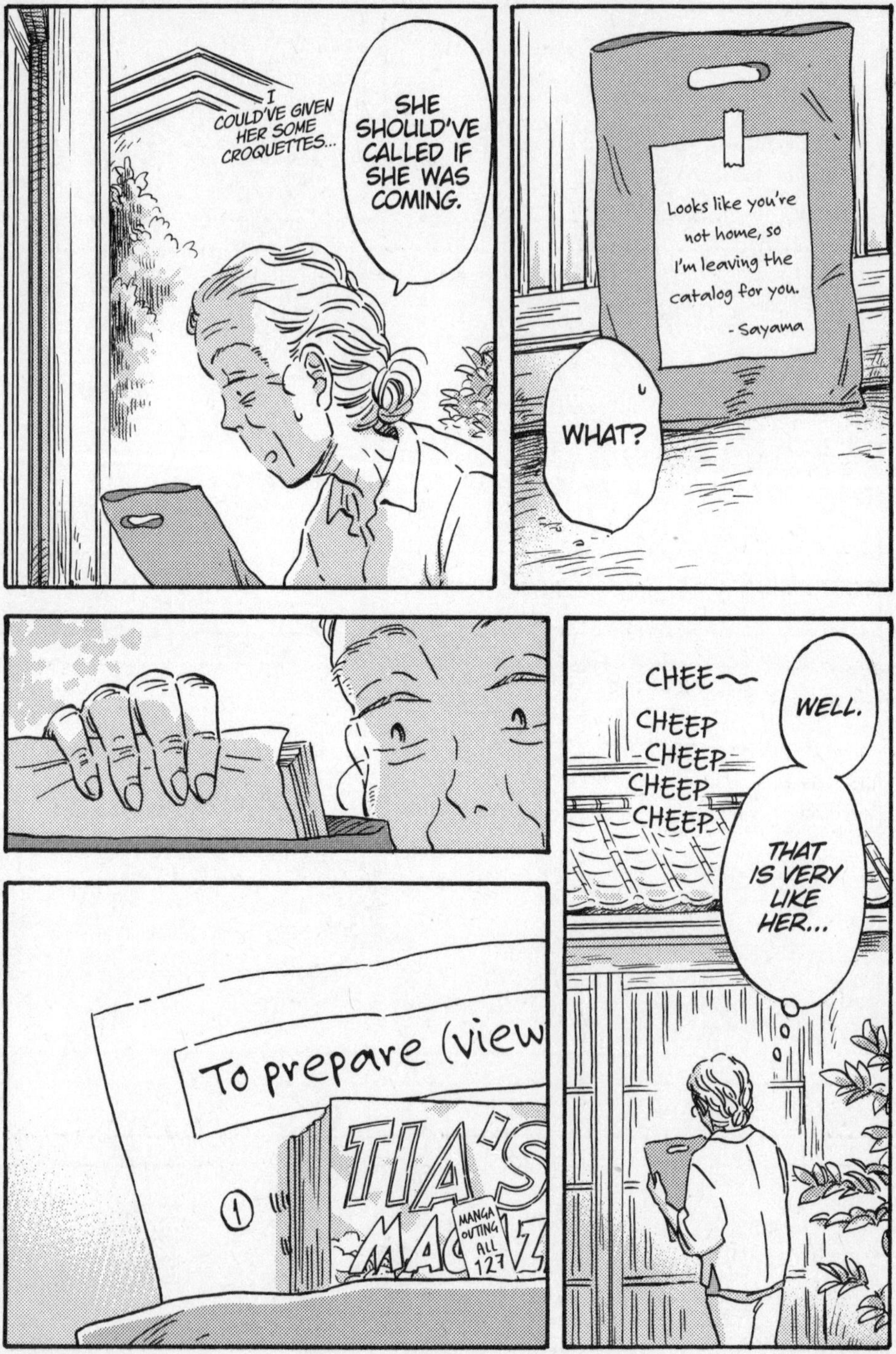

Looks like you're not home, so I'm leaving the catalog for you. - Sayama
WHAT?
SHE SHOULD'VE CALLED IF SHE WAS COMING.
I COULD'VE GIVEN HER SOME CROQUETTES...
WELL.
THAT IS VERY LIKE HER...
CHEE~
CHEEP CHEEP CHEEP CHEEP
To prepare (view
① TIA'S MAG
MANGA OUTING ALL 127

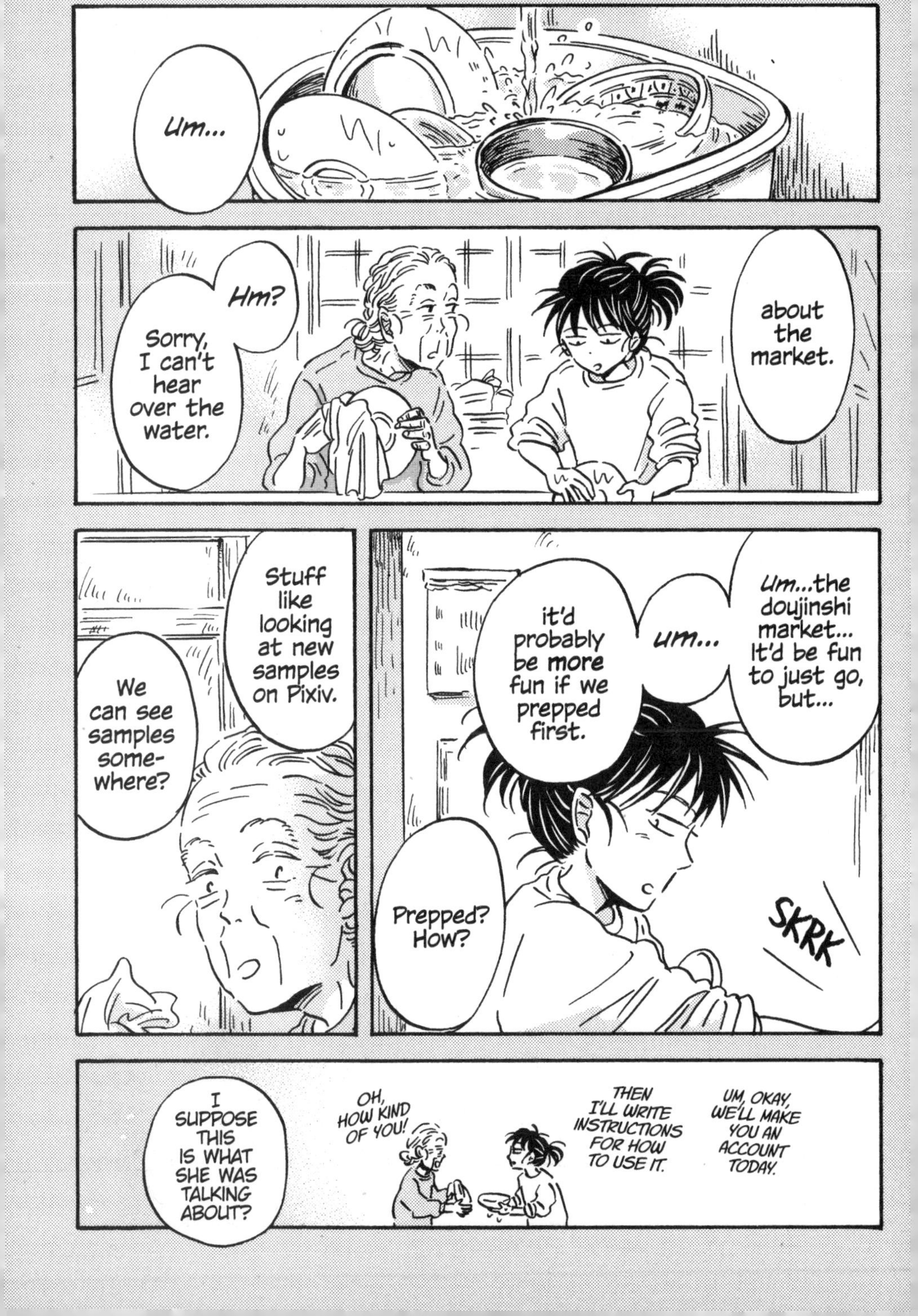
Um...
about the market.
Hm?
Sorry, I can't hear over the water.
Um...the doujinshi market... It'd be fun to just go, but...
um...
it'd probably be more fun if we prepped first.
Prepped? How?
SKRK
Stuff like looking at new samples on Pixiv.
We can see samples somewhere?
UM, OKAY, WE'LL MAKE YOU AN ACCOUNT TODAY.
THEN I'LL WRITE INSTRUCTIONS FOR HOW TO USE IT.
OH, HOW KIND OF YOU!
I SUPPOSE THIS IS WHAT SHE WAS TALKING ABOUT?

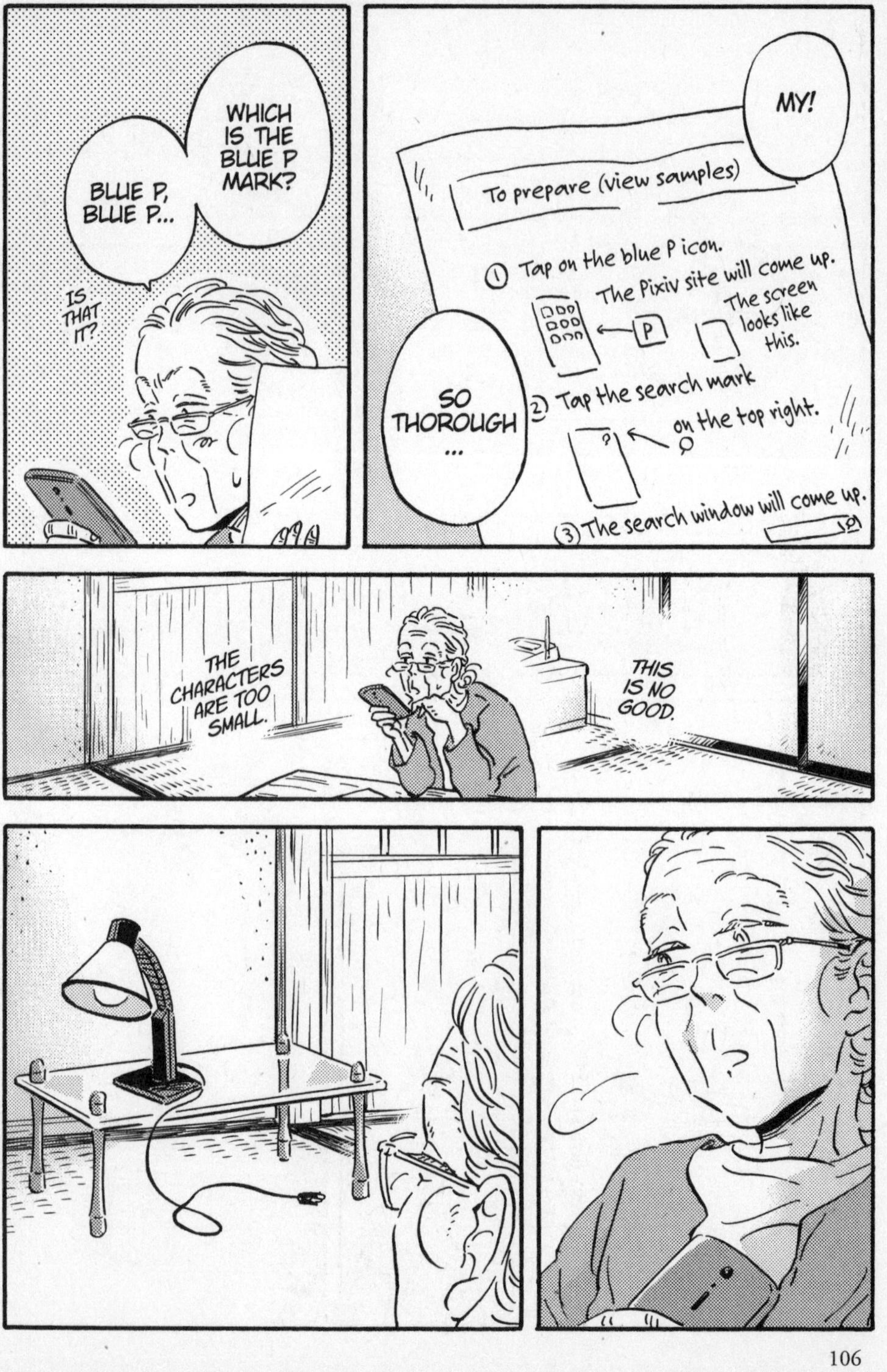
MY!
To prepare (view samples)
① Tap on the blue P icon.
The Pixiv site will come up.
The screen looks like this.
② Tap the search mark on the top right.
③ The search window will come up.
SO THOROUGH ...
WHICH IS THE BLUE P MARK?
BLUE P, BLUE P...
IS THAT IT?
THIS IS NO GOOD.
THE CHARACTERS ARE TOO SMALL.

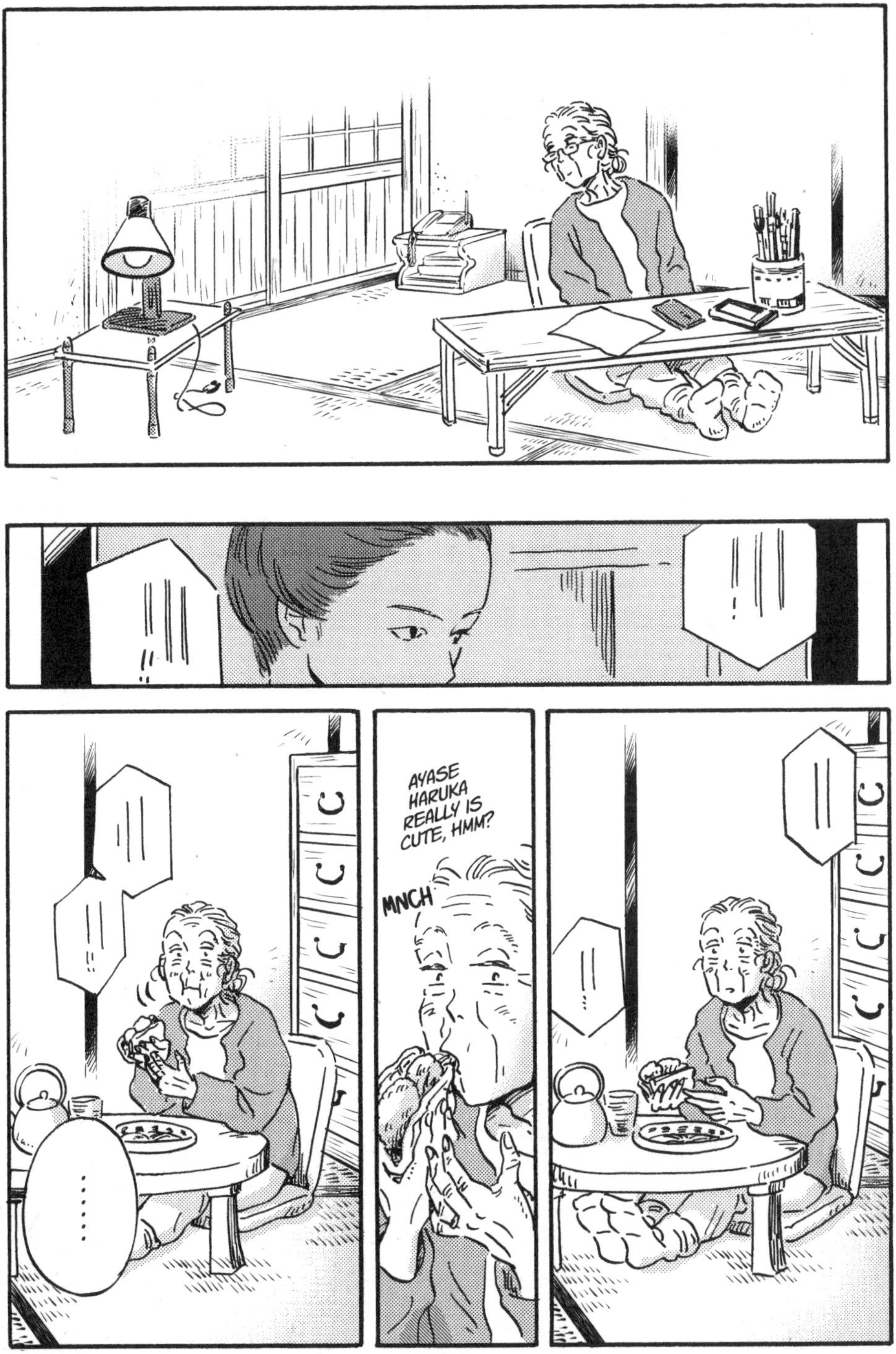
AYASE HARUKA REALLY IS CUTE, HMM?
MNCH
......

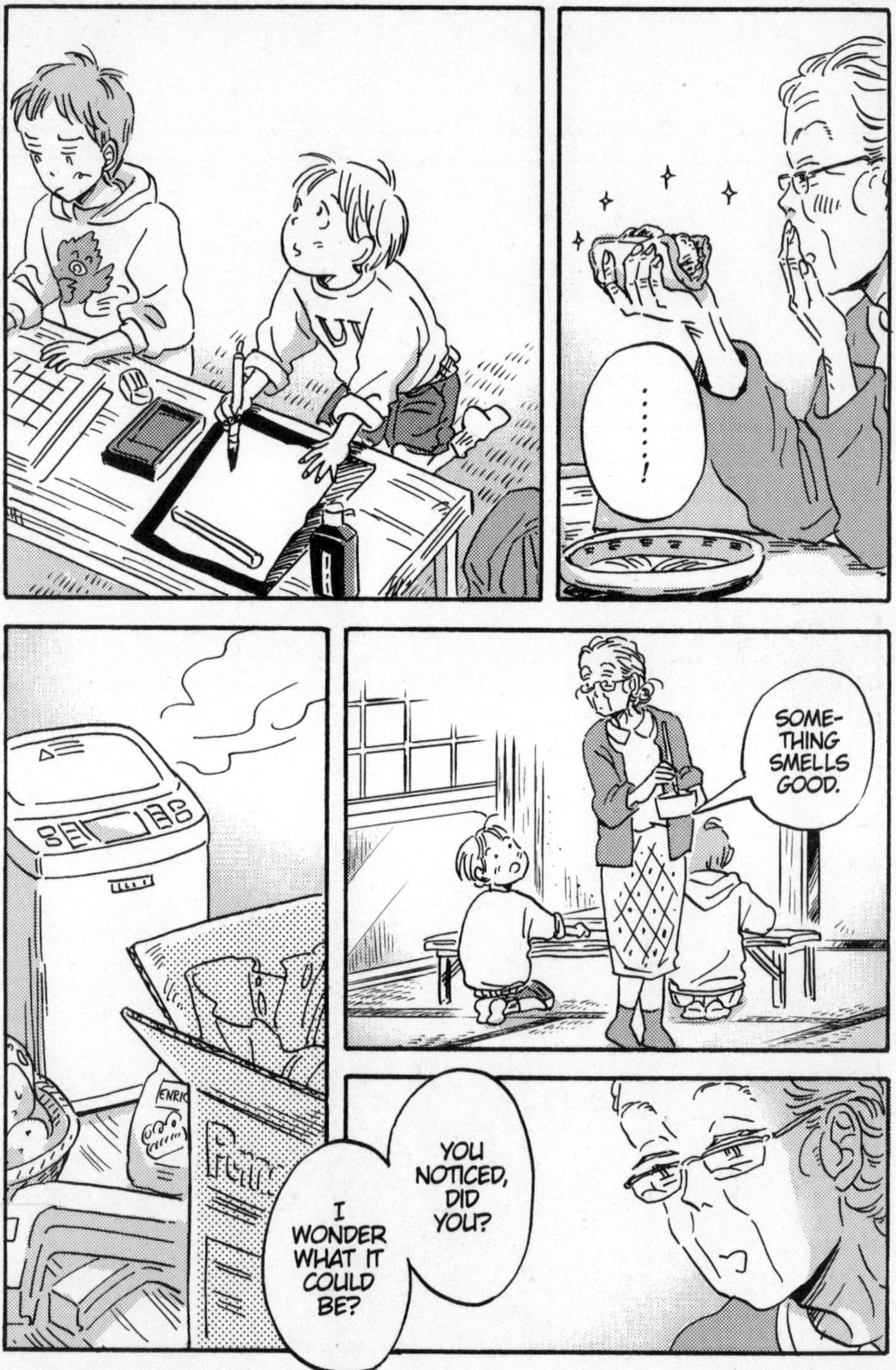
......!
SOME-THING SMELLS GOOD.
YOU NOTICED, DID YOU?
I WONDER WHAT IT COULD BE?

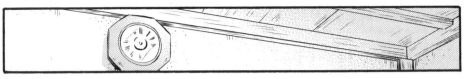

HOT!

HOT, HOT!

KSSH

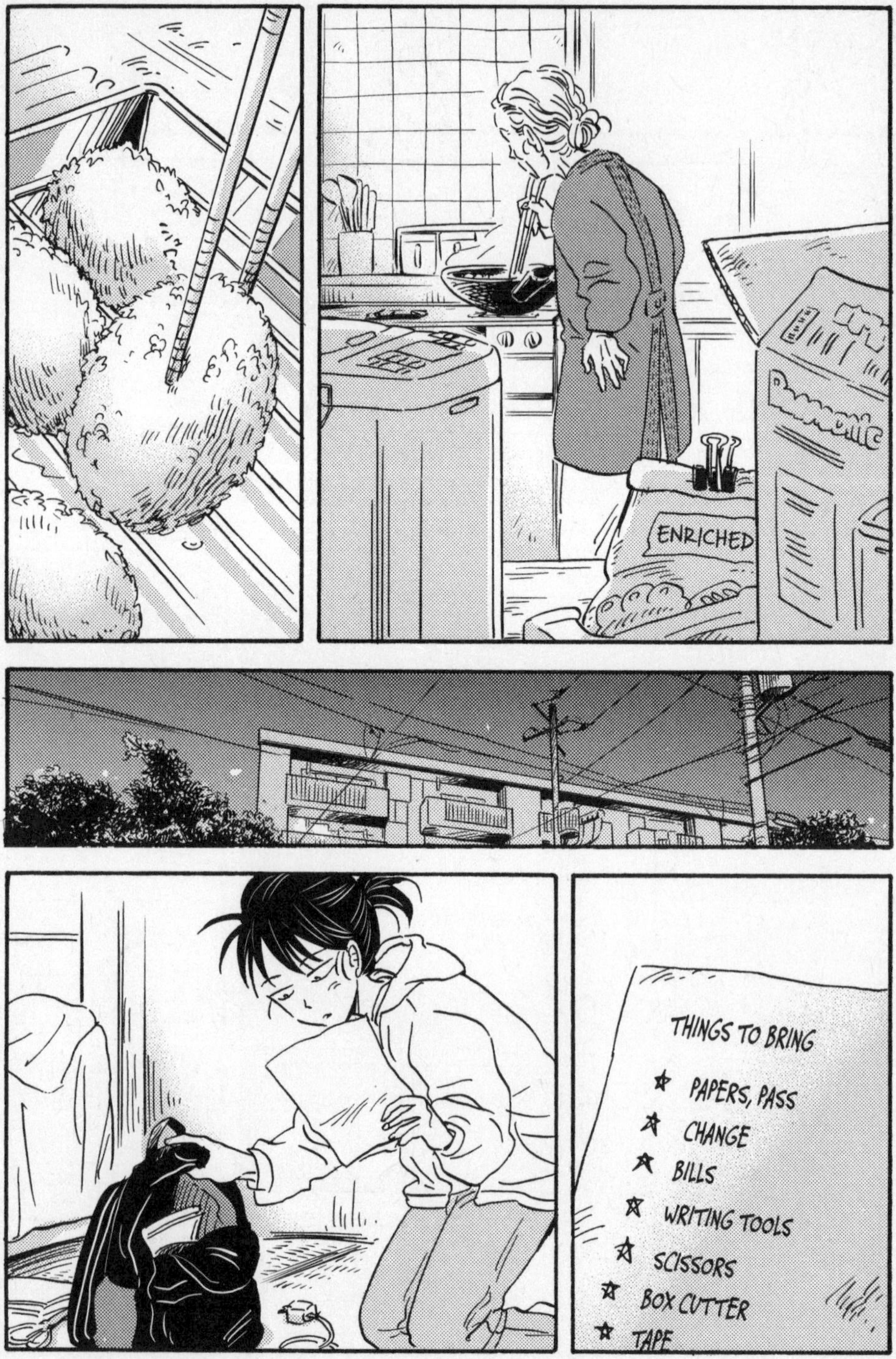
ENRICHED
THINGS TO BRING
☆ PAPERS, PASS
☆ CHANGE
☆ BILLS
☆ WRITING TOOLS
☆ SCISSORS
☆ BOX CUTTER
☆ TAPE

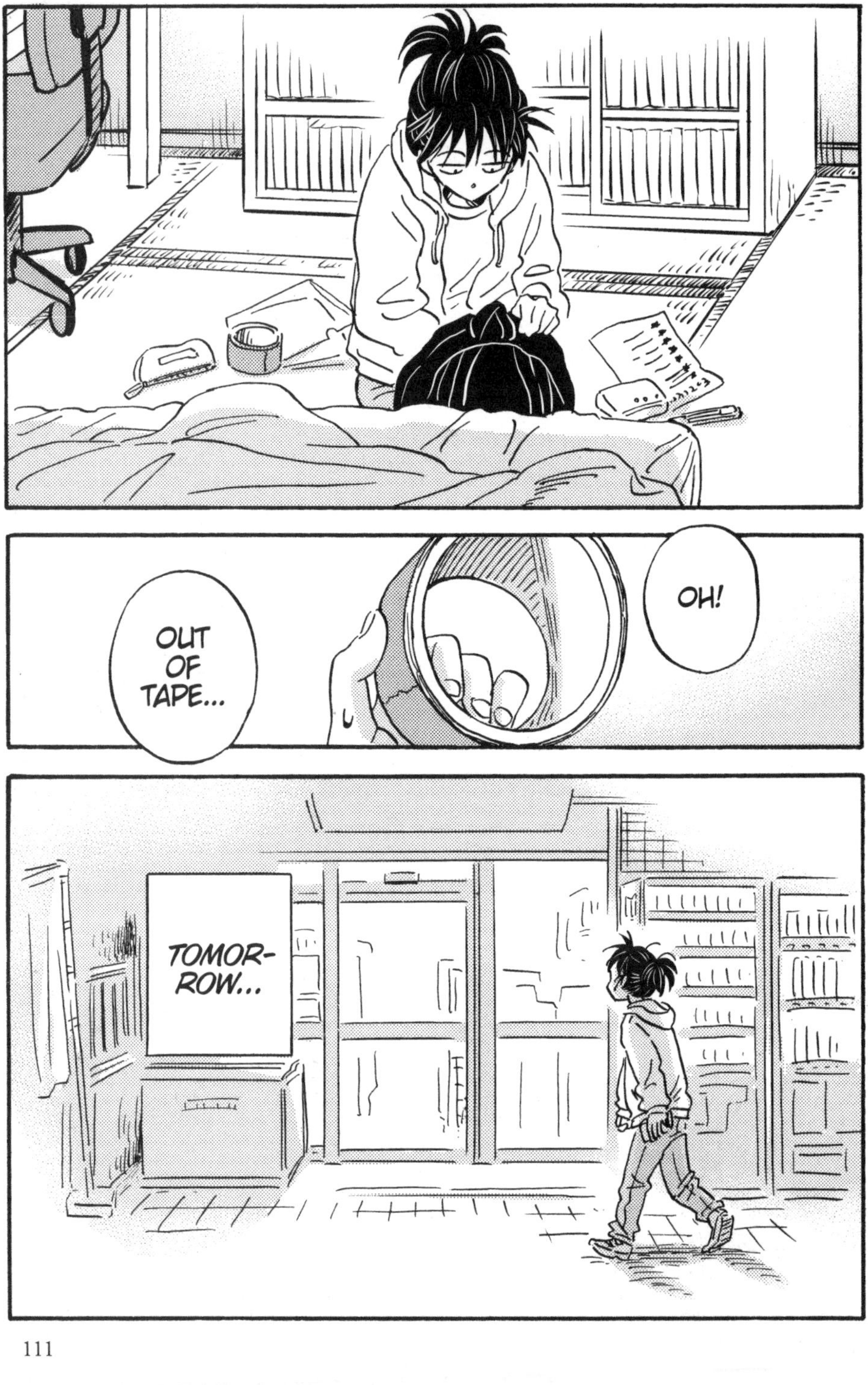
OH!
OUT OF TAPE...
TOMORROW...

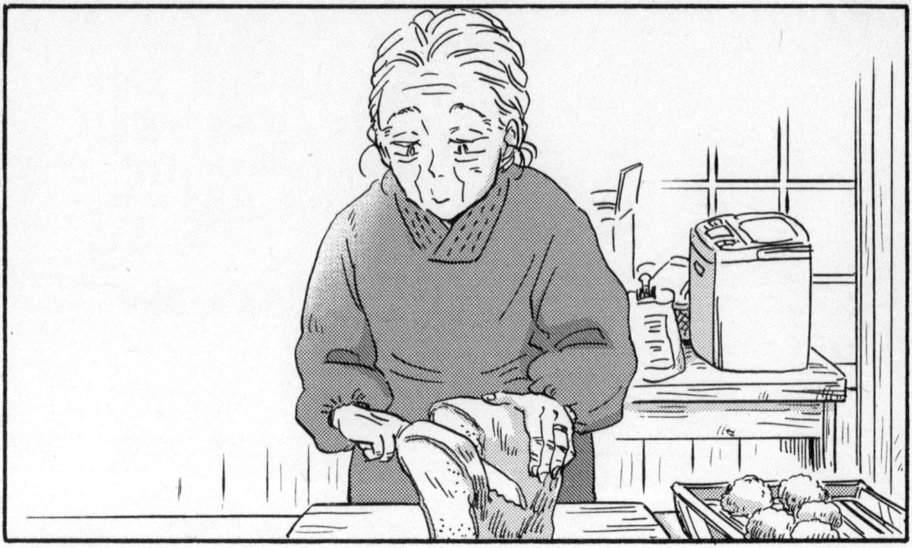

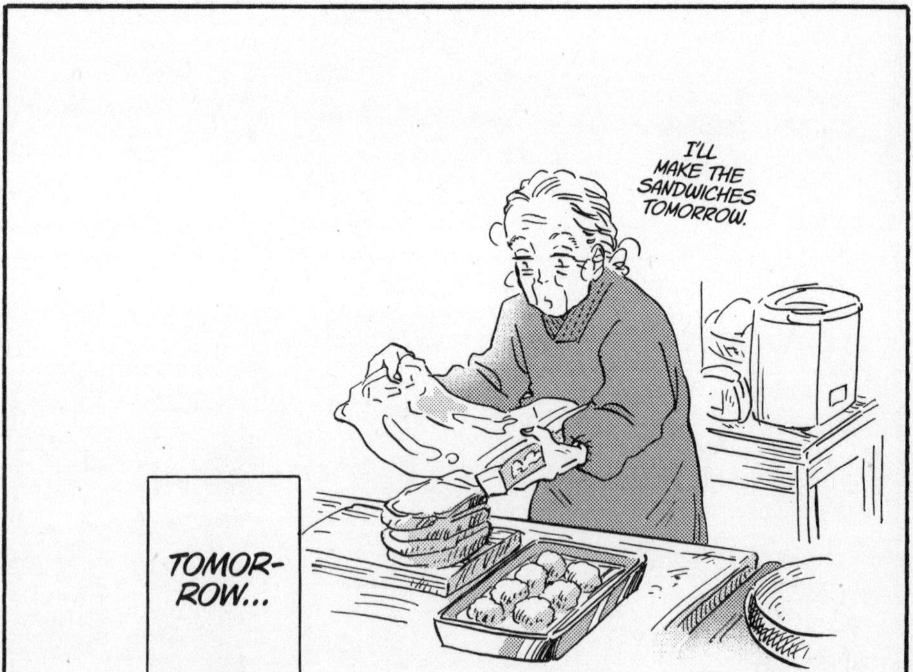
I'LL MAKE THE SANDWICHES TOMORROW.
TOMOR-ROW...

metamorphosis

Chapter 39

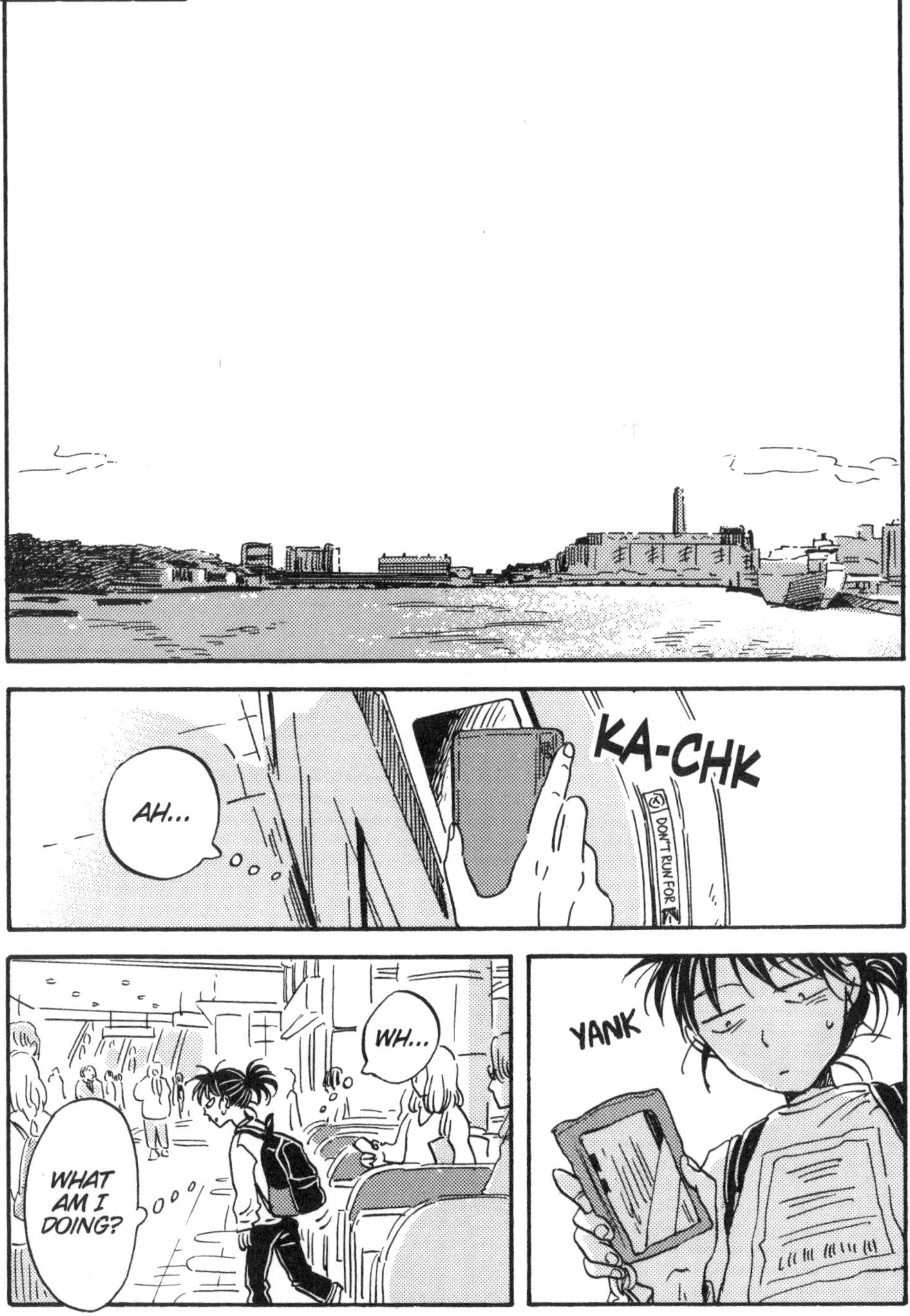
KA-CHK
DON'T RUN FOR
AH...
YANK
WH...
WHAT AM I DOING?

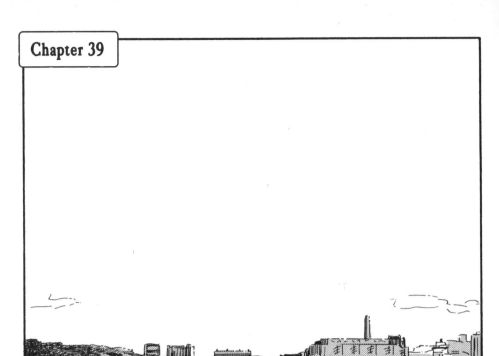

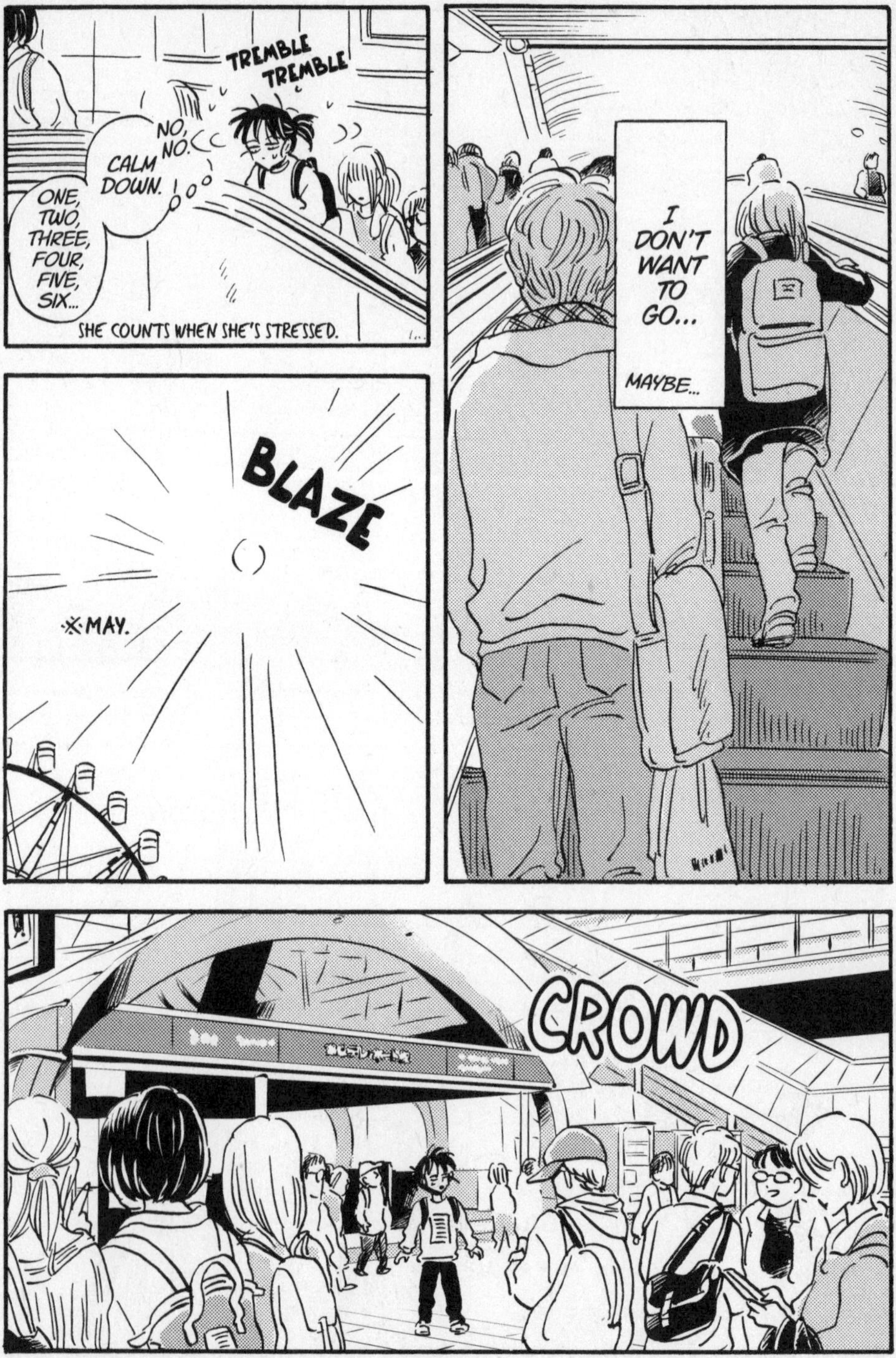
I DON'T WANT TO GO...
MAYBE...
TREMBLE TREMBLE
NO, NO.
CALM DOWN.
ONE, TWO, THREE, FOUR, FIVE, SIX...
SHE COUNTS WHEN SHE'S STRESSED.
BLAZE
※MAY.
CROWD

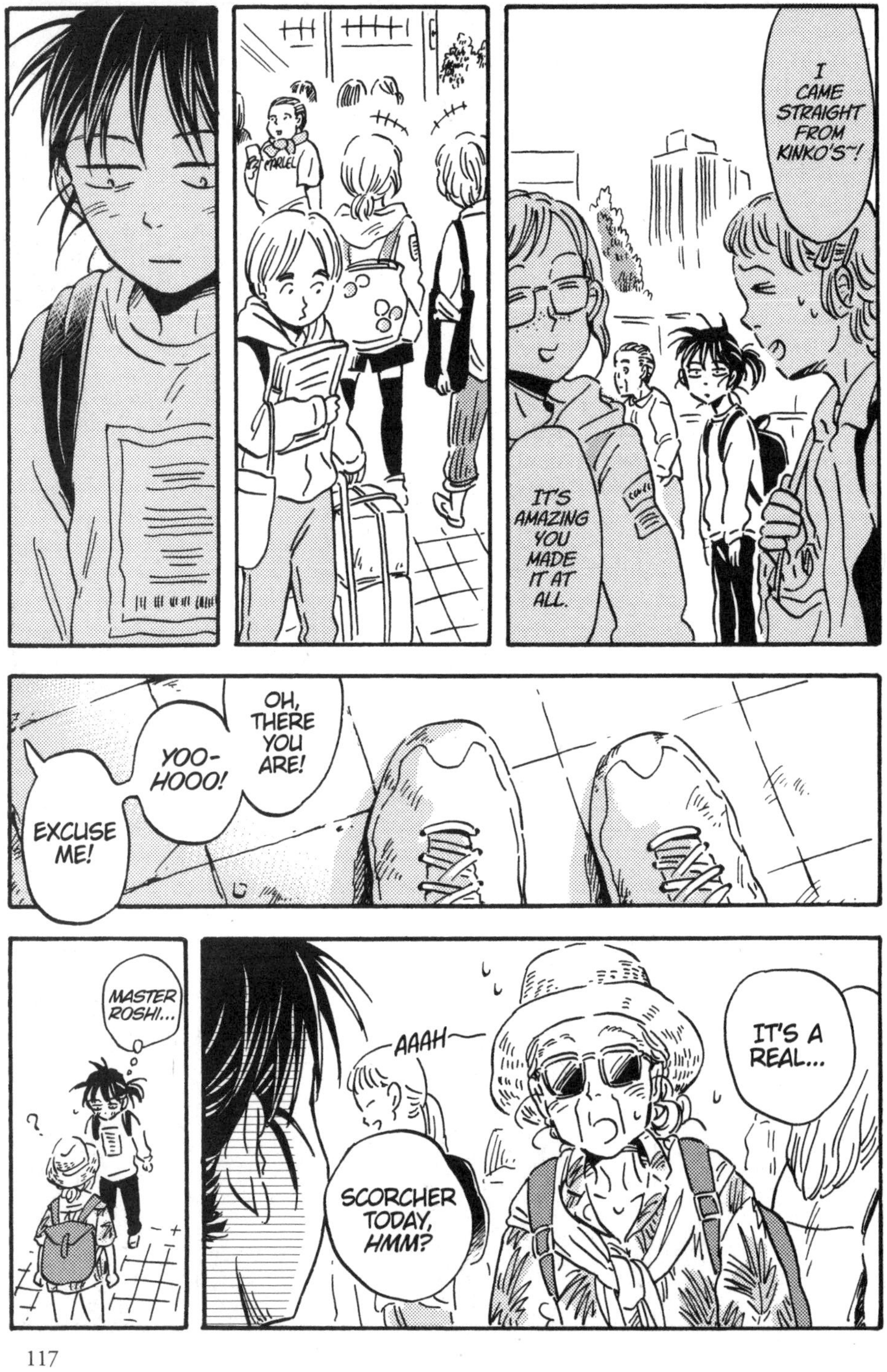
I CAME STRAIGHT FROM KINKO'S~!
IT'S AMAZING YOU MADE IT AT ALL.
OH, THERE YOU ARE!
YOO-HOOO!
EXCUSE ME!
IT'S A REAL...
AAAH~
SCORCHER TODAY, HMM?
MASTER ROSHI...

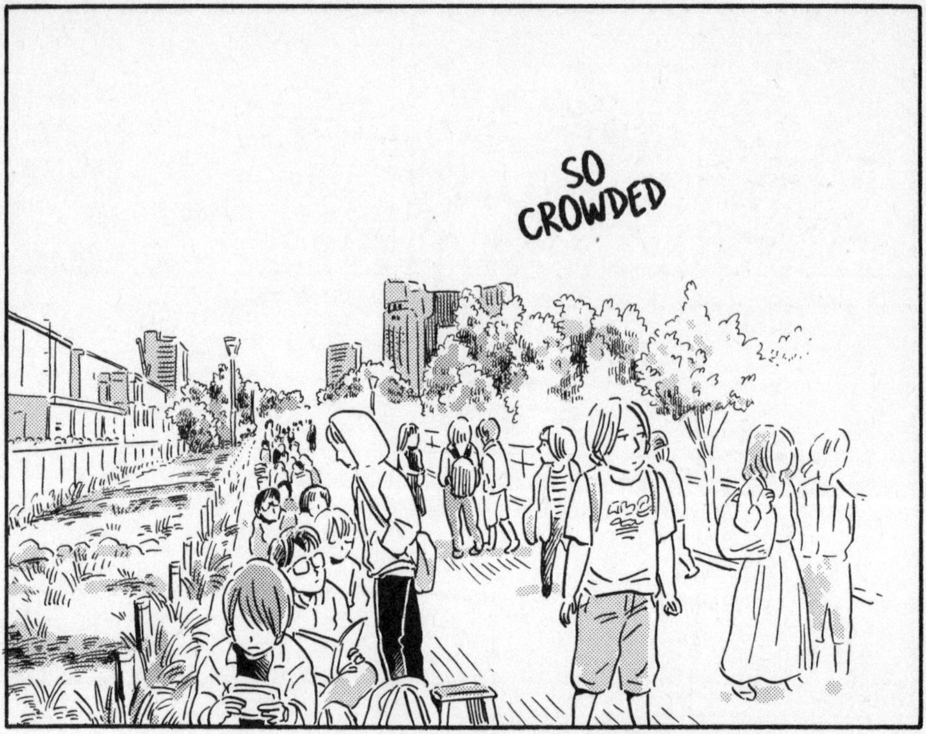
SO CROWDED

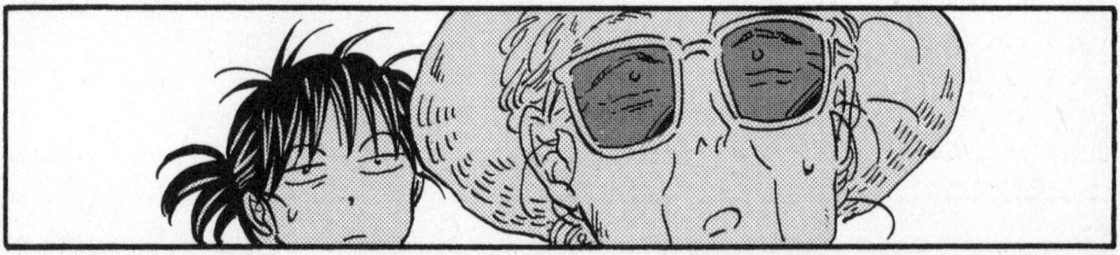

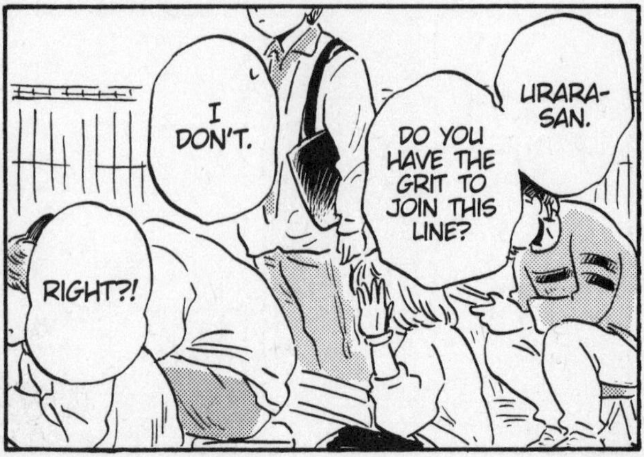
URARA-SAN.
DO YOU HAVE THE GRIT TO JOIN THIS LINE?
I DON'T.
RIGHT?!

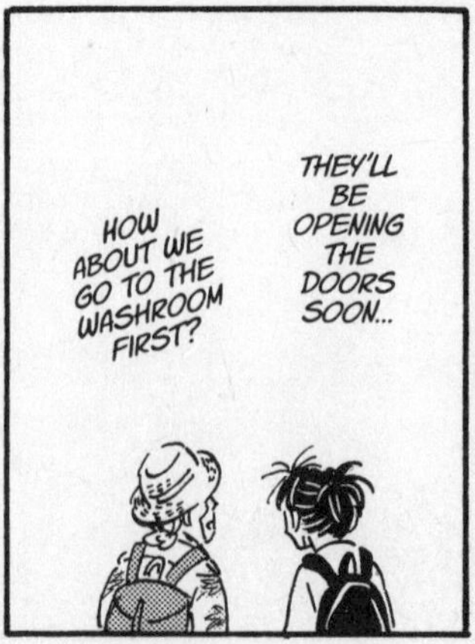
THEY'LL BE OPENING THE DOORS SOON...
HOW ABOUT WE GO TO THE WASHROOM FIRST?

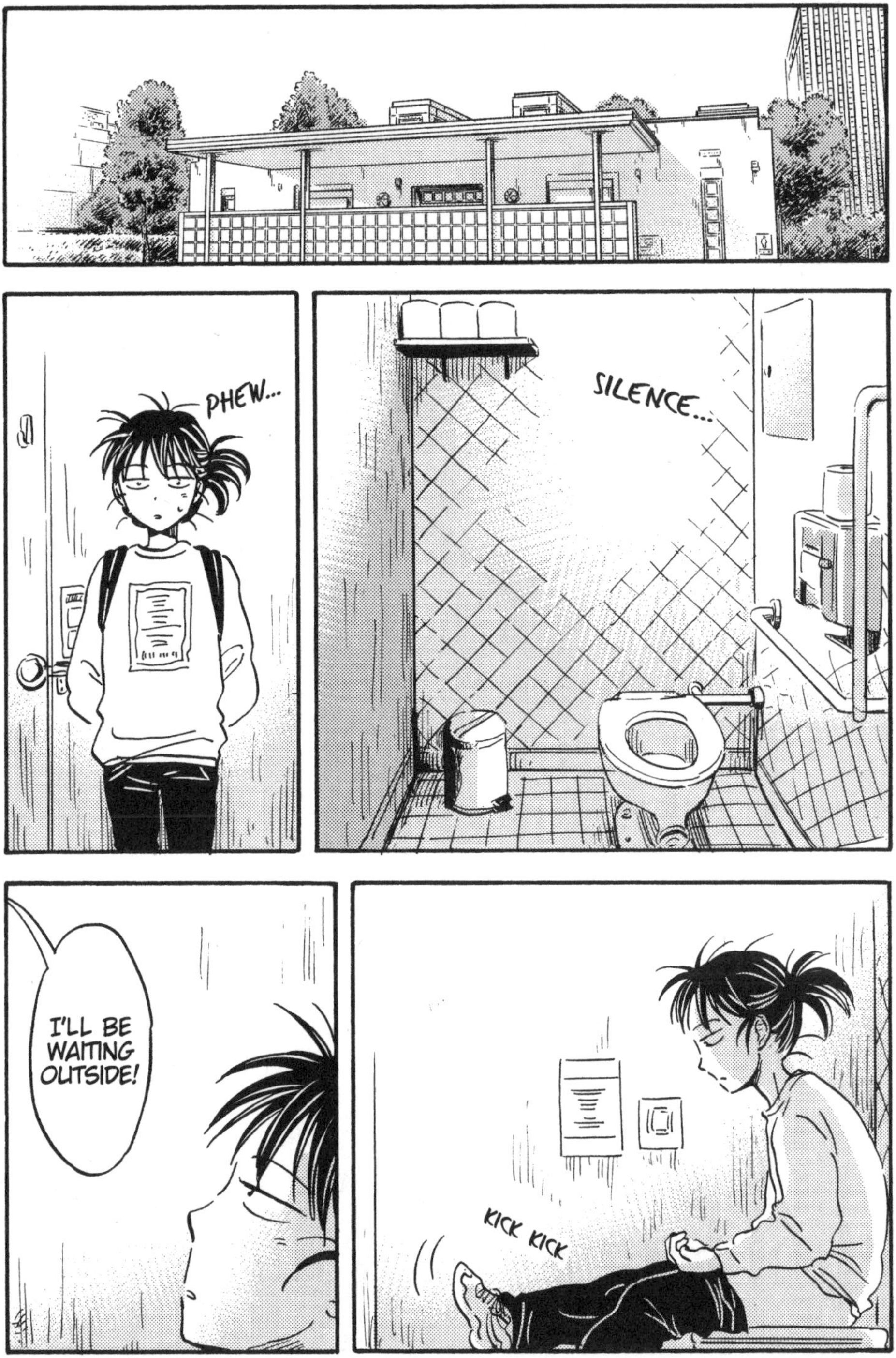
SILENCE...
PHEW...
KICK KICK
I'LL BE WAITING OUTSIDE!

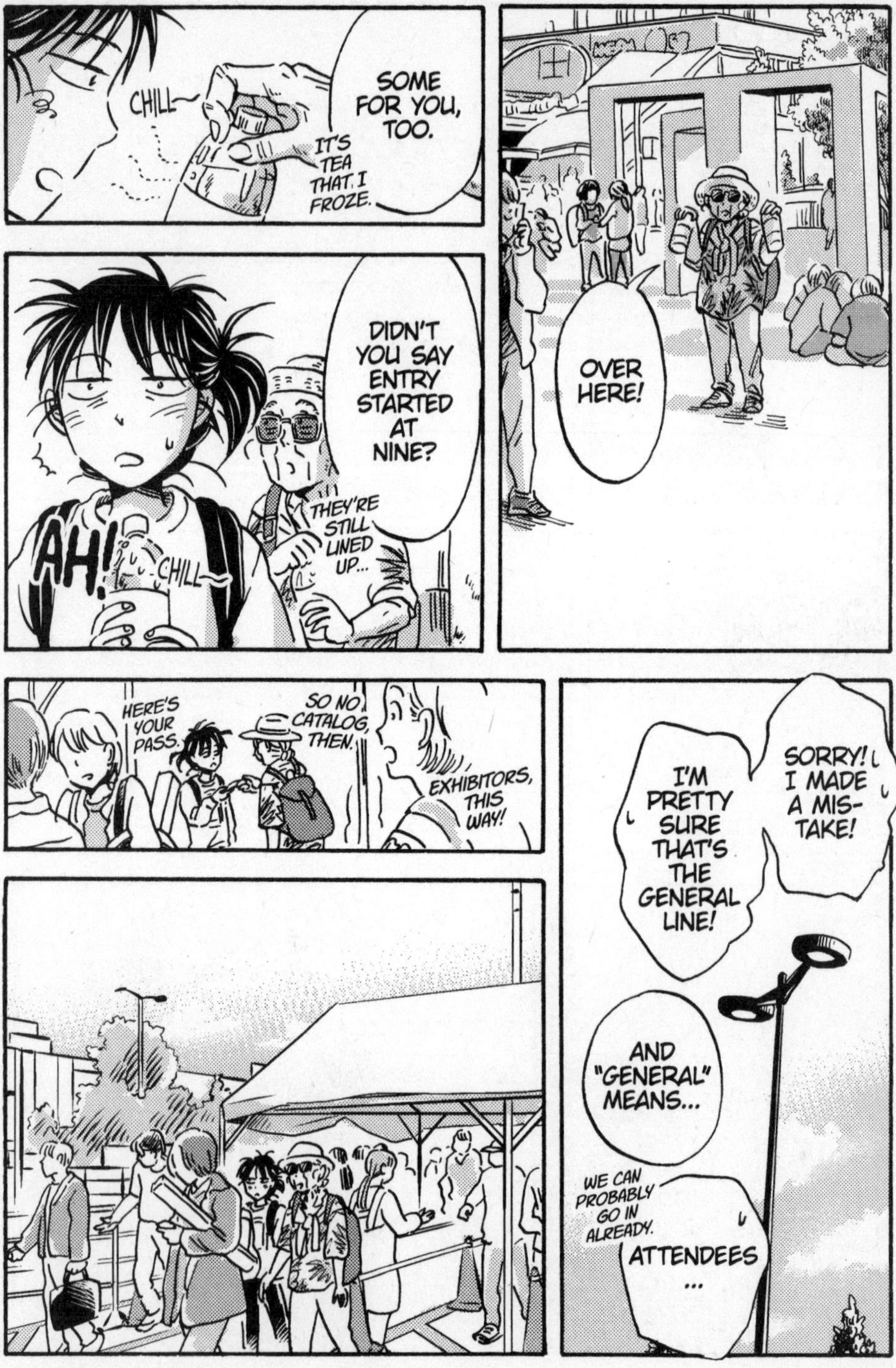
OVER HERE!
SOME FOR YOU, TOO.
IT'S TEA THAT I FROZE.
CHILL~
DIDN'T YOU SAY ENTRY STARTED AT NINE?
THEY'RE STILL LINED UP...
AH!
CHILL~
SORRY! I MADE A MIS-TAKE!
I'M PRETTY SURE THAT'S THE GENERAL LINE!
AND "GENERAL" MEANS...
ATTENDEES ...
WE CAN PROBABLY GO IN ALREADY.
EXHIBITORS, THIS WAY!
SO NO CATALOG, THEN.
HERE'S YOUR PASS.

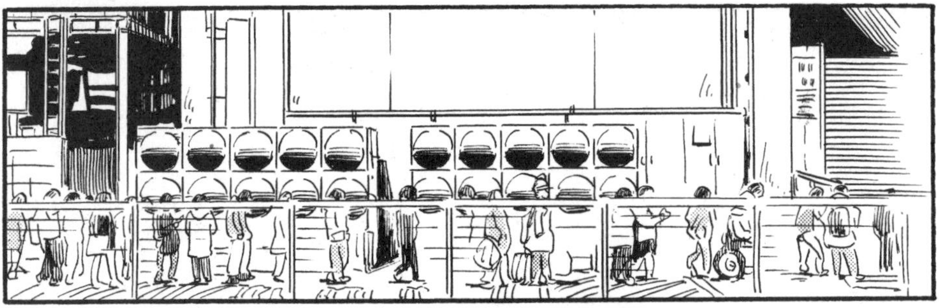
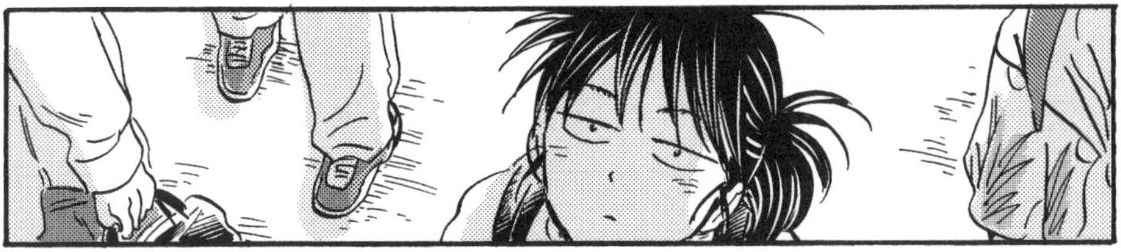
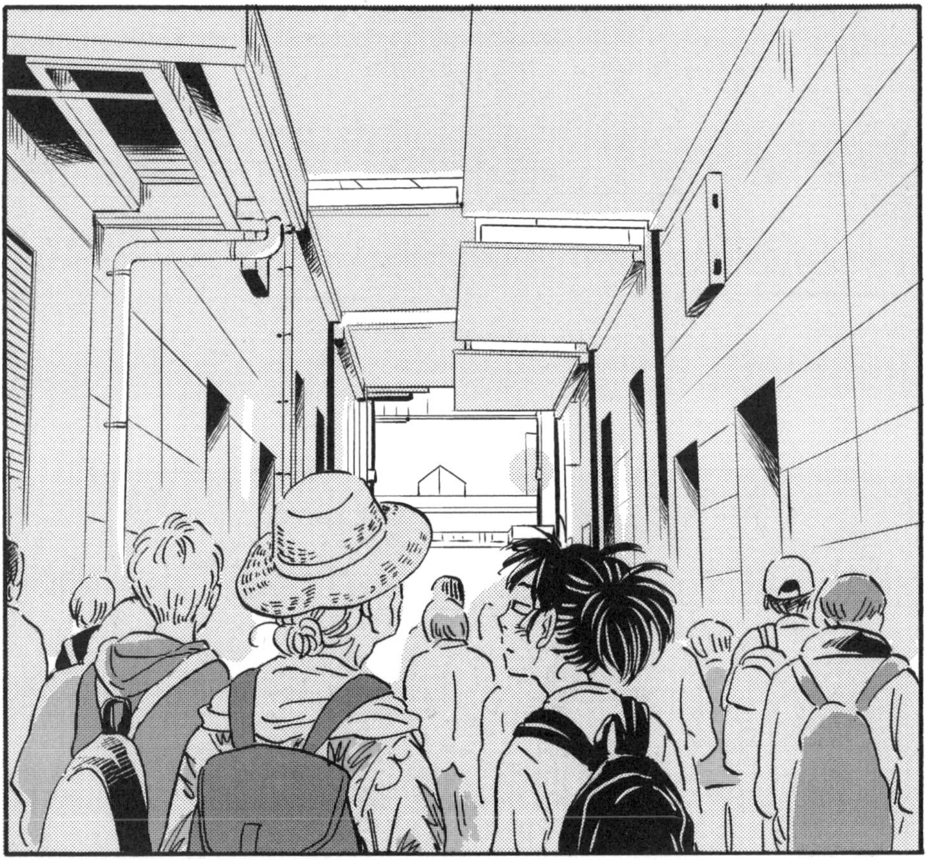

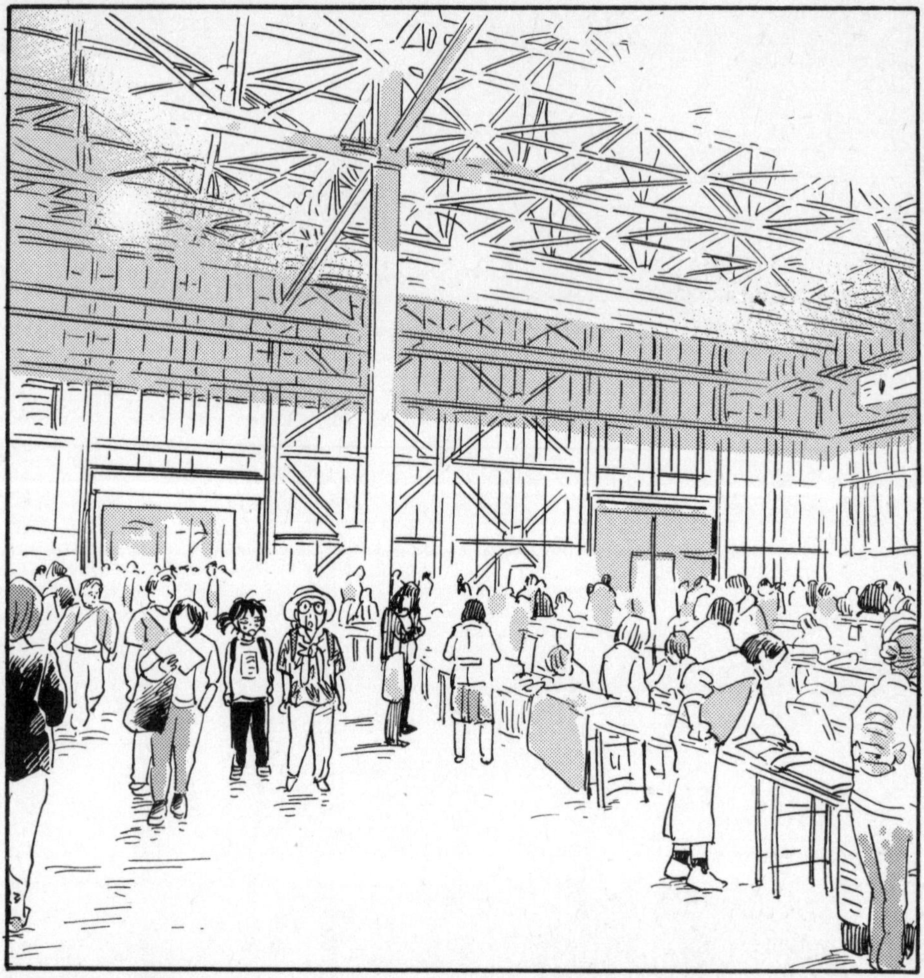

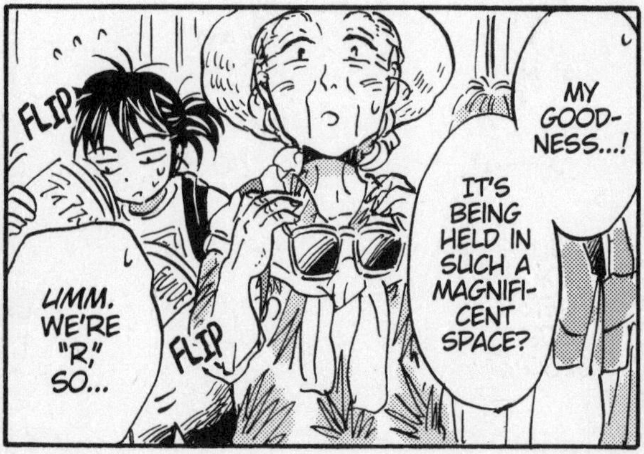
MY GOODNESS...!
IT'S BEING HELD IN SUCH A MAGNIFICENT SPACE?
FLIP
UMM. WE'RE "R," SO...
FLIP

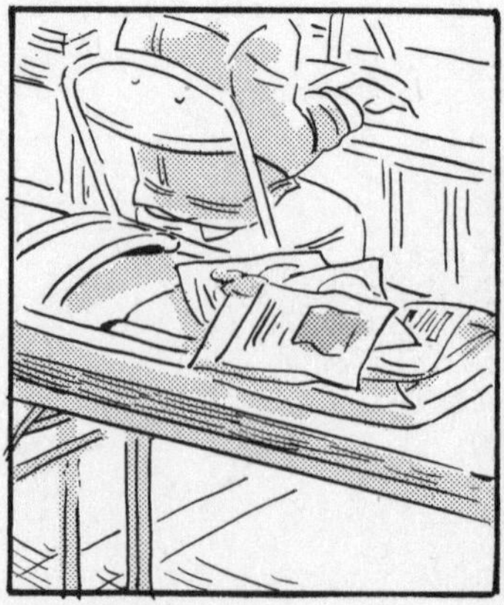

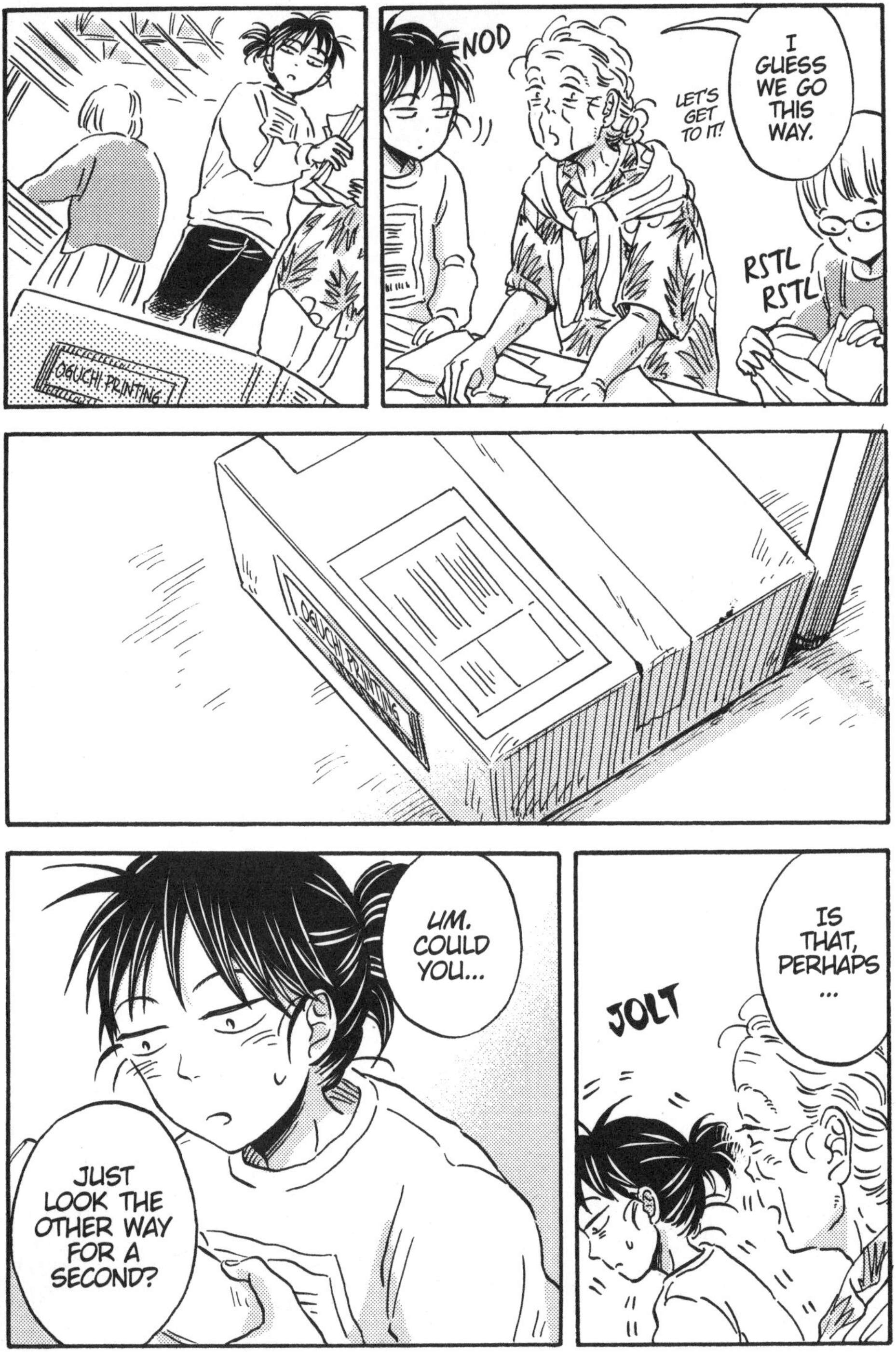
I GUESS WE GO THIS WAY.
LET'S GET TO IT!
NOD
RSTL RSTL
OGUCHI PRINTING
OGUCHI PRINTING
IS THAT, PERHAPS ...
JOLT
UM. COULD YOU...
JUST LOOK THE OTHER WAY FOR A SECOND?

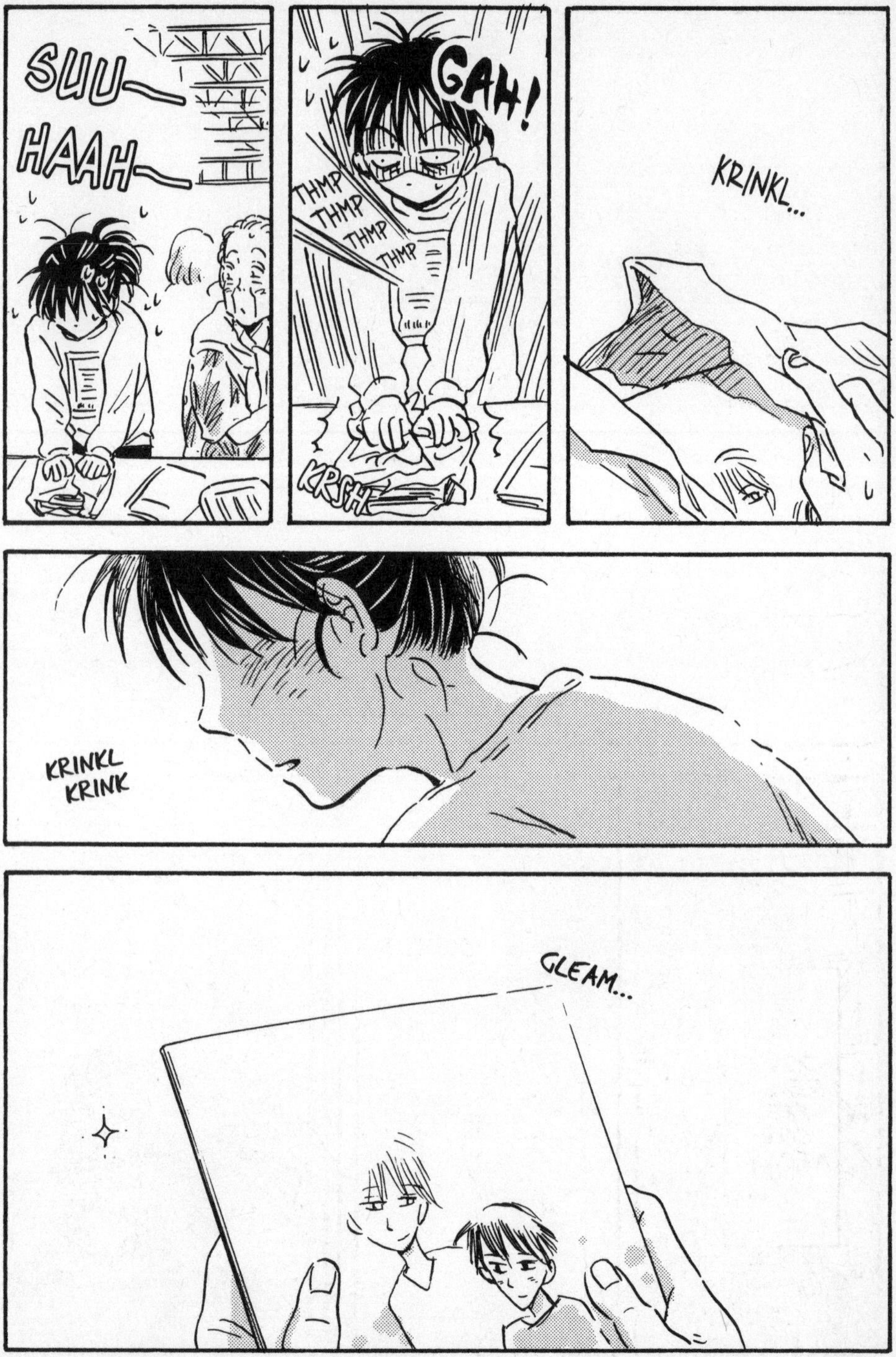
SUU—
HAAH—
GAH!
THMP THMP THMP THMP
KRSH
KRINKL...
KRINKL KRINK
GLEAM...

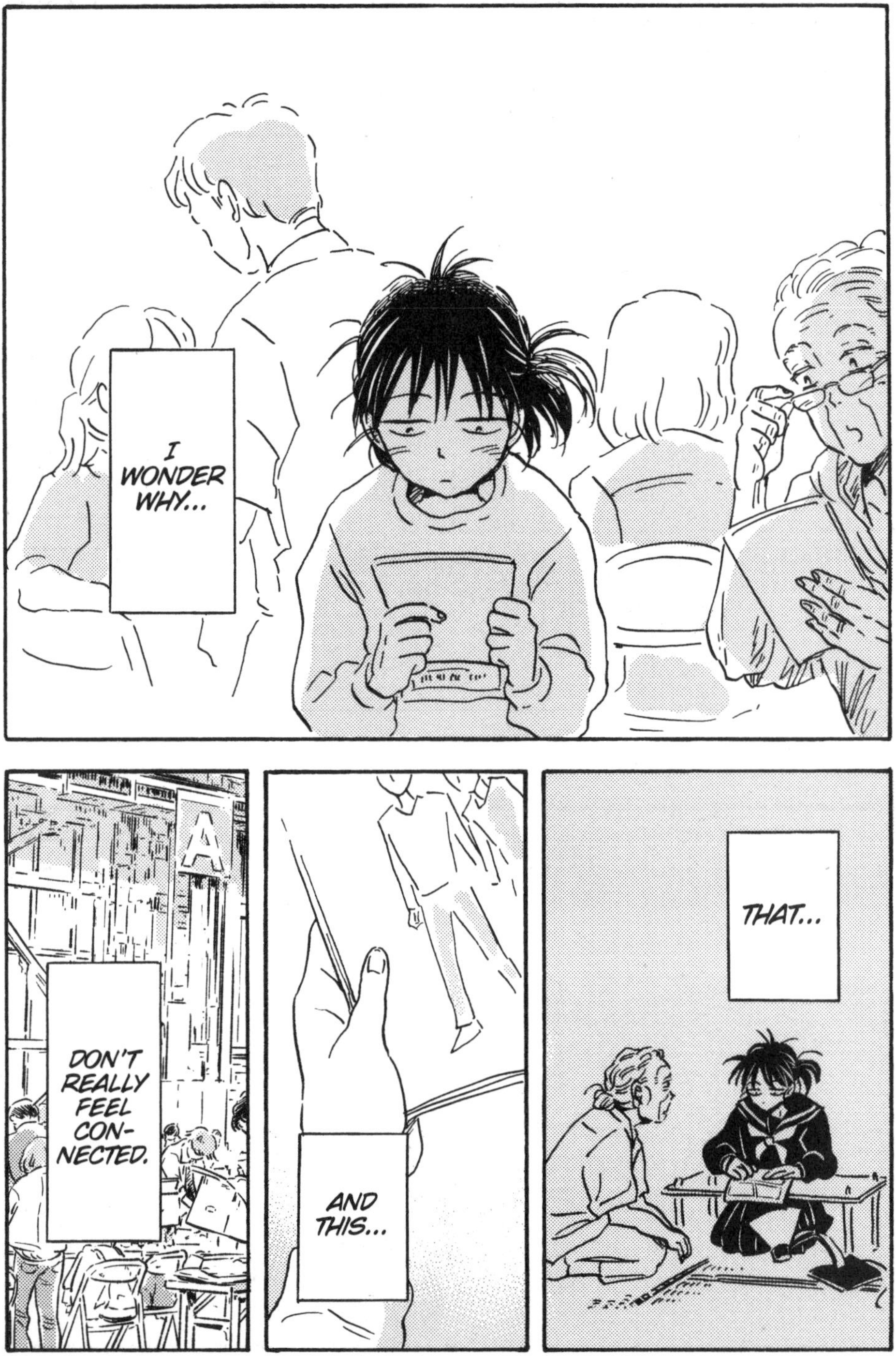
I WONDER WHY...
THAT...
AND THIS...
DON'T REALLY FEEL CON-NECTED.

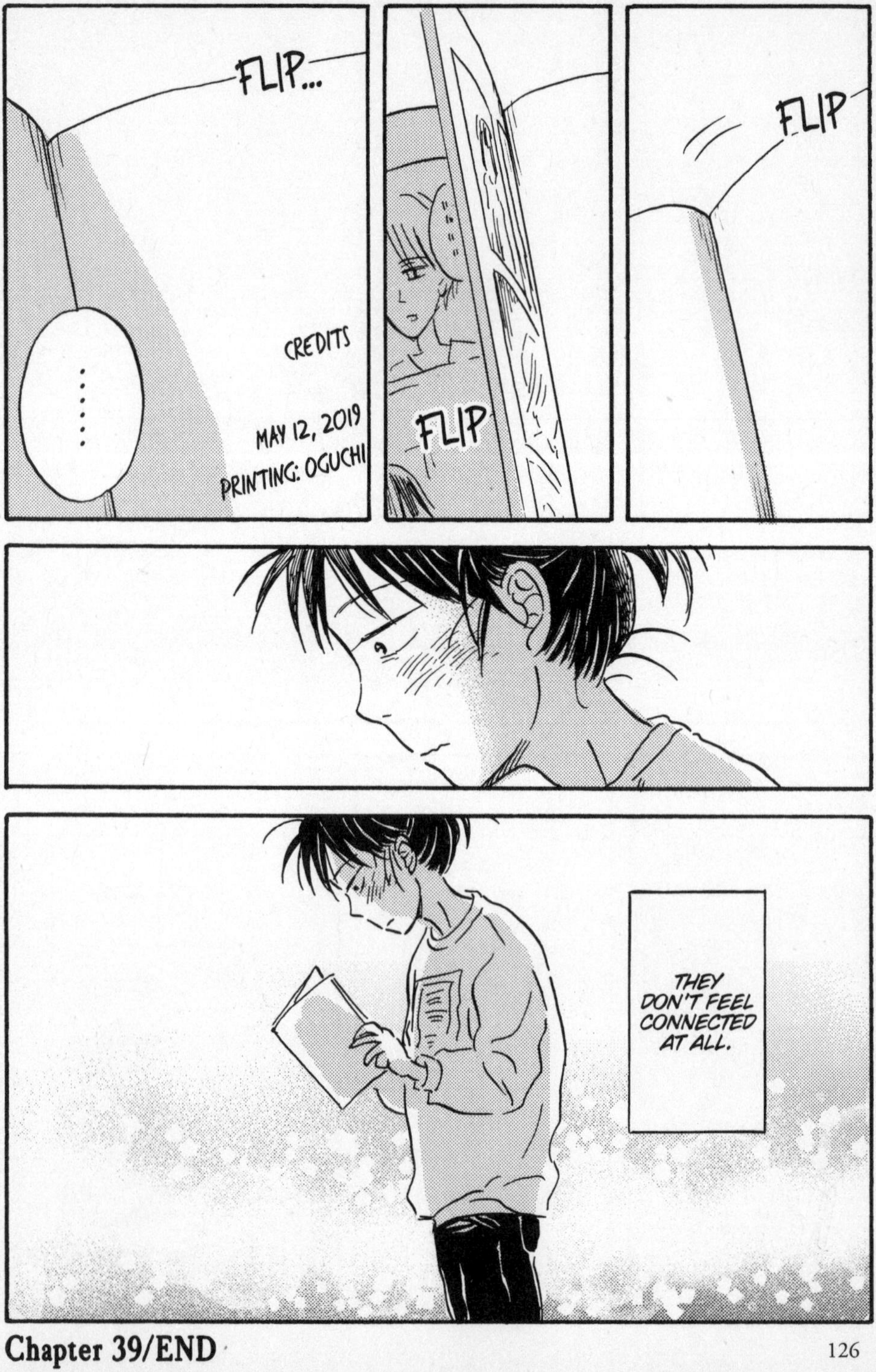
FLIP
FLIP
FLIP...
CREDITS
MAY 12, 2019
PRINTING: OGUCHI
......
THEY DON'T FEEL CONNECTED AT ALL.

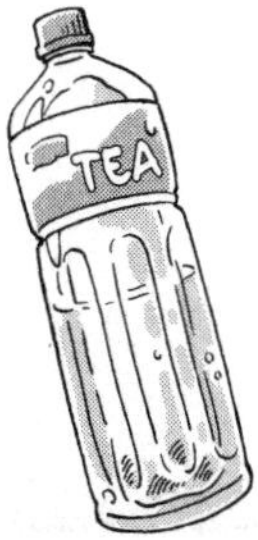
TEA

metamorphosis

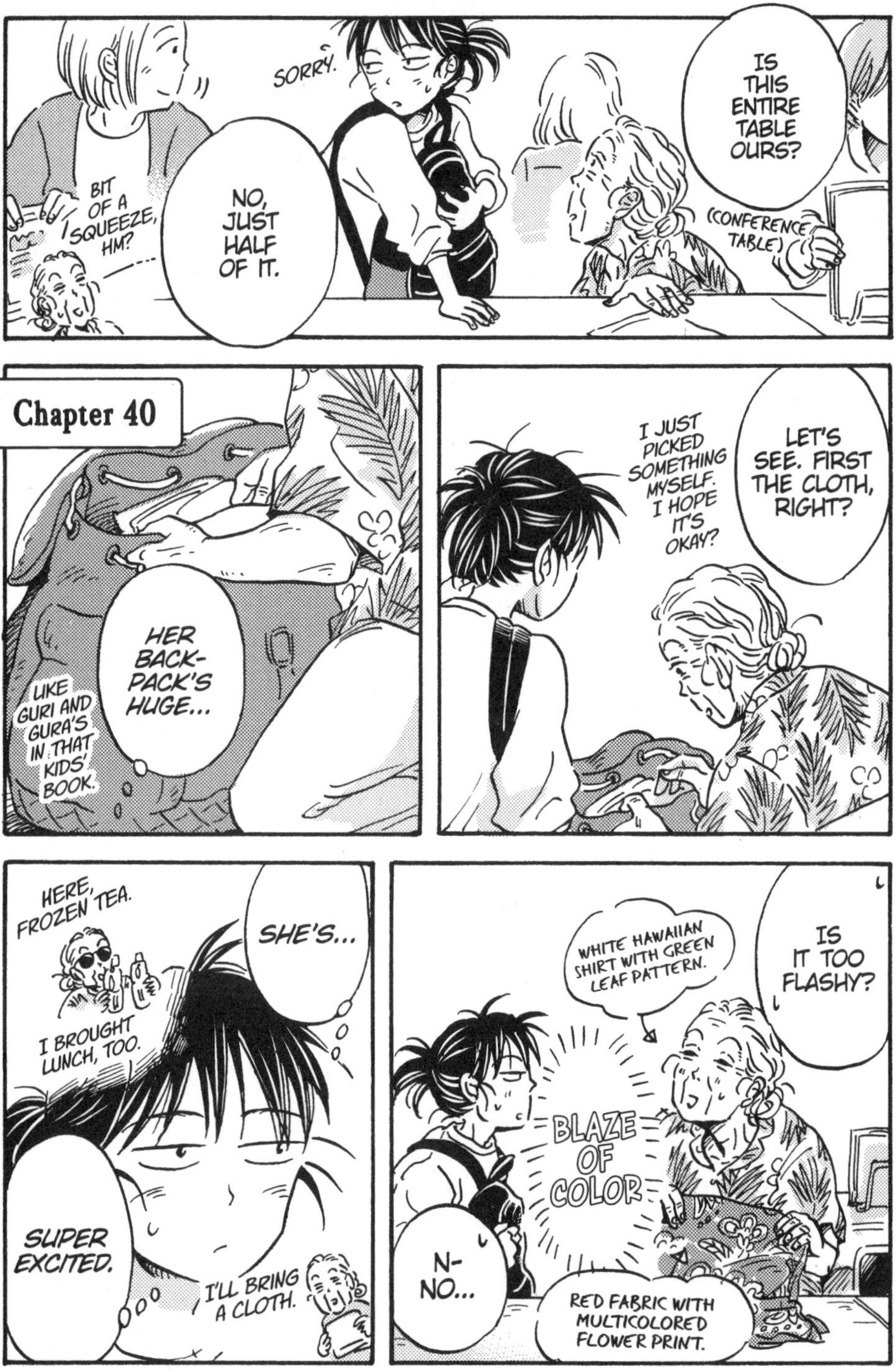
IS THIS ENTIRE TABLE OURS?
(CONFERENCE TABLE)
NO, JUST HALF OF IT.
SORRY.
BIT OF A SQUEEZE, HM?
LET'S SEE. FIRST THE CLOTH, RIGHT?
I JUST PICKED SOMETHING MYSELF. I HOPE IT'S OKAY?
Chapter 40
HER BACKPACK'S HUGE...
LIKE GURI AND GURA'S IN THAT KIDS' BOOK.
IS IT TOO FLASHY?
WHITE HAWAIIAN SHIRT WITH GREEN LEAF PATTERN.
BLAZE OF COLOR
N-NO...
RED FABRIC WITH MULTICOLORED FLOWER PRINT.
SHE'S...
HERE, FROZEN TEA.
I BROUGHT LUNCH, TOO.
SUPER EXCITED.
I'LL BRING A CLOTH.

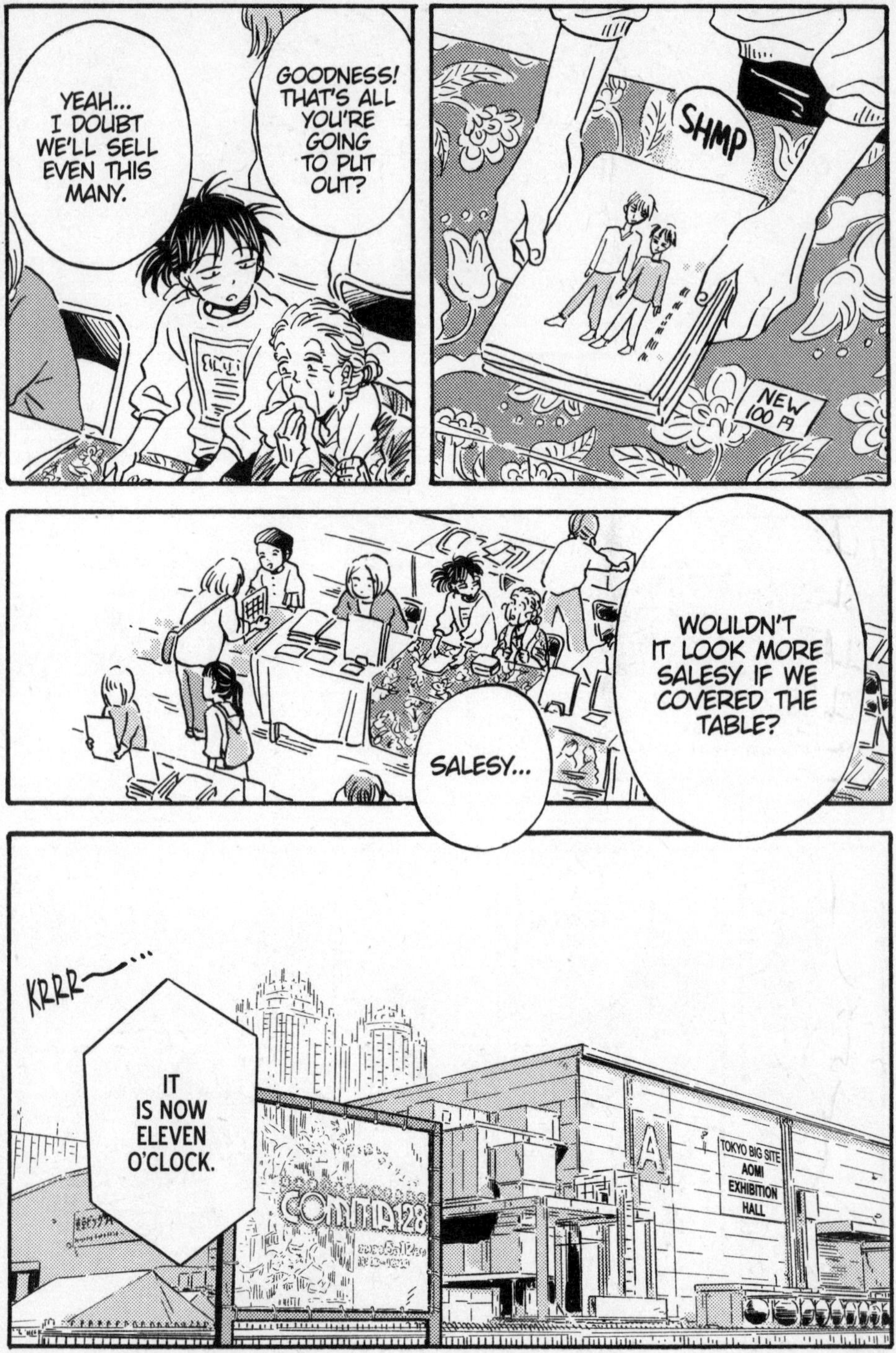
SHMP
NEW 100円
GOODNESS! THAT'S ALL YOU'RE GOING TO PUT OUT?
YEAH... I DOUBT WE'LL SELL EVEN THIS MANY.
WOULDN'T IT LOOK MORE SALESY IF WE COVERED THE TABLE?
SALESY...
KRRR~...
IT IS NOW ELEVEN O'CLOCK.
TOKYO BIG SITE AOMI EXHIBITION HALL
A
COMITIA128

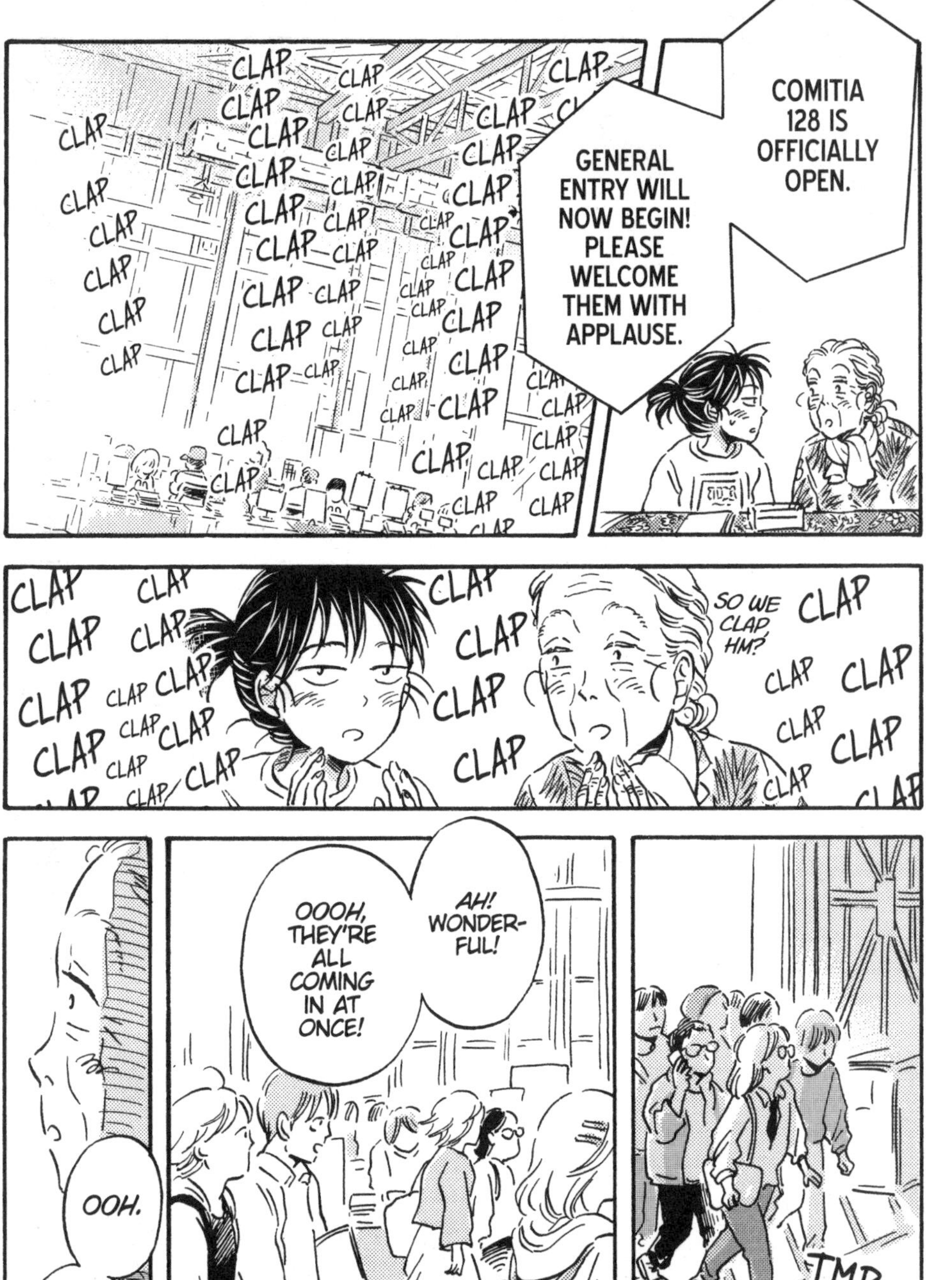
COMITIA 128 IS OFFICIALLY OPEN.
GENERAL ENTRY WILL NOW BEGIN! PLEASE WELCOME THEM WITH APPLAUSE.
CLAP CLAP CLAP CLAP CLAP CLAP CLAP CLAP
SO WE CLAP, HM?
CLAP CLAP CLAP CLAP CLAP CLAP CLAP CLAP
TMP
AH! WONDERFUL!
OOOH, THEY'RE ALL COMING IN AT ONCE!
OOH.
THIS...

I'M AT THE
STATION.

READ

I'M AT THE
STATION.

THAT'S THE
WRONG STATION!

POMG

THE VENUE IS AT TOKYO
TELEPORT STATION.

WHAT?!

SITE AOMI
EXHIBITION HALL

KA-SNAP～

⋯⋯⋯⋯

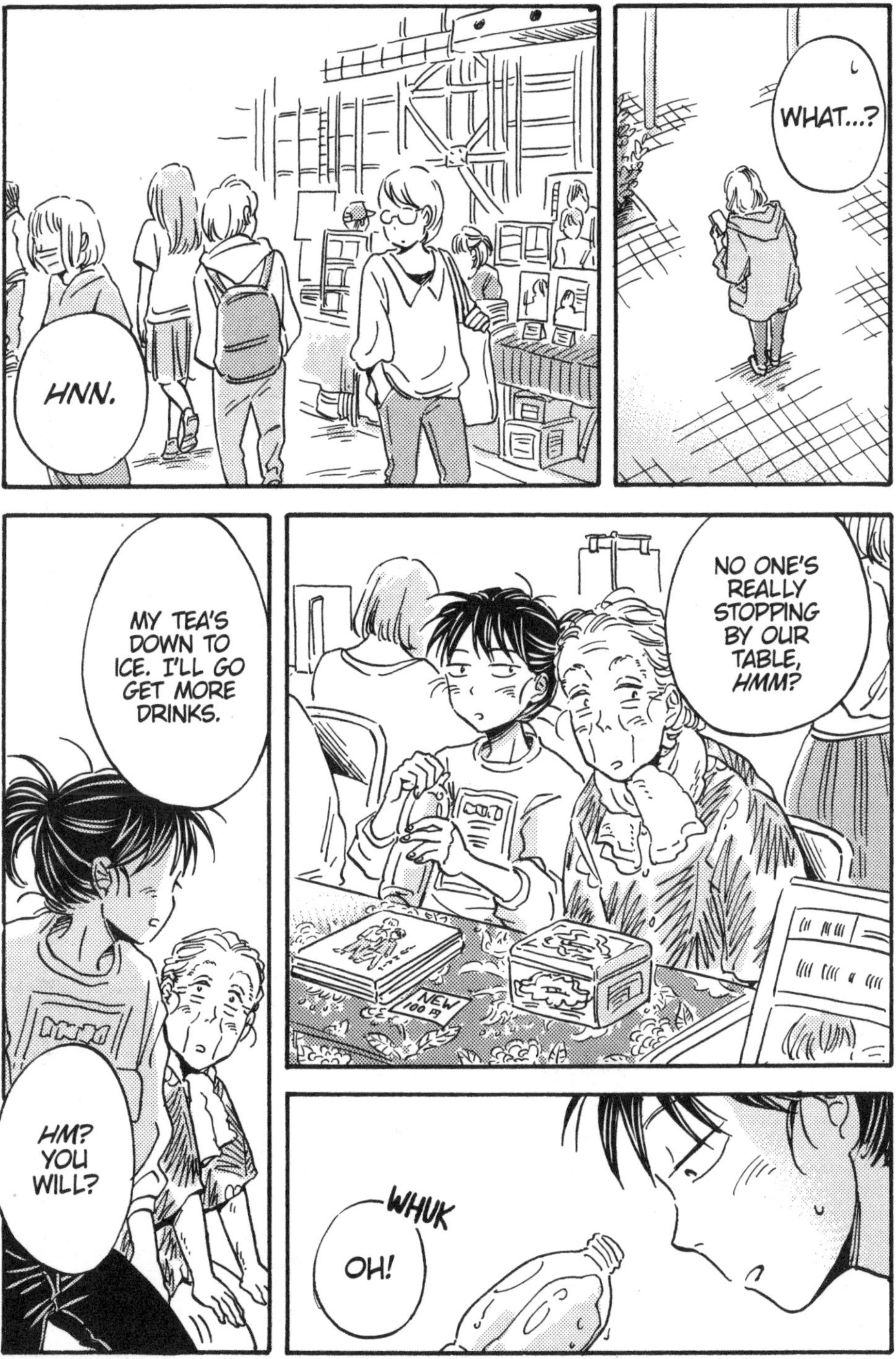
WHAT...?
HNN.
NO ONE'S REALLY STOPPING BY OUR TABLE, HMM?
WHUK
OH!
MY TEA'S DOWN TO ICE. I'LL GO GET MORE DRINKS.
HM? YOU WILL?

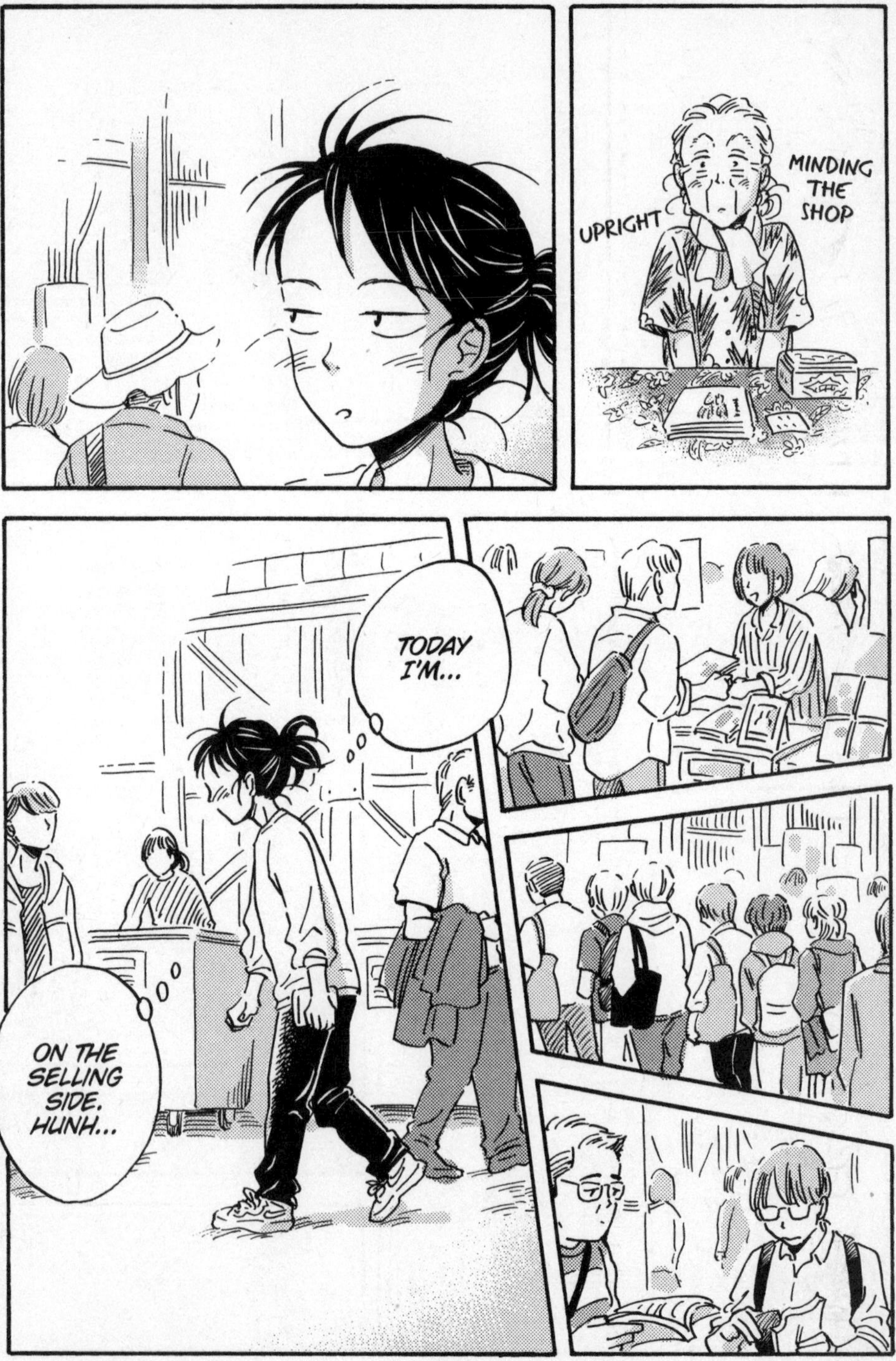
MINDING THE SHOP
UPRIGHT
TODAY I'M...
ON THE SELLING SIDE. HUNH...

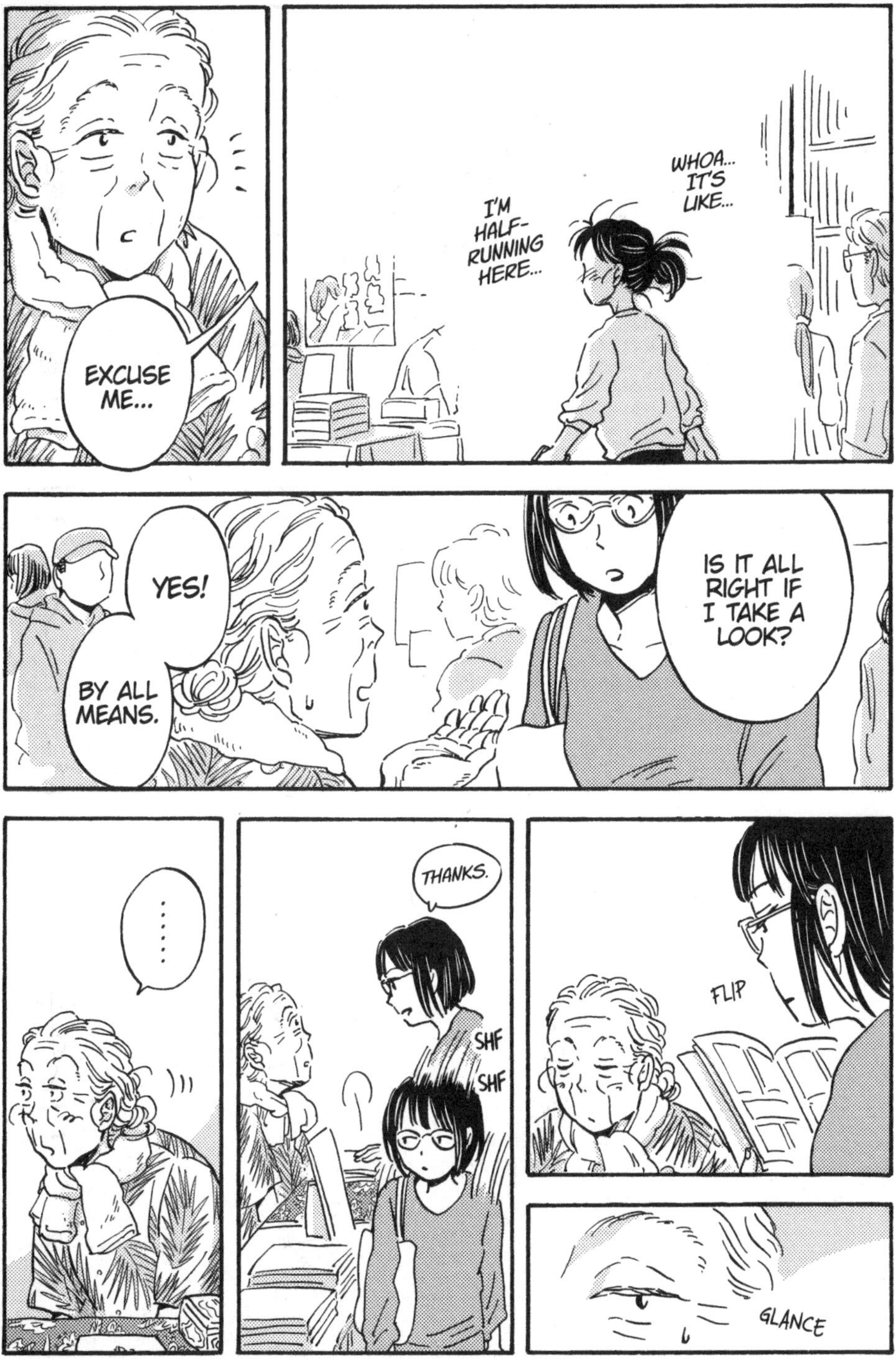
WHOA... IT'S LIKE...
I'M HALF-RUNNING HERE...
EXCUSE ME...
IS IT ALL RIGHT IF I TAKE A LOOK?
YES!
BY ALL MEANS.
FLIP
GLANCE
THANKS.
SHF
SHF
......

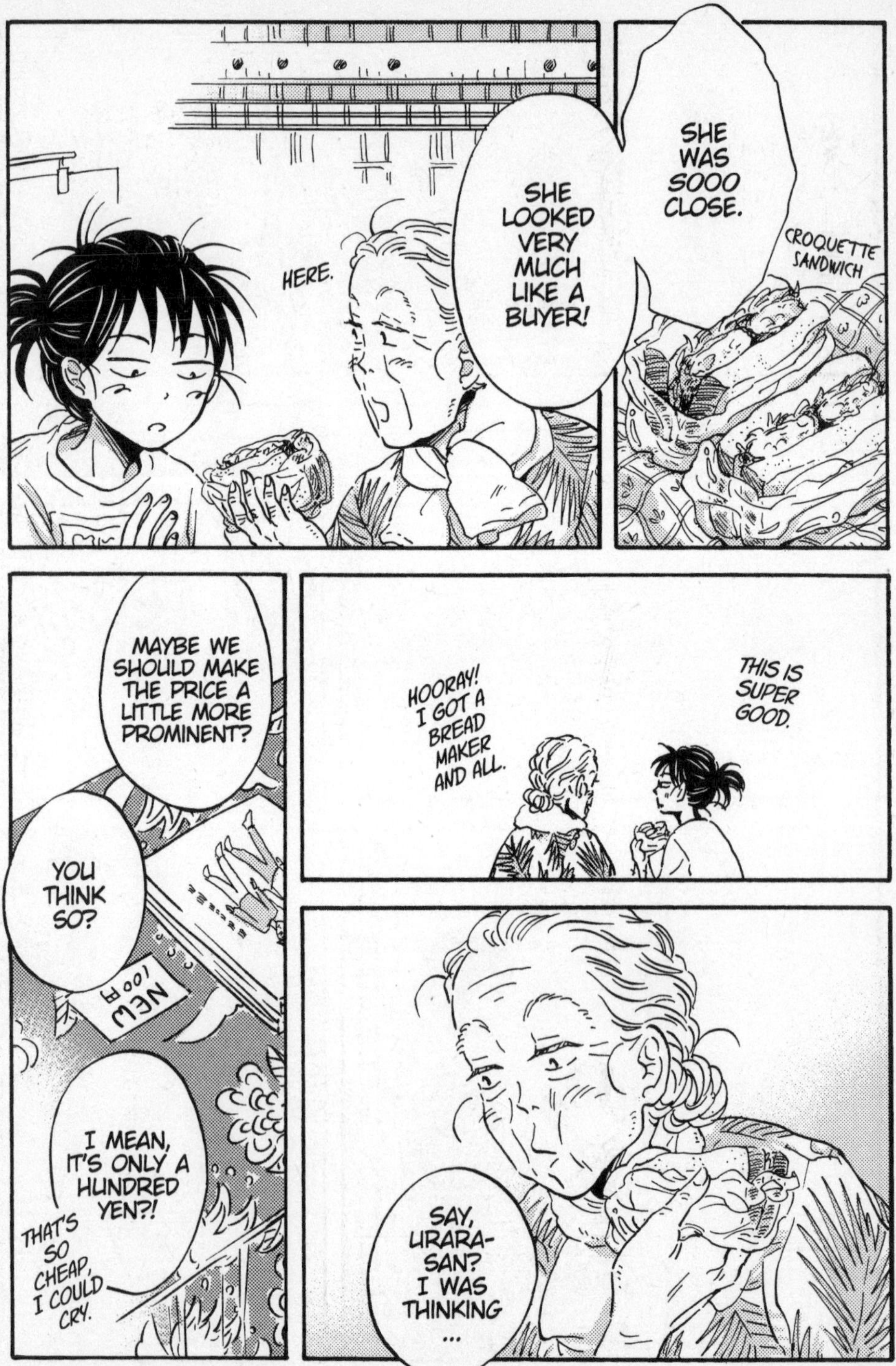
SHE WAS SOOO CLOSE.
CROQUETTE SANDWICH
SHE LOOKED VERY MUCH LIKE A BUYER!
HERE.
THIS IS SUPER GOOD.
HOORAY! I GOT A BREAD MAKER AND ALL.
SAY, URARA-SAN? I WAS THINKING ...
MAYBE WE SHOULD MAKE THE PRICE A LITTLE MORE PROMINENT?
YOU THINK SO?
NEW 100円
I MEAN, IT'S ONLY A HUNDRED YEN?!
THAT'S SO CHEAP, I COULD CRY.

WE'VE COME ALL THIS WAY! YOU DO WANT SOMEONE TO BUY A COPY, DON'T YOU?
AT LEAST MAKE IT SO THE PEOPLE WALKING BY CAN SEE IT.

I GUESS YOU'RE RIGHT.

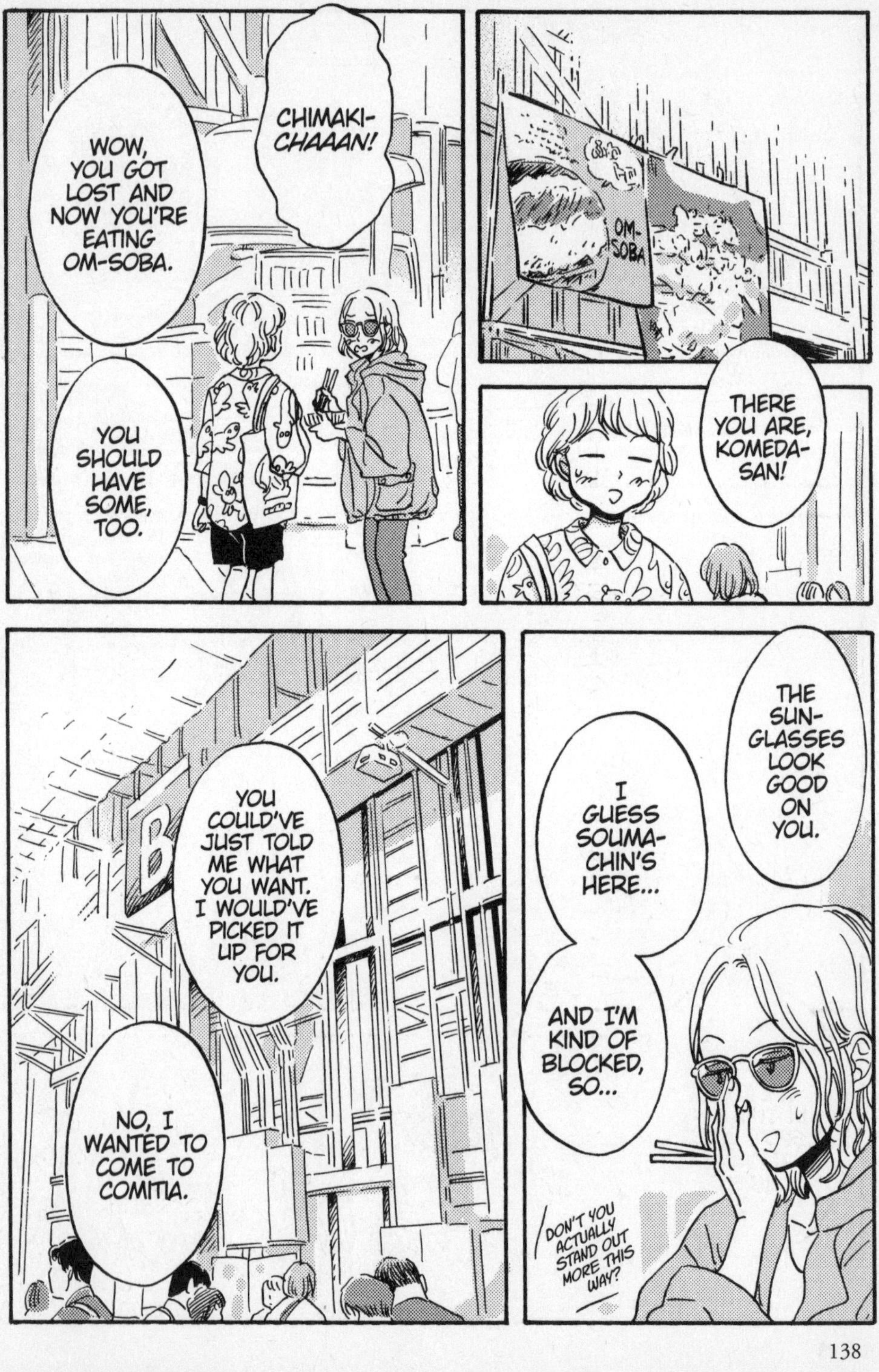
OM-SOBA
THERE YOU ARE, KOMEDA-SAN!
CHIMAKI-CHAAAN!
WOW, YOU GOT LOST AND NOW YOU'RE EATING OM-SOBA.
YOU SHOULD HAVE SOME, TOO.
THE SUN-GLASSES LOOK GOOD ON YOU.
I GUESS SOUMA-CHIN'S HERE...
AND I'M KIND OF BLOCKED, SO...
DON'T YOU ACTUALLY STAND OUT MORE THIS WAY?
YOU COULD'VE JUST TOLD ME WHAT YOU WANT. I WOULD'VE PICKED IT UP FOR YOU.
NO, I WANTED TO COME TO COMITIA.

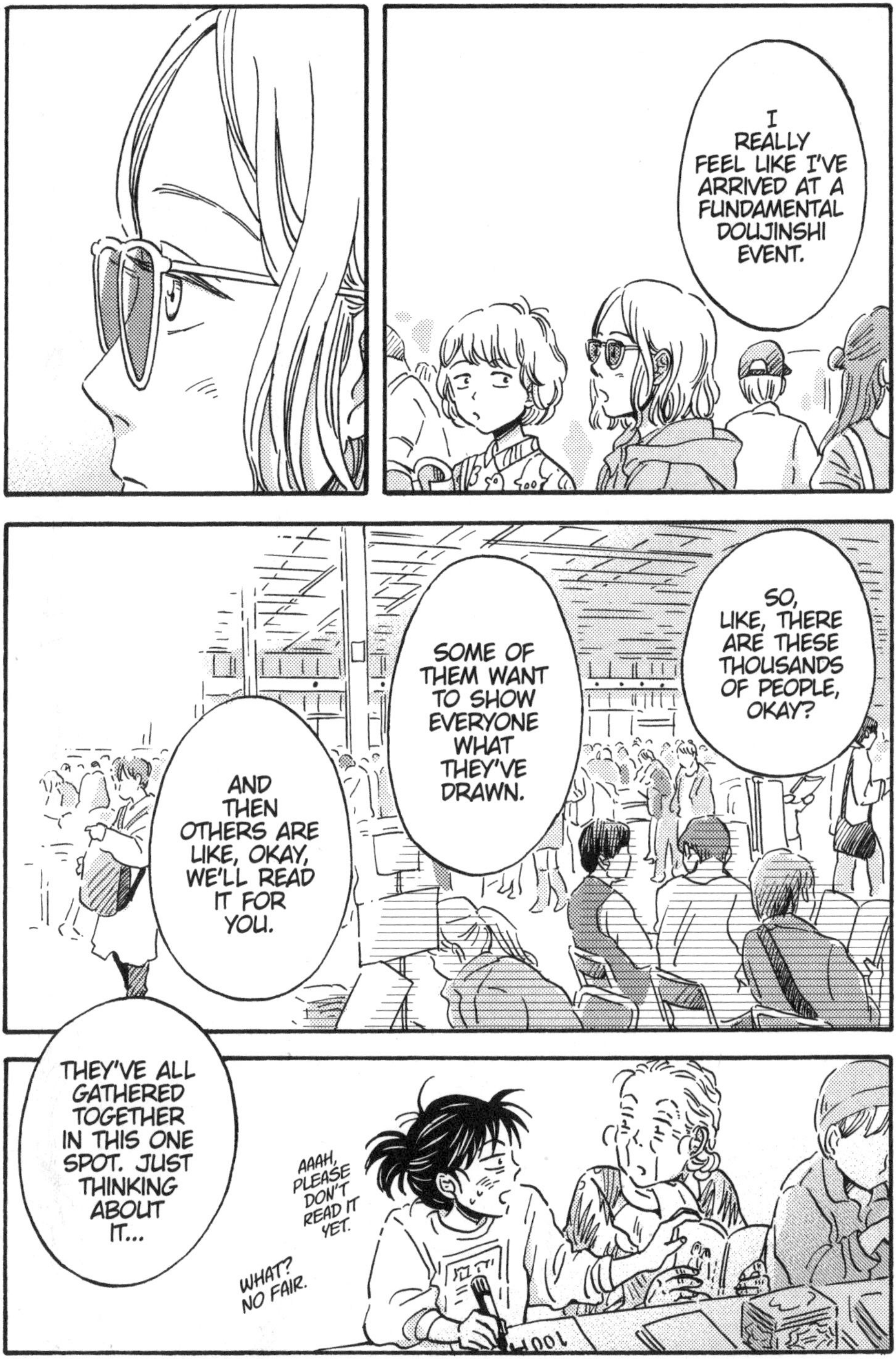
I REALLY FEEL LIKE I'VE ARRIVED AT A FUNDAMENTAL DOUJINSHI EVENT.
SO, LIKE, THERE ARE THESE THOUSANDS OF PEOPLE, OKAY?
SOME OF THEM WANT TO SHOW EVERYONE WHAT THEY'VE DRAWN.
AND THEN OTHERS ARE LIKE, OKAY, WE'LL READ IT FOR YOU.
THEY'VE ALL GATHERED TOGETHER IN THIS ONE SPOT. JUST THINKING ABOUT IT...
AAAH, PLEASE DON'T READ IT YET.
WHAT? NO FAIR.

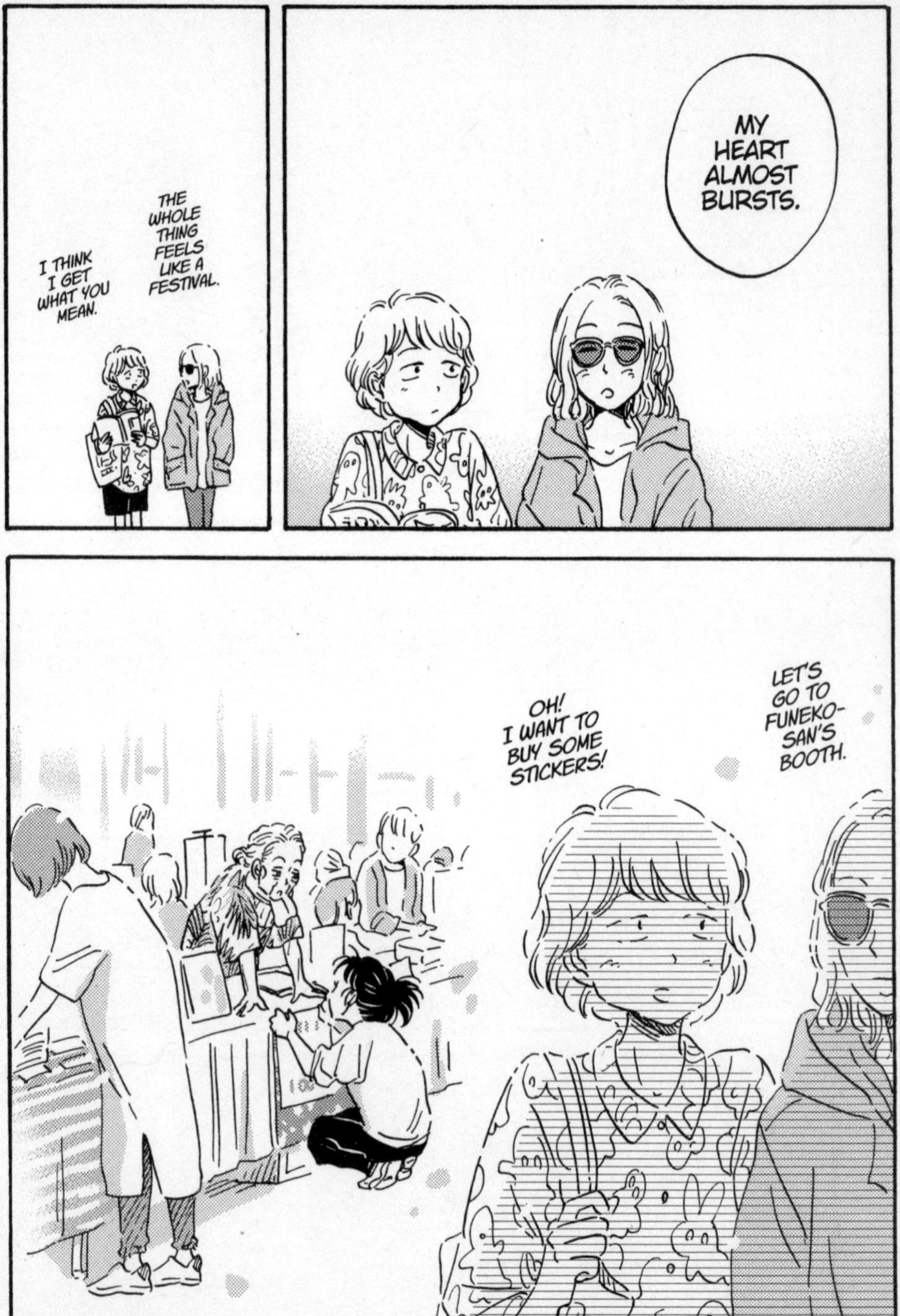
MY HEART ALMOST BURSTS.
THE WHOLE THING FEELS LIKE A FESTIVAL.
I THINK I GET WHAT YOU MEAN.
LET'S GO TO FUNEKO-SAN'S BOOTH.
OH! I WANT TO BUY SOME STICKERS!

Chapter 40/END

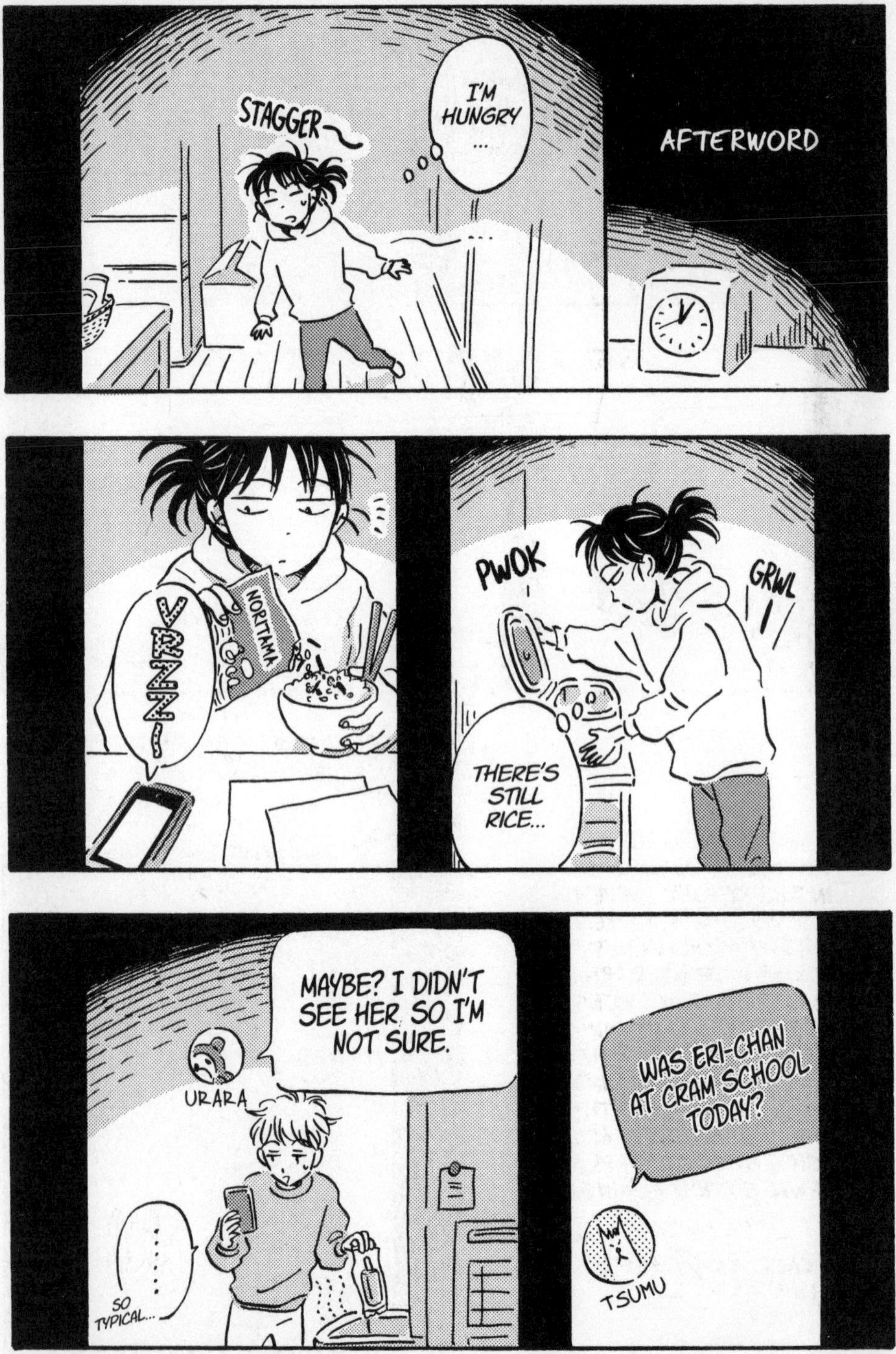
AFTERWORD
I'M HUNGRY ...
STAGGER~
GRWL
PWOK
THERE'S STILL RICE...
NORITAMA
VRZZZ
WAS ERI-CHAN AT CRAM SCHOOL TODAY?
TSUMU
MAYBE? I DIDN'T SEE HER, SO I'M NOT SURE.
URARA
......
SO TYPICAL...

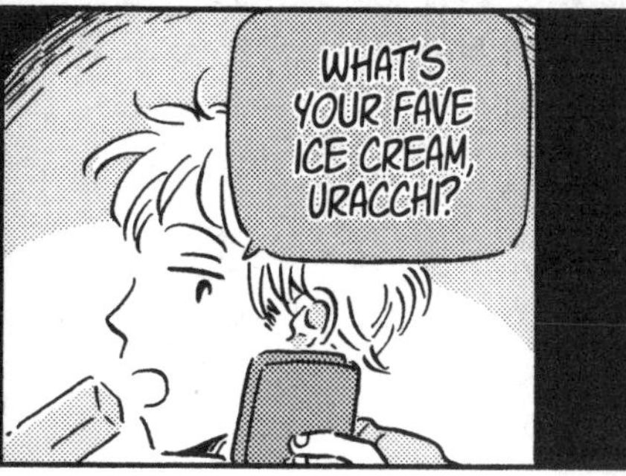
WHAT'S YOUR FAVE ICE CREAM, URACCHI?

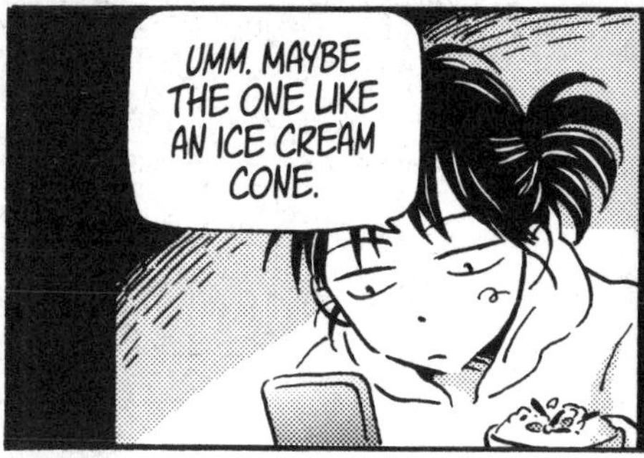
UMM. MAYBE THE ONE LIKE AN ICE CREAM CONE.

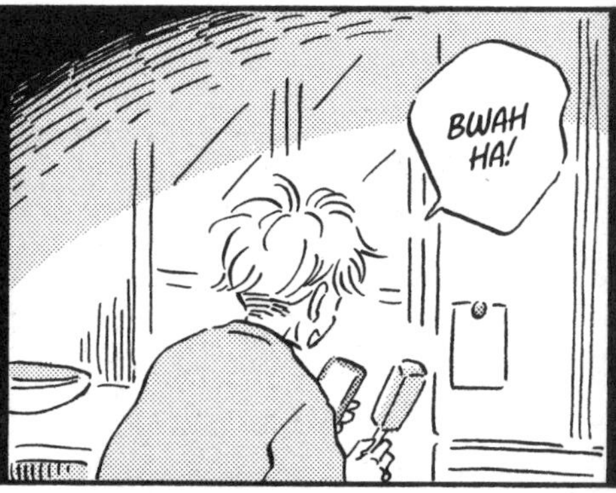
BWAH HA!

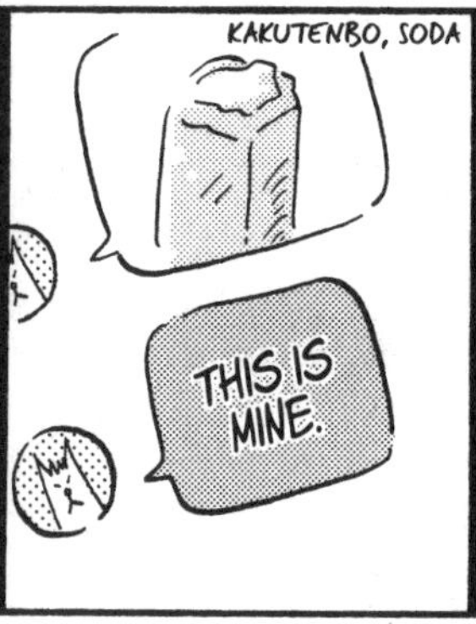
KAKUTENBO, SODA
THIS IS MINE.

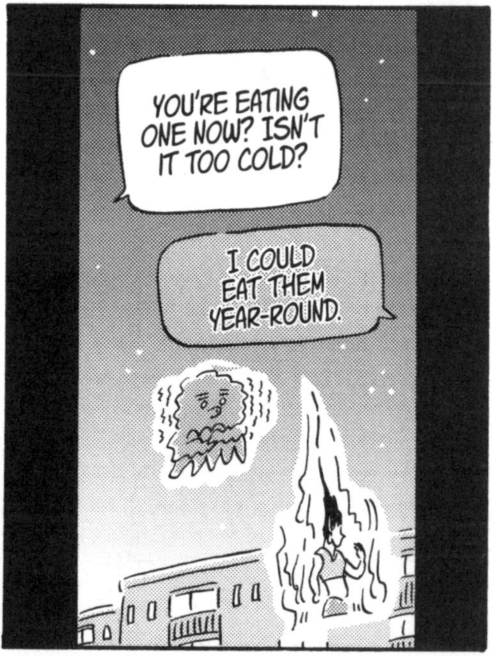
YOU'RE EATING ONE NOW? ISN'T IT TOO COLD?
I COULD EAT THEM YEAR-ROUND.

THANK YOU FOR PICKING UP VOLUME 4! IN THE READER SURVEY FOR VOLUME 3, I ASKED ABOUT YOUR KEENEST MEMORIES WITH YOUR FRIENDS. ALL THE REPLIES WERE THESE FASCINATING THINGS THAT WOULD TOTALLY HAVE NEVER CROSSED MY MIND. IT MADE ME REALIZE THAT THERE REALLY ARE ALL KINDS OF FRIENDSHIPS. IT WAS OVERWHELMING.

KAORI TSURUTANI
JANUARY 14, 2020

COVER DESIGN
Kohei Nawata Design Office

STAFF
Lucy Tokuyama
Katsuhito Fujiya
Mayumi Tsuge
Keiko Nagatomo

EDITOR
Masayasu Noguchi

SPECIAL THANKS
Comitia executive committee
Nimo Printing, LLC
Shogaku Asagaya branch

SEVEN SEAS ENTERTAINMENT PRESENTS

BL metamorphosis

story and art by KAORI TSURUTANI   VOL. 4

TRANSLATION
Jocelyne Allen

ADAPTATION
Ysabet Reinhardt MacFarlane

LETTERING
Ray Steeves

COVER DESIGN
Nicky Lim

LOGO DESIGN
Ki-oon

PROOFREADER
Dawn Davis
Danielle King

EDITOR
Jenn Grunigen

PREPRESS TECHNICIAN
Rhiannon Rasmussen–Silverstein

PRODUCTION MANAGER
Lissa Pattillo

MANAGING EDITOR
Julie Davis

ASSOCIATE PUBLISHER
Adam Arnold

PUBLISHER
Jason DeAngelis

Seven Seas press and purchase enquiries can be sent to Marketing Manager
Lianne Sentar at press@gomanga.com. Information regarding the distribution
and purchase of digital editions is available from Digital Manager CK Russell
at digital@gomanga.com.

Seven Seas and the Seven Seas logo are trademarks of
Seven Seas Entertainment. All rights reserved.

ISBN: 978-1-64505-995-0

Printed in Canada

First Printing: March 2021

10 9 8 7 6 5 4 3 2 1

FOLLOW US ONLINE: **www.sevenseasentertainment.com**

READING DIRECTIONS

This book reads from *right to left*, Japanese style.
If this is your first time reading manga, you start
reading from the top right panel on each page and
take it from there. If you get lost, just follow the
numbered diagram here. It may seem backwards at
first, but you'll get the hang of it! Have fun!!

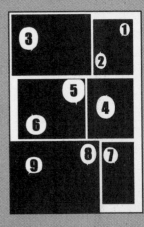